Economics
and Economic Policy

ALSO BY ALEC CAIRNCROSS

Introduction to Economics *(1944; 6th edn 1982)*
Home and Foreign Investment, 1870–1913 *(1953)*
Monetary Policy in a Mixed Economy *(1960)*
Economic Development and the Atlantic Provinces *(1961)*
Factors in Economic Development *(1962)*
Essays in Economic Management *(1971)*
Control of Long-term International Capital Movements *(1973)*
Inflation, Growth and International Finance *(1975)*
Snatches *(Poems) (1981)*
Sterling in Decline *(with Barry Eichengreen; 1983)*
Years of Recovery *(1985)*
The Price of War: British Policy on German Reparations
1941 to 1949 *(1986)*

Economics and Economic Policy

ALEC CAIRNCROSS

Basil Blackwell

First published 1986
First published in USA 1987

Basil Blackwell Ltd
108 Cowley Road, Oxford OX4 1JF, UK

Basil Blackwell Inc.
432 Park Avenue South, Suite 1503
New York, NY 10016, USA

British Library Cataloguing in Publication Data

Cairncross, *Sir*, Alec
Economics and economic policy.
1. Economic policy
I. Title
330.9 HD87

ISBN 0-631-15233-4

Library of Congress Cataloging in Publication Data

Cairncross, Alec, Sir, 1911–
Economics and economic policy.

Bibliography: p.
Includes index.
1. Economics 2. Economic policy.
3. Macro-economics. I. Title.
HB171.C17 1987 338.9 86-11751
ISBN 0-631-15233-4

Phototypeset in 10/12pt Sabon by Dobbie Typesetting Service, Plymouth, Devon
Printed in Great Britain by T. J. Press Ltd, Padstow, Cornwall

Contents

Preface

The papers included in this book were prepared over the last ten years either as occasional lectures to audiences in Britain or abroad or as contributions to a *Festschrift* or similar symposium. They are not intended as a commentary on the changing problems of the day but as a synopsis of one economist's reflections on the abiding issues of economic policy.

The subjects dealt with fall under four headings. The first two papers discuss the role of economists as contributors to economic policy; these are followed by four papers on various aspects of economic planning and three on economic development and growth; the volume then concludes with four papers on the aims and instruments of macro-economic policy. Although some prior familiarity with elementary economics is obviously desirable, even the layman will, I hope, find the level of treatment such as to make the drift of each paper readily intelligible.

Three papers – those on 'Planning and decision-taking under conditions of uncertainty', 'Is there a general theory of economic development?' and 'The rise and fall of employment policy' – have not been published hitherto. The others are either not readily accessible or are scattered over many different types of publication.

I am grateful to Methuen and Co. for permission to reprint 'Academics and policy makers' from *Changing Perceptions of Economic Policy*; to Oxford University Press for permission to include a revised version of 'The market and the state' from the volume with that title; to the Macmillan Press for permission to include 'Keynes and the planned economy' from *Keynes and Laissez-faire* and 'The limitations of shadow rates' from *Employment, Income Distribution and Development Strategy*; to Leeds University Press for permission to include a revised version of 'Reflections on innovation' from *Inflation Development and Integration*; and to Allied Publishers Private Ltd for permission to reprint the paper on 'The role of technology and natural resources in the development process' from

Reflections on Economic Development and Social Change. I have also to thank the American Economic Association for allowing me to reprint my Richard Ely Lecture on 'Economics in theory and practice'. The remaining three papers are published with the agreement of the Open University, the British Academy and the *Three Banks Review*.

My intellectual obligations in the preparation of these papers are far too extensive to be listed here. I must, however, express my indebtedness to Ely Devons even if it is now 20 years since his death, long before any of these papers was written. My ideas on technology and technical change owe much to Michael Fores. I should like also to acknowledge the benefit I derived from chairing a series of meetings some years ago on the relation between monetary and fiscal policy under the auspices of the Institute of Fiscal Studies. Finally, my thanks are due to Walter and Michael Salent and to Professor Thomas Wilson for helpful comments on a draft of 'Economics in theory and practice'.

I am also indebted to Mrs Anne Robinson for converting my hesitant hieroglyphics into beautifully clear typescript.

Alec Cairncross

1

Economics in theory and practice

Do you not know, my son, with how little wisdom the world is governed?
Oxenstierna

Let's face it. Whatever economics was in the past, it is now virtually an industry. It stretches from the building of new models by the theorists to the supply of advice, forecasts, proposals, and programmes by the practitioners, and caters mainly for a market of policymakers in business and government. In the economics business, market forces work feebly, particularly at the level of theory. The competitive process derives little benefit from price adjustments, and suppliers are often remote from the market and unaware of market pressures. But the usual phenomena of growth and development are all at work: investment, economies of scale, and the interaction between technical innovation and market expansion. Some of our colleagues confine their activities to production while others occupy themselves with the business of packaging and marketing. Division of labour has made rapid progress, both horizontally and vertically. On the one hand, we have specialists in different branches of economics: macro-economics, industrial economics, transport economics, health economics, international economics, mathematical economics, etc., etc. On the other hand, we have a lengthening chain of intermediaries between the priestly who live in clouds of theory and the lay brethren in Washington, Whitehall, and elsewhere, who do battle in the corridors of power. Where so many labour, their efforts merit scrutiny as yet another branch of economics.

I do not propose today to embark on so ambitious a task as an exposition of the economics of economics. Having spent half my working life in a

Richard T. Ely Lecture delivered at the Annual Meeting of the American Economic Association at Dallas, December 1984.

succession of government departments and international bodies, I thought it best to set myself a more modest task and draw on my own experience as an intermediary in the market for economic advice. I propose to limit myself to an examination of the links between theory and practice, between the theorists who seek to trap the inner secrets of the economy in their models and the practitioners who live in a world of action where time is precious, understanding is limited, nothing is certain, and non-economic considerations are always important and often decisive.

Action can take two forms. It may go no further than policy recommendations, or it may consist in taking policy decisions. When I speak of practitioners I shall normally have in mind those who busy themselves with what the policy should be, whether professional economists or not, rather than those who take the final decisions on policy. But I may on occasion feel obliged to refer to the difficulties of the decision-taker in making use of economic advice as opposed to those of his economic advisers in formulating it.

When one looks around, theory and practice are often far apart. In many countries there is even a physical separation: the theorists remain in their universities, the practitioners in their departments of government, with little contact between the two. And since ideas circulate most freely through personal contact, the physical segregation carries with it an intellectual segregation. The thinking of advisers on policy proceeds largely in isolation from the thinking of the academics. Even in countries where there is some circulation between universities and government, and some mixing of one set of economists with the other, there is a strong tendency for the thinking of each to stay within its own orbit, the insiders pursuing lines of thought independently of contributions from outside, and vice versa.

It is hardly surprising that there should be some divorce between theory and practice when their starting points are so different. As in medicine, engineering and other human activities, one can ask either: 'what is the truth of the matter?' or: 'what ought I to do?' according as one's interest is in theory or practice. An economist entering a business concern or a government department, unless consigned to the outer darkness of a research section, finds himself in an atmosphere where action takes precedence over intellectual speculation. The question at issue for the practitioner is always: 'what is to be done?' That is a question which the pure theorist may decline to answer because he feels that he has no special competence to do so. He may share the view of Nassau Senior that 'the conclusions of the economist, whatever their generality and truth, do not authorize him in adding a single syllable of advice'.[1] But it is not a question that can be evaded; and presumably a training in economics is of some help in answering it.

How much help does theory provide? Sometimes the honest answer is 'very little'. It may elucidate, but certainly does not resolve, controversial issues of economic policy. An obvious example is the controversy in Britain in the early 1970s over the desirability of joining the Common Market, with half the academic economists signing a letter in favour, and the other half signing a letter against. Or one can point to the conflict of view between those who put their faith in monetary policy and those who regard it as a broken reed, or between the advocates and opponents of floating rates of exchange, or between those in favour of and those against a statutory incomes policy. Even when the theorists are in agreement, the issue of policy remains undecided. There is widespread agreement that in theory an expenditure tax is preferable to an income tax. But so far as I am aware, the Finance Ministries of the world have remained unmoved. There has been no rush to change over to an expenditure tax and the only countries which did, India and Sri Lanka, gave up the experiment almost at once.

The limitations of economic theory were brought home to me when I was asked to organize a course of instruction for senior administrators who had come to Washington for six months to learn as much as possible about the kind of economic policies their countries ought to pursue. They did not want to study economic theory as such, and had indeed no time in which to master it, but were interested in the practical upshot of economic thinking and speculation about economic development. They asked quite simple questions – some of them with a familiar ring – such as: 'can inflation assist or does it retard economic development? How much can one safely borrow abroad? What tax system is most likely to favour economic development?' I found, as you might expect, that economic theory was indispensable for analysing their problems, but that it very rarely allowed one to arrive at policy conclusions with any confidence.

Later I encountered a similar group who had come to study investment appraisal and had become well versed in the theory of discounted cash flow. But investment appraisal involves a lot more than economic theory. I asked the group what rate of interest they would use on their return home. There was a long pause until one bold spirit suggested 'Bank Rate'. Nobody Nobody contradicted him. Nobody had other suggestions to offer.

An earlier occasion on which I asked myself to what use I would be able to put my knowledge of economic theory was when I joined the British War Cabinet Secretariat in 1940. There could be no doubt of the profound influence on policy in wartime of a comparatively small group of professional economists. And yet I never saw much use made of the more refined and esoteric parts of economic theory. I concluded, as my colleague, the late Ely Devons put it, that 'in so far as economic theory is useful in enabling us to understand the real world and in helping us to take decisions on policy, it is the simple, most elementary and, in some ways, the most obvious propositions that matter.[2] But, as he was careful to add, before the simple propositions become part of normal processes of thinking and cease to be 'kept in a separate compartment labelled "economic theory",'[3] familiarity with the subject needs to advance well beyond the elementary level. Lionel Robbins said much the same when he argued that

> . . . the most useful economic principles, when stated in their most general form, seem often mere banalities, almost an anti-climax after the formidable controversies amid which they have emerged. Yet experience seems to show that, without systematic training in the application of such platitudes, the most acute minds are liable to go astray.[4]

I found that two or three rather elementary economic concepts, which I had assumed would be familiar to everyone, were often not at all well understood by non-economists but were of particular value in policy formulation. Among these concepts I should include as of first-rate importance the idea of the interaction of supply, demand, and price; the concept of opportunity cost; and the marginal theory of value. Later, I concluded that it was even more important to be able to think of market forces operating within an economic *system,* and to recognize the coordinating function of the price mechanism. Many other elementary concepts, particularly at the macro level, were equally fundamental, but these examples are enough for purposes of illustration.

Non-economists have rarely sorted out in their mind how supply and demand operate on market prices and have no instinctive appreciation of the virtues – indeed the indispensability – of the price mechanism. On the contrary, their bias is almost always towards an organizational or political approach to economic problems. They like fixed prices because they seem to inject an element of stability and predictability. During and after World War II, when something became scarce the immediate reaction of businessmen or bureaucrats was nearly always in favour of control and rationing without any thought for the contribution that *some* rise in price might make to relieving or ending the shortage. The pricing of coal, for example, at the time of the nationalization of the industry in Britain in 1947, paid not the slightest regard to the chronic shortage of fuel and the danger that that shortage would arrest industrial recovery, as in the end it did. The pricing of foreign exchange, in much the same way, was divorced from market pressures and continued to be regarded by ministers as a moral or organizational issue: they believed that planning and control could do all that devaluation of the currency could do.

Of course, economists may fall into the opposite error and think that market forces, left to themselves, will always do the trick. At the end of World War II, when practically every country except the United States was running a balance of payments deficit, there were those who regarded the dollar shortage as an invention of governments that were determined to prolong the shortage by overvaluing their currencies. How far rates might have to fall and what the consequences of such a fall might be were matters rarely explored. In the early postwar years, with demobilization in progress and production well below capacity, it was not at all self-evident that a general realignment of currencies and a consequential revamping of the price structure would do much to restore balance of payments equilibrium, however necessary it might prove later on. On the contrary, there was good reason to take direct action to limit imports, encourage exports, develop alternative sources of supply and restrict the export of capital, that is, to make use of planning rather than prices.

Similarly, at the outbreak of war the necessary reallocation of manpower cannot easily be brought about by market forces alone. It might be possible in theory to work through variations in the funds at the disposal of different departments and agencies, but if the government means to impose its priorities on the market it will achieve quicker and more predictable results by direct methods. Where a major upheaval is required, market forces operate slowly and blindly.

Opportunity cost is another concept that does not come naturally to the non-economist. Few people have given thought to the inner meaning of 'cost', or habitually decide on a course of action on the basis of the alternatives that might be adopted. Yet in my experience the concept is indispensable in policy analysis and lends itself to very wide applications. This is equally true of the idea of the margin: the average man thinks of averages rather than increments and often goes off on the wrong tack for this reason, particularly in relation to pricing and investment decisions.

Both concepts, however, need careful handling. Marginal theory is usually taught in terms of a single margin when in fact there are a great many. No businessman thinks of output and prices as his only variables, and even when he does, has to consider the repercussions of changing either of them over a whole series of time horizons. With opportunity cost there is a similar danger of neglecting the full range of possibilities. Lord Kaldor has recently used the concept to justify keeping open high-cost coal mines under conditions of heavy unemployment. But the logical conclusion of his line of argument is that so long as there is substantial unemployment, no firm should ever be allowed to close down and no one should ever be sacked, since it is better to have some output than none. The alternatives compared have to have regard to the full consequences, not just the immediate ones.

When I read the literature on shadow prices I have a rather similar reaction that the idea of opportunity cost can be carried too far. The notional prices corresponding to the opportunity cost of capital, labour, or foreign exchange may be enforceable on the limited sector of the economy under the government's control; but that introduces distortions between the controlled and uncontrolled sectors, which may thwart the government's intentions. Besides, the enforcement of shadow prices that diverge widely from market prices is far from easy, even within the controlled sector. Subordinate authorities are apt to take little notice of a hypothetical test rate of discount in deciding on their investment programme and do their sums on the basis of the rate they have to pay on borrowed money, diluted by any subsidies from the central government. To make a shadow rate take effect throughout the public sector, the central government is unlikely to get very far by directives unsupported by offers of capital at the shadow rate.

The biggest single advantage that economists have is their way of thinking. It comes naturally to them to think in terms of alternatives and to trace the implications of alternative lines of action within the logical framework of an economic system. They are alive to the interaction of economic forces within that system and hence to the full economic impact of policy decisions. They are not at a loss, like Prime Minister Attlee, to understand how it is that when activity is so brisk at home there should be so much trouble with the balance of payments. They do not need to be persuaded like Lord Radcliffe – perhaps the most outstanding lawyer of his day – that an enquiry into the working of the monetary system may involve a study of the working of the capital market (though I must admit that there are professional economists who even now seem to share Lord Radcliffe's view).

The importance of an adequate framework of thought was strikingly illustrated in the controversy over central economic planning after World War II. Administrators and politicians alike tended to overlook the role of the price mechanism in their enthusiasm for planning. Two of the most outstanding figures of the period, Sir Oliver Franks and Sir Stafford Cripps – one a top administrator and later Ambassador in Washington, the other a memorable Labour Chancellor of the Exchequer – published expositions of the case for central planning without any hint that there are always powerful forces at work to close any gap between supplies and requirements and that it may be well to pay regard to these forces.[5] Few administrators or politicians, unless trained in economics, perceive that there can be no question of relying exclusively on government planning, or alternatively on the price mechanism, and that the real problem is always how to combine the two.

It can happen, as in wartime, that the price mechanism plays only a minor part because the government's priorities must take precedence over those of individual consumers; and in the wake of such circumstances the role of prices may be overlooked. It can also happen that economists are so mesmerized by the price mechanism that they limit their vision to the study of market forces when the phenomena of government planning merit equal attention. Just as administrators may fail to understand the workings of the price mechanism, so economists are apt to disregard organizational influences on economic activity. What goes on *inside* the firm, *inside* the government department, *inside* the Cabinet, is often left on one side. Yet it cannot make sense to pursue the study of market failure and undertake no systematic analysis of the weaknesses of alternative agencies of coordination.

To the four elementary economic concepts I have just discussed – supply and demand, opportunity costs, the margin and the economic system – I could add some familiar maxims such as 'Bygones are forever bygones', or 'There is no such thing as a free lunch'. These, too, are very helpful in coping with muddled thinking in high places. They form a small but indispensable part of the economists' stock-in-trade. Where the full range of tools is most likely to be brought into play is in economic forecasting. Here indeed the practitioner has to keep in close touch with current theory. The relationship between theory and practice in economic forecasting raises many interesting questions, since those who prepare the forecasts and are perhaps best equipped to judge the risk of error may have little contact with those who use them and run their risks on the basis of the forecasts. But economic forecasting is much too large a subject for me to do more than touch on.

I turn instead to examine some of the reasons why economists find difficulty in bringing their theoretical apparatus to bear on practical problems. As Jacob Viner, who had plenty of experience, emphasized years ago, 'the list of handicaps of the economic theorist as a participant in public policy . . . is discouragingly long'.[6] Some of these handicaps arise from the practical difficulties that attend the use of economic theory in trying to work out an appropriate policy; others relate to the presentation of the policy so that it carries conviction and obtains support; others again derive from the need to marry economic with non-economic considerations in making a policy acceptable. Let me take these in turn.

LIMITATIONS OF ECONOMIC THEORY

Economic theory is fundamentally an exploration of models and conceptual relationships couched in hypothetical terms and necessarily abstracts from many features of the real world. Without abstraction and simplification it would not be possible to begin thinking about economic problems. There is no option but to leave out what may seem to some people highly important. As Wicksell pointed out, it is not to be expected that economic theory should attach significance to the features of the real world according to their prominence in the eyes of the layman since 'it is not the purpose of science to describe the obvious in elaborate terms'.[7] But abstraction can be carried too far. The theorist may follow paths that lead him further and further from the real world and expose him to the danger of what one economist has called 'theoretic blight'.[8] He may be tempted to select problems that lend themselves to sophisticated technical analysis rather than on grounds of practical importance; and become lost in admiration of the conceptual schemes he has developed without regard to the unrealistic premises on which they are constructed. He may also make the common mistake of getting things the wrong way round; or leave out what really does matter or can only be left out provisionally. He may then be deceived into thinking that he understands how things work when in fact the model is misconceived. Theory, as someone once put it, can be 'an organized way of going wrong with confidence'. To be a useful guide it has to separate correctly what is adventitious from what is truly significant.

Economic policy, on the other hand, has to deal with practical problems and specific situations. While it is possible to develop a branch of economics bearing on these problems and situations and call it applied economics, such a branch is still part of economic theory. It still consists of a set of logically consistent propositions and abstracts from many of the circumstances that may in practice govern the policy pursued. What is to be done is never a simple corollary of theoretical conclusions.

The need for care in drawing conclusions from theory was brought home to me in Berlin in the winter of 1945–46 when I took part in a discussion between Sir Paul Chambers (later Chairman of ICI) and General William H. Draper (then Economic Adviser to General Clay). Sir Paul, challenged as to the accuracy with which he had been able to forecast budgetary revenue as Director of Statistics and Intelligence in the Inland Revenue, gave us a short exposition of the theory of probability. 'If you toss a penny and it comes down tails ten times in succession,' he said, 'that doesn't affect the probability that it will come down heads next time. The chances remain fifty-fifty.' 'Shall we test that?' said General Draper, producing a penny. 'Will you call?' Ten times Sir Paul called heads and each time the penny came down tails. Before tossing it again, General Draper revealed that the exercise of a little sleight of hand might be affecting the behaviour of the penny. It is always necessary to enquire whether the assumptions of theory are valid in the case at hand before applying it; and if the facts do not conform to theoretical expectations it may be the facts that need looking into, not the theory.

Whatever the limitations of economic theory, it is very powerful stuff, more powerful the more general it comes. We certainly cannot dispense with it in trying to understand any economic system. If we enter a maze we need a thread to guide us in it and the purpose of theory is to furnish that guide. On the other hand, we cannot hope to get very far with theory alone and there are serious dangers in moving from the world of theory to the real world without regard to the difference between the two. One danger is that the theory may be obsolete. It isn't just the practical man who may become the slave of some defunct economist. Even professional economists, deeply immersed in their everyday duties in some government department, have to live on an intellectual capital that is rapidly depreciating and need an opportunity of rebuilding it in an academic environment. There may also be times when the boot is on the other foot and it is the practitioner who is alive to truths disregarded in current theory. Theory may suffer from a distortion of emphasis or a quirk of intellectual fashion that throws into prominence the wrong variables, the wrong problems or the wrong formulations of them; attention may then be diverted from the things with which theory should be occupying itself. When that happens, economic theory must be accounted not just irrelevant, but bad: for the primary purpose of theory is to assist us in posing questions, and if we are moved to ask the wrong questions theory has failed us.

The most serious problem for the practitioner is that the theorists differ, even on technical economic issues. There is no agreement on how the economy works – on what governs the level of output or employment or prices. Where the disagreements go so deep as they do nowadays it is difficult to speak with authority on technical economic issues. I need not dwell on the problems this creates in advising on policy.

And yet there are times when I wonder whether the disagreements between economic theorists, even now, go so deep as their solidarity when confronted with the heresies which so often shape the policies of governments. To take an extreme case, we may debate whether the money supply is too great or too small: but what of governments – and there have been some – that try to do away with money altogether or come to power, like the Social Credit party, preaching that there is never enough? Or, to come nearer home, what of the comment made to me on the Radcliffe Committee by the President of the National Union of Mineworkers, one of Arthur Scargill's predecessors: 'You fellows seem to worry about what the rate of interest should do. But my members don't see why there should be a rate of interest at all.' Or, still on the subject of interest rates, what are we to make of Chancellors of the Exchequer who exclaim like Hugh Dalton: 'You can't allow higher interest rates while resisting higher wage rates.' It can sometimes be easier to reach agreement between economists on what should be done than on matters of theory.

A further difficulty facing the practitioner relates not to theory but to economic information. Economic theory has always to be mixed with a large dollop of fact before prescriptions for action can be framed; but the facts are usually obscure, disputed, seen through different eyes against a different experience of life and stretching far beyond the limited economic context within which the economist seeks to analyse them.

The theorist moreover is in control of his starting point, since he is free to make his own assumptions; but the practitioner is never quite sure where he is. As Lord Roberthall, who was Economic Adviser to the British government for fourteen years, used to say: 'it's very hard to forecast where you are now.' Indeed, you don't even know where you *were*. The official statisticians are busy rewriting history from the word 'go'; and they don't stop. When I look back at the British balance of payments deficits in the three years after World War II, for example, I find that the figures for the current account first published added up to £1245 million, were revised by 1953 to show a total of £740 million, and continued to be revised over the next thirty years until they dwindled to £585 million. Instead of working out at exactly the level assumed in the Washington Loan Negotiations in 1945, the cumulative deficit is now put at less than half and British capital exports over the period are consequently estimated at a total higher than was thought at the time by $2½, that is, by two-thirds of what was borrowed from the United States. Another example is the way in which the UK monthly index of industrial production in 1964 was completely flat in the nine months up to September – a General Election was due in October – but was revised over the next two years so that it was sloping steeply upwards in official publications in 1966 and then was further revised until now it is flat again, as in 1964.

I cite these changes, which could easily be multiplied, to show that if the future is uncertain, so also is the past. I have often been intrigued to see how patiently economists apply themselves to explaining what, if later information is to be trusted, never occurred and how figures of assorted reliability are given equal treatment by those who do not live among them. The practitioner, recognizing the uncertainty of the information at his disposal, can have only a limited grasp of what is going on. He has to make the best of incomplete, inconsistent, and changeable data, relying on human judgement to derive a plausible, self-consistent picture of the existing situation. He is quite likely to find, as I have found, that the best way to reconcile the data is to begin by making a forecast of the future as a way of deciding on the underlying trends and then work backwards to a consequential interpretation of the present. The judgement he makes – as in the examples I have cited – may be crucial to the choice of policy. If for instance, you think the economy is stuck, you opt for policies very different from those appropriate to a rip-roaring expansion.

A further difficulty is that the economy never works in quite the same way for very long. You may feel confident that you can explain how it worked in the recent past and set your conclusions down in equations with all the coefficients, lags, etc., carefully estimated. But, as Keynes put it, human behaviour is not 'homogeneous through time.'[9] Whether you realize it or not, you are always working with relationships that are obsolescent without knowing just how obsolescent they are. One day you can count on people spending more when prices go up; then you find them spending less. One day the unemployment figures go up when the vacancy figures come down; then they both go up together. It is always necessary to be on the look out for some departure from normal patterns and pay attention to straws in the wind. They may reveal, earlier than any statistics, new forces at work or a strengthening of existing forces. Analysis of these forces has to be coupled with a good eye for straws.

Then there is the limitation imposed by the need to be specific: in particular, to deal in specific magnitudes and at specific points in time. Many of the more important generalizations in economics make no reference to magnitudes or time. They may be of assistance to a government that wants to know in which direction it should be operating; but they do not, in their general form, offer much help to a government wanting to know how far to go.

For example, it may be possible on general grounds to indicate that the government should be thinking in terms of increasing taxation. But the question that has operational significance is, how much should the increase be? This requires immersion in a mass of statistical detail and the working out of far more definite views of the functioning of the economy than found their way into the traditional textbooks in economics some years ago.

Then there is the content of the tax package. What *taxes* should be increased? What effect will the increases have? What other action, if any, should accompany the increases in tax or be contemplated for introduction later?

Another set of issues relates to timing. When should the government act? When will it be possible to judge whether the action has been effective? Is it likely to be necessary to take further action later?

It takes time to become aware of changes in the situation, to size up the strength of the forces at work, to prepare the appropriate response. One cannot wait for certainty, but it is also a mistake to act prematurely when the diagnosis may prove to be quite wrong. Delay may be inescapable. After the devaluation of sterling in November 1967, there was a great burst of consumer spending and a clamour for early action to restrain it. The right time to act was of course in November, but when that opportunity was missed it was not easy, for technical reasons, to redeem the error by imposing additional taxation in the weeks immediately before Christmas. In January it seemed better to put all possible effort into a battle for lower government expenditure and by the end of the month the budget was already in sight only a few weeks away. So although the need for action was not in dispute, it was four months before a suitable package of measures could be introduced.

Another source of difficulty is that many of the questions on which advice is sought from economists have very little to do with conventional economics. Cabinet ministers, I found, don't ask the questions you are ready to answer. They want to know how people will react, both to events and to their policies. Will there be a strike or won't there? Will the rate of exchange weaken or strengthen? Will it be possible to get backing for this or that line of policy?

I concluded that attitudes were just as important as prices and that economic policy had to embrace efforts to change attitudes, not just efforts to make better use of market forces. Just as economic events and policies may have their biggest impact outside the functioning of the economy – as world depression could clear the way for Hitler – so the most effective levers of economic policy sometimes bypass the market and operate on confidence and opinion, expectations and attitudes. In the same way as economists so often neglect goodwill in discussions of industrial economics, so they tend to neglect the prestige, credit, standing, authority – call it what you will – of governments and the ways in which morale and endeavour are affected by factors other than pay.

PRESENTATIONAL DIFFICULTIES

Let me turn next to presentation. This raises problems at two levels, that of the theorist and that of the practitioner.

Theorists may confine themselves to the business of producing theories without much regard to the market for them. But in applying economics in practice, it is impossible to overlook the importance of the consumer. This is obviously true in the short-run sense that one has to have regard to the chances that any attention will be paid to suggested lines of action by those who have it in their power to act on them. It is true also, in a much wider sense: that those parts of economic theory that do not supply useful answers tend to receive little attention in business or government, while those that purport to throw light on practical problems, and point in the direction of specific ways of dealing with them, command respect and interest.

Practitioners face a rather different problem of presentation. Governments are almost as much concerned about what to say and how to say it as about what to do. Indeed, what they say may have more effect on the markets than what they do. They may be given credit for cutting public expenditure by simply announcing that that is their intention even when, as in the first four years of Mrs Thatcher, it continues to increase. Similarly they may be given credit for mastering inflation when all they have done is to contribute to an international depression that brings down import prices. The public reacts to the declared aims of government as presented in speeches, often without close enquiry into the success with which these aims are pursued. This being so, economists can neither ignore how policies are presented nor how market opinion may narrow the scope for government action. Against the extra leverage that skilful presentation of policy may provide must be set the danger that the government may become the prisoner of market opinion, forced to conform to the role assigned to it by that opinion, and so transmuting into rational expectations what would otherwise have no rational foundation.

The issue of presentation is obviously highly important when any major change of policy takes place. If, for example, a more restrictive policy is proposed involving higher taxes, the Minister of Finance needs to see the case presented in persuasive terms so that the government, in turn, can be persuaded and the new policy defended in public debate. There is always a question how the higher taxes can be presented with the minimum damage to the credit and authority of the government and its capacity to carry through the rest of its programme. What is to be said and how is it to be said? The handling and presentation of the decision is part of the decision itself and cannot be dismissed as irrelevant to it. It is partly because this is so that it becomes difficult to find a use for those parts of economic theory that are not easily translated into simple language.

Taxation provides many illustrations of the problem of presentation. I can remember Chief Festus of Nigeria recounting how he had to withdraw a tax on cosmetics because, as he explained, holding up a large, pudgy hand, 'I burnt my fingers'. In Britain the Selective Employment Tax introduced in 1965 was withdrawn six years later, in part at least because the refined economic logic by which it was justified did not make sense to the general public. Or take corporation tax. Economists might agree that there is no strong case in theory to have a corporation tax at all.

But a proposal to abolish the tax would certainly be laughed out of court by politicians and would be unintelligible to the general public.

In stressing presentation and acceptability, I should not want to be interpreted as defending mere sycophancy and time-serving, automatic approval of any act of policy that is likely to gain popular approval and command a Parliamentary majority. Neither Parliament nor the public has any prerogative of wisdom in economic affairs, whatever democratic theory may imply, and the test of sound policy can never be made on acceptability alone. On the contrary, the economist is wise to be on his guard, as Marshall emphasized, when his views are popular and all men speak well of him.[10] He owes it to his profession to speak up for what he thinks right, to denounce policies that he thinks mistaken and to try to persuade those in power of the dangers they run if his advice is neglected. But if he wishes to be heard, he has to learn when to keep his peace and when to press his point. There are times when policies have to be ruled out because the political leadership required for their adoption simply does not exist; and when indeed the policies that seem right to the economist in his study might provoke adverse reactions, of which he has taken little or no account, but would make nonsense of the policies. There are other times when new ideas could fill a political vacuum, and what was previously unacceptable can be taken down from the shelf and put on sale.

In practice, political choices are rarely a matter of good and bad, black and white. They usually turn on a balance of considerations among which economic factors are not decisive. I don't know what undergraduates make of the questions they are asked to decide in three-quarters of an hour in final examinations. But if they have difficulty in coming to firm conclusions they are in good company. One can make a case – and generally quite a respectable case – for a variety of economic policies at any point in time and argument is unlikely to destroy every case but one and leave the surviving case as indisputably 'right'. Economists do notoriously disagree. So what they have to square with their conscience is usually not failure to demonstrate the error of some politician's ways but failure to offer the right degree of resistance, to do battle with the right degree of conviction, to use what Lord Roberthall once designated 'the right tone of voice'. Like the lawyer, the economist comes to see the case that can be made for and against, and loses the campaigning spirit with which he set out. He has to be forever pointing out that things are not quite so simple as politicians suppose, forever dwelling on the hidden snags. Policies cease to be right or wrong, but just better or worse, and often only marginally so. The occupational disease that he has to fight is not time serving but atrophy of conviction and the sense of commitment.

NON-ECONOMIC FACTORS IN ECONOMIC POLICY

I come next to the implications of the obvious fact that the policies of governments are by definition a political matter. If you are considering what governments should do, you can hardly avoid taking account of what sort of government you have, and how much government you want. It makes quite a difference whether you have been brought up to regard the government as Santa Claus, Stalin, or a dog fight. One government may be benevolent, another dictatorial, a third incapable of making up its mind. All of them have the failings of their human components, ministerial and bureaucratic.

Governments are political animals, moved by political considerations. They have to ask themselves what they *can* do and this may rule out many otherwise attractive lines of action. There are commitments by which they are bound – to other governments, to particular interests, to the party supporting them in office. They hesitate to fly in the face of prevalent attitudes and opinions. They are more conscious of immediate pressures and short-term considerations than of what is desirable in the long run and usually prefer to put off the evil day. Even when they are anxious to do the 'right' thing, as a surprising number are, or when they give priority to long-term objectives over short, they tend to do so with an obstinacy fatal to their hopes: either because they lack understanding of the appropriate sticking-points, or because they hesitate to give ground for fear of unsettling opinion and losing the support they need. One of the most difficult problems in policy making is to know how far to persist and when to bend. Overcommitment can be worse than opportunism.

In any event, the economist has to recognize that policy does not take shape in a vacuum but within a machine that has several well-defined organizational characteristics with which he would do well to become acquainted. Government is not a simple optimizing activity that can be reduced to a second differential in a mathematical equation. It is more likely to be a collection of bald-headed and somewhat bewildered men sitting round a table, harassed and short of time, full of doubts and dogmatism, with all the strengths and failings of successful politicians. Such men may survive for a long time without any policy at all except in the form of a series of specific responses to matters forced on their attention and calling for immediate decision.

If, therefore, the economist wants to influence policy and asks where policy is formed, the answer may be either anywhere or nowhere. It is not unknown for political theorists studying a government department to come to the conclusion that no intelligible answer can be given to the question: 'who forms policy?' A succession of battles on a succession of issues may rage within or between departments, involving different groups at different times, and there may be no consistency in the outcome of their debates except what is imposed in ignorance by some later historian. Or decisions may be taken low down in the hierarchy by someone who is unaware that he has taken any decision at all (such as the decision to do nothing); and although the matter may be fought out at increasingly exalted levels until it reaches the Cabinet, ministers may have no option but to accept the inevitable, even if so little disposed to recognize their own impotence that they go through the charade of further debate and carefully minuted decision. It is one of the curiosities of government how frequently what is plainly due to the force of events is attributed to free and deliberate choice.

This is not to say that policy itself is a hallucination and not worth bothering about. What governments do can hardly be discussed in such a ludicrous fashion. The point is rather that one has to understand the scope for policy, the times at which it may be influenced, and the pressures that govern it. Similarly, one has to have some awareness of the bureaucratic atmosphere within which economic problems arise and have to be tackled. That atmosphere is somewhat different from the comparative calm of university life. Many years ago I described how 'the various divisions in many government departments (were) loosely geared together, uncertain of the limits of their responsibilities, losing and gaining staff almost every week, themselves dissolving from time to time into new divisions or subdivisions, and facing an avalanche of fresh problems on which to advise, fresh cases to decide, and fresh policies to apply'.

No doubt that exaggerates a little; but it brings out some of the features of life with Leviathan that an academic economist might overlook. These features condition the way in which economic theory impinges on policy and limit in particular the chances of drawing on highly complex bits of theory.

Allowance has to be made next for the political setting: the need, if one is in business, to guess what the government will do next, or, if one is in a government department, what is likely to prove feasible and acceptable to a government wishing to stay in office. A wise decision on what should be done cannot be based on economic reasoning or models that pay no regard to the distribution of political power, the frame of mind of the public, or the political ambitions and anxieties of the party in office.

Suppose, for example, that one thinks, like one of my distinguished Cambridge colleagues, that the economic situation calls for the use of import restrictions. One may begin by setting out the economic arguments.

Then one has to reflect on the political situation. If on January 1, 1973, Britain has just joined the European Economic Community, one has to ask whether it makes sense to urge ministers *a week later* to introduce import restrictions that will fall heavily on imports from Common Market countries. If in June 1975 a referendum is to be held on continued membership of the Community and the Cabinet is split down the middle on the issue, one has again to ask if it makes sense to press the Chancellor, just ahead of the referendum, to budget in April for import restrictions, especially if the identical remedy was appropriate two years earlier in very different circumstances. If the advice is accepted and an international row brings on a run on the pound, how is the Chancellor to explain to the IMF that he acted in the interests of greater stability in the exchange rate, and how is he to put it to his continental colleagues – most of them struggling with heavier unemployment than Britain – that he felt compelled by the intolerable level of unemployment to set aside his treaty obligations.

It is not only the organizational and political setting that is important. Economic problems have also to be seen in their institutional setting. It is (or should be) impossible to discuss monetary policy without regard to the kind of banking system and methods of credit control in operation, just as it is or should be impossible to discuss wage theory without regard to the way in which wage bargains are struck and bringing in various kinds of legislation affecting bargaining power (for example, in relation to minimum wages, the powers and practices of trade unions and employers' associations, redundancy, labour mobility, and so on).

Frank Knight in his latter days used to agonize over the futility of being an economist. He doubted whether society would ever take advantage of anything he had to contribute to the solution of its problems. Others like Max Planck have turned away from economics because of its appalling complexity. Others again have given up in despair of arriving at finality: they are repelled by the inconclusiveness of the subject – what Wicksell called 'the permanent state of war'[11] between diametrically opposed views neither of which is ever vanquished or disappears from the field as would happen with the natural sciences. There is no received body of doctrine – only a 'technique of thinking'.

In spite of what I have said about the limitations of economic theory as a guide to policy, the contribution it can make seems to me none the less invaluable. Any doubts on that score are soon quelled by life among non-economists in positions of power. Moreover, the very inconclusiveness of economics has its value as a preparation for the world of affairs where the same inconclusiveness rules. In government and business there is rarely a conclusive answer; instead there is an equally enduring 'state of war'.

The evidence on which an answer might be reached, even on matters of fact, tends also to be inconclusive since there is rarely any finality in the statistical data that purport to summarize the facts. It is necessary to decide between alternatives in the light of uncertain and often contradictory evidence. The decision, it is true, rarely turns exclusively on economic considerations. But it is a great advantage to be able to assess the force of these considerations, just as it is also a great advantage to be able to test the data with the kind of insight into the underlying relationships at work that economic theory engenders.

In the application of economics to practical problems, that kind of insight needs to be reinforced by imagination and accurate observation. Imagination is kindled by good theory but is powerless or mischievous if fed with inadequate or inaccurate information. In the social sciences there is no substitute for getting the facts right, and observation ranks at least as high as logic. Most theoreticians tend to treat far too lightly the difficulty of obtaining and presenting the information necessary to a sound decision. If you want to understand how the economy works, you need to have an eye for the information that matters; and since the unexpected keeps happening you need very up-to-date information. An economist like Keynes may owe his reputation to his originality as a theorist; but in my judgement he stands out from the other economists of his time at least as much for his flair in picking on significant statistics, often from relatively obscure sources before anybody else, and piecing them together by conjectural arithmetic to reveal a danger not then fully appreciated. Other economists of the first rank commonly have a similar power to startle with unfamiliar figures that give a new perspective to events.

Those who have done their homework thoroughly, and have mastered every scrap of information likely to be of assistance will be of little use, however, without the imagination to conceive of alternative policies and visualize the reasons why they may not work as expected. They may fail to make use of available information because they do not appreciate its relevance and overlook or misconstrue important relationships. For example, price control is obviously not enough by itself to remove the danger of inflation in wartime. But it required considerable imagination in World War II to invent three new devices for that purpose: postwar credits (an acceptable form of forced saving); points rationing (the circulation of a new currency to be used exclusively for the purchase of rationed goods); and subsidies to stabilize the prices of key commodoties, making up a kind of iron ration. All these were expedients, not intended to last indefinitely, but they did contribute to a general stabilization of incomes and prices.

CONCLUSIONS

It has been part of my theme that economics has more to offer by way of analysis than prescription. So it is hardly surprising that I should have few proposals for improving the state of affairs I have described. I have three rather modest suggestions.

The first can be put in a word: circulate. The practitioners need to mix with the theorists and vice versa. More than that – the practitioners need to be given a chance to catch up with theoretical developments by release from time to time from their duties. They should be offered sabbatical leave, or enabled to attend conferences or at the very least given time to read the journals. They also need encouragement and opportunities to make their own contributions to current theoretical controversy. Conversely, the academics need a modicum of experience of policy formulation. A spell in government or business can do wonders in changing the outlook of a theorist on the best way of spending his time, on the choice of problems to study, and on the limits within which action can be taken. In some countries, however, including my own, it has become more difficult to move in and out of government. Twenty years ago a remarkably high proportion of top British economists had had experience of service in government. Today there is very little circulation. That seems to me a step in the wrong direction.

Secondly I think we need to revalue and upgrade the work of intermediaries between the profession and the public. Financial journalism, for example, is an increasingly demanding skill and has become both more sophisticated and professional and more influential since the war. The press also carries articles by professional economists, and a number of specialized publications reprint (or commission) articles by them that help to illuminate current issues. But the mass media are largely untouched by this trend. It may be that nothing can be done about this. But there does seem to me great scope for those economists who have a gift for conveying the thinking of the profession, with all its doubts and dissensions, to the man in the street.

Finally, don't let us be overwhelmed by our disagreements: we have also plenty to agree about. As I have tried to show, it is often the most elementary propositions in economics, on which we all agree, that matter for practical purposes. Similarly, we should not underrate the value of the habits of mind that are nourished by economic analysis, even if they yield no common programme of action. Where we continue to disagree, let us try to understand and narrow our differences, remembering always that we have a duty to our fellow citizens to offer them the best advice we can.

NOTES

1 John Jewkes, 'The economist and public policy', *Lloyds Bank Review*, 28 (April 1953), p. 29.
2 Ely Devons, 'Applied economics – the application of what?', in *Essays in Economics* (George Allen and Unwin, London 1961), pp. 13–14.
3 Devons, 'Applied economics – the application of what?', pp. 25–26.
4 Alec Cairncross, *Essays in Economic Management* (George Allen and Unwin, London, 1971), p. 203.
5 Sir Oliver Franks, *Central Planning and Control in War and Peace* (London School of Economics, London, 1947); Sir Stafford Cripps' exposition appeared anonymously in the *Economic Survey for 1947* (Cmd 7046).
6 Jacob Viner, *The Long View and the Short* (Free Press, Glencoe, 1958), p. 109.
7 Knut Wicksell, *Lectures on Political Economy*, Vol. 1 (George Routledge and Sons, London, 1934), p. 19.
8 E. R. Walker, *From Economic Theory to Economic Policy* (Chicago University Press, Chicago, 1943), p. 57.
9 Keynes to Harrod, *Collected Writings* (1973, pp. 296–297), quoted in Bernard Corry, 'Keynes in the history of economic thought', in *Keynes and Laissez-Faire* (Macmillan, London, 1978), pp. 5–6.
10 Cited by A. C. Pigou, *Memorials of Alfred Marshall* (Macmillan, London, 1925), p. 89.
11 Knut Wicksell, *Selected Papers on Economic Theory* (George Allen and Unwin, London, 1958), p. 52.

2

Academics and policy makers

Economic policy making is an activity like any other activity which involves producers competing to supply a market and consumers hoping to find their wants supplied. Economists may produce ideas and their ideas may be drawn upon at the official or the ministerial level. But what guides policy may have very little to do with the ideas that economists put forward. It may be dominated by non-economic considerations or by the views of non-economists or by doctrines refuted long ago or in widespread disrepute. What economists have to say may be neglected because its bearing on policy is obscure, contested, ambiguous, or insufficiently precise; because economists' conclusions rest on mistaken or inappropriate assumptions; because they are not adapted to the needs of the policy maker; or because, for that or any other reason, they simply fail to gain a hearing. Policy makers, as a rule, are slightly deaf: there is too much noise.

In a seller's market, in which economists are credited with the capacity to change the world and enjoy the prestige that comes with success, these non-economic resistances to the spread of their ideas may be submerged or attenuated. But when events are clearly in the saddle and economists seem impotent, they lose the favour and attention they were previously accorded. Such swings in fashion, so apparent since World War II, are a commonplace of competitive markets.

Market resistances of another kind may also come to the fore through product differentiation. Competition in the supply of a homogeneous product is one thing: economic advice grounded in a common orthodoxy may find unchallenged acceptance. But when economists compete with one another in brands of theory, their hold tends to be confined to their own special market which may or may not embrace the centres of policy making.

Paper delivered at conference on *Changing Perceptions of Economic Policy* at St. Peter's College, Oxford, in 1981, and published in volume with that title (Methuen, London, 1981).

It is easy for economists to bury themselves in research and development and lose themselves in admiration of their products regardless of any link with policy. But product development, whether it relates to stabilization and demand management or to the labour market, or any of the matters discussed in the papers to be presented at our conference, is only part of the business. If we are to master our trade thoroughly we need to study the market and its characteristics, the way in which policies take shape and gain acceptance, the changes that are in progress among producers and consumers and the role of intermediaries between the two.

THE MARKET IN 1911

Let us start by looking at the consumers. Seventy years ago their requirements were modest. Ministers felt in no need of the services of professional experts. The objectives of government were limited, readily translated into policy measures and essentially long term so that there was ample time for debate of the underlying issues and the decisions to be taken were infrequent and lacking in complexity. There was no suggestion that the government should manage the economy, which was seen as fundamentally self-regulating. Since market forces were taken to be almost wholly beneficent there was correspondingly limited scope for government intervention to promote economic growth; the idea of using public works in order to stabilize employment had just surfaced; inflation was a matter for the (privately owned) Bank of England rather than the Treasury; protection and subsidies to particular industries were alike anathema; the welfare state lay almost entirely over the horizon.

The limited scale of government operations seventy years ago is evident from the size of the budget. In 1911 the rate of income tax had only recently been raised dramatically by Lloyd George from 1/- to 1/2d. Current expenditure by public authorities, central and local, was running at £200 million, a year – about 10 per cent of GNP – and about half of that went in paying for past wars in debt interest or possible future wars in defence expenditure. It would have been unthinkable that manual workers should be asked to pay income tax (though not at all unthinkable that they should pay indirect taxes or that indirect taxes should be the main source of government revenue).

The same point can be made in terms of employment. The central government employed 1.5 per cent of the working population (excluding the armed forces which were rather more numerous) and the local authorities employed just over 3.5 per cent (including teachers, police, etc.). There were less than a million workers, full-time and part-time, in the two groups together. But things were changing fast, for in the previous twenty years the number had more than trebled.[1]

Under these circumstances it is hardly surprising that in 1911 practically no government or government department had ever knowingly hired a professional economist. The central government machine in Britain (as in India) was minuscule. Governments employed few administrators and were even more sparing in their use of experts of any kind. There were years, even in the 1930s, when there were no new entrants to the Administrative Class of the British Civil Service. The Treasury got along before World War I with an administrative staff of twenty (many of whom survived into their nineties). It is true that they included Hawtrey and for a time Keynes. But neither Hawtrey nor Keynes ever sat a university examination in economics and neither would have described himself in 1911 as an economist.

The same absence of demand was apparent in business. The typical business was small and felt little in need of advice from economists. The first multinationals had just been born; macro-economics had not. The market environment, uncomplicated by sporadic and widespread government intervention, was more stable, more predictable, and above all, more comprehensible.

The lack of demand was mirrored on the side of supply. Virtually no British economist (except Bowley?) held a PhD or other higher degree in economics before World War I. In the 1930s when Cambridge was the leading centre of economic study in the world, no member of the staff had a higher degree in economics and at the beginning of the decade there was no living PhD in economics of the University. Indeed when Ronald Walker was awarded the degree in 1933, the research students who had come up the previous year gave him a dinner to celebrate. The number of chairs in economics in the entire country was not more than about twenty, some universities having none at all. Had the government set out to recruit a dozen trained economists of academic standing it would have had a hard time.

Not that the government thought of doing any such thing. Economists busied themselves teaching and the government went on administering, without any interchange between the two except in wartime. Now and again an economist would be appointed to a committee of inquiry or a Royal Commission and the report might be acted upon after the usual lag of a generation. Communication was either at the personal level, or through the press. There might be contact at meetings of the Royal Statistical Society or of the Political Economy Club. But in general the few economists who took an interest in policy had to content themselves with a letter to *The Times* if they wanted to bring their views to the attention of the public.

The economic and financial press was less rudimentary. Business news was carried in the more serious newspapers and the subject of comment in the daily press, in *The Economist* and *The Statist* among the weeklies and in some of the magazines and journals like *The Banker*. But there was very little that would pass as economic analysis and nearly all the commentators with any detailed knowledge were interested in specific industries or specific problems. None of the financial journalists would have claimed any standing as an economist except possibly Sir Robert Giffen (who gave up financial journalism long before 1900), Hartley Withers, the editor of *The Economist*, or his successor Walter Layton.

The fact is that contemporary issues of policy rarely called for refined economic analysis. In any event, economics as a subject was not designed for immediate application to practical issues. The matters of controversy in economic policy had been largely confined to issues about the currency (paper money and the return to gold in 1821, regulation of the banks, bimetallism, centralization of the gold reserves) or protection (the Corn Laws, Imperial Preference) or income distribution (the relief of poverty, progressive taxation, etc.). Many of these controversies had been forgotten or were regarded as settled and those that were still active were highly political. Few of them featured in what textbooks there were, and there were very few. Economics did not supply ready-made answers to the problems posed in these controversies. It was essentially 'a moral science and not a natural science' in that it employed 'introspection and judgements of value'.[2] It was a preparation for thinking about economic problems through the construction of models from which the real values of the variables were necessarily missing. As customarily taught and studied, it was an exercise in logic that was almost always long-term logic and had little or no bearing on the day-to-day problems confronting government.

An important reason for the abstract character of economics was the limited availability of statistics. Indices of prices and wages were in their infancy; production statistics, as Giffen complained, hardly existed (the results of the first Census of Production were just appearing); calculations of the national income and the balance of payments were primitive and unfamiliar; nobody had ever heard of the terms of trade, or domestic capital formation, or the public sector borrowing requirement. A large proportion of the available statistics were annual or even decennial. Any picture of what was happening to the economy from month to month would inevitably have been impressionistic and non-quantitative. Even what data existed were rarely pieced together so as to introduce some degree of coherence and consistency.

THE MARKET TODAY

Things have obviously changed a great deal since 1911. The pace has been set by demand but, as usual, demand and supply have interacted on one another. Economists have been diligent in proposing new activities for government, in detecting weaknesses within both the private and public sector, and in propounding the need for management of the entire economy, whatever the line of division between the two sectors. We need not enquire here into the reasons for the enlargement and growing complexity of government operations nor detail the part played by economists in the changes that have occurred. We need only note the contrast with seventy years earlier. Government expenditure now absorbs half the national income. Nearly half the capital investment of the country is public investment. The aims of government have become far more ambitious, its responsibilities far heavier, its influence enormously more extensive. Governments control or seek to control the level and direction of economic activity. They are involved, in an increasingly detailed and complex manner, in almost every kind of economic activity in the discharge of one or more of their various functions: either in carrying on the activity itself or in regulating the terms on which it can be carried on or in buying the product or in taxing any profit that is made or in many other ways.

They are involved because they have an active economic policy in pursuit of the objectives of growth, stability, greater economic equality, etc. for which previously they took little or no responsibility. It is not only that the scale of their activities has grown. It is that these activities are largely dominated by economic factors, that it is increasingly difficult to secure consistency and coherence in the whole range of activities, and that many of the issues calling for decision are highly complex. The more control over the economy is centralized the greater the need for expert analysis of these issues; and naturally economists regard themselves as equipped to fill the role. We shall discuss later how far that self-confidence is justified.

But of course it is not only in government that the need for expert advice on complex economic issues arises. Business is faced with the same problems, largely because it has to reckon with the activities of government. While the economists in government seek to unravel the mysteries of the private sector and what it will do, business economists bend to the even heavier task of unravelling the mystery of what governments will do. Economists come to be recognized as the great map readers of the modern economy, without whom navigation is far more difficult and, as a result, the demand for their services expands steadily.

There has also been an expansion in export demand and in distribution. If economic management was in its infancy before the war, international economic management had not even been born. In the last generation new international agencies by the dozen have sprung up, the multinationals of the economics business. Since their functions are almost exclusively economic, it is hardly surprising if they have raided the economics profession throughout the world for staff. In addition, an important export industry has grown up: the advanced countries supply economic advisers to the less developed and offer in their universities and institutes training in economics for foreign students.

Another type of expansion takes the form of intermediation. If policy is dominated by economics and framed by economists, the public has a natural curiosity in what is going on. There is a need for economists who can translate what their fellow economists are saying into language intelligible to the layman and communicate their contentions through the press, on the radio, on television, and in other ways.

It is not a long step from intermediation to missionary activities. The economist in government is looked to for a gospel that will permit consensus. The economist in business is expected to provide a rationale for the life of the businessman. The economist abroad is welcomed as an up-to-date replacement for the medicine man. The economist employed by the media is supplied with a pulpit and asked to produce a weekly flow of sermons.

We turn next to the impact on economics and on economists of the new market environment. The main effect can be summed up as professionalization. It is now increasingly taken for granted that a professional economist will have a higher degree in the subject. Where not so long ago a chair in economics might be filled by someone without even a first degree, now applicants are expected as a rule to have a second. Very little that an economist had to say seventy years ago was unintelligible to the layman. Now very little is intelligible. The expansion of the market has also had the usual effect on the division of labour. Separate markets break off and are supplied by transport economists, health economists, monetary economists and a long list of other specialists. More and more journals cater for each group of specialists; and more and more use a language, including the language of mathematics, that confines the readership to a priestly few even when the issue under discussion affects the lay multitude. However, a parallel process allows each issue to be treated in ascending order of professional sophistication in the daily press, the trade press, the bank review, the conference paper and the learned journal. Communication is still possible between different groups of economists and between them and the weaker brethren in politics, business or ordinary life.

At the same time the sharp division between those on the inside and those outside the policy making machine has been greatly softened. There was a time in many countries – and it remains true in some – that economists in the universities were concerned primarily with ideology and eternal verities. A visitor to Japan would be asked on arrival whether he was a Marxist or a Keynesian as if economics were a form of religious belief. On the other hand, the Bank of Japan and the Ministry of Finance employed economists whose work was indispensable to economic policy making. In Britain in the interwar period there might be a few grandees within the machine who held the title of Economic Adviser, one or two like Sir Sydney Chapman who were academic economists and others like Sir Frederick Leith Ross who were not. The beginnings of an association between economists in academic posts and the business of economic advising go back to the Economic Advisory Council and the Committee on Economic Information which emerged from its entrails. In war and postwar years the Economic Section of the Cabinet Office (from 1953 of the Treasury) brought academic economists within the administrative machinery of government much as, in the United States, the Council of Economic Advisers marked a decisive change. But the existence of the Economic Section did not by itself guarantee movement between academic life and government. That movement on a regular footing came later, when in the 1950s and 1960s provision was made for recruitment of economists on a two to five year basis and when, under the Labour government of 1964–70, large numbers of economists entered government departments, usually on temporary appointments.

There is therefore, in Britain and other countries, an increased reliance on expert economic advice, tendered by people who regard themselves as professional economists and may expect to resume an academic career in due course. In some countries, however, there is no deliberate segregation of economists from other administrators and efforts are made to ensure that those who discharge economic functions have at least an elementary knowledge of economics.

Whatever the position in government, banking (and especially central banking) and big business generally make extensive use of staff trained in economics and no longer confine such staff to the assembly of economic information, speech writing, etc. A large and growing component of management in every sphere is literate or numerate in economics. And there is far more coming and going between the universities, business, banking and government than there used to be.

If economists have come to regard themselves more as practitioners, they have also had to recast their subject in more operational terms. This means, first and foremost, an increased preoccupation with problems of the short term; secondly, an enormous expansion in data analysis via econometrics; and thirdly, an effort to narrow the gulf between the empyrean of pure logic and the nitty gritty of the real world. Success in all these efforts is of course contingent on a recognition that economics is by no means the whole story and that there are other studies of human behaviour with which economics has to make common cause. There is space for only a few illustrations of how these changes are working out and how the teaching of the subject still fails to prepare economists for the realities of economic policy making.

An example of the first is economic forecasting. The horizon of such forecasting is usually limited to eighteen to twenty-four months so that the models on which the forecasts rest incorporate short-term relationships. These relationships had not been the subject of any extensive investigation before the 1930s partly because much of the necessary data did not exist but more fundamentally because the focus of government policy was traditionally long term. It is hardly necessary to point out that the kind of economic analysis used in, say, the *Economic Review* of the National Institute of Economic and Social Research or the *Economic Outlook* of the London Business School is almost entirely postwar.

The need for economic forecasting arose out of the change in government objectives after the White Paper on Employment Policy (Cmnd 6527) in 1944. Forecasting is a tool of management indispensable to the framing of policy; and it was the development of economic management under the influence of Keynesian ideas that produced so much emphasis on economic forecasting. Whether Keynes himself would have approved of this emphasis is another matter.

So far as the training of young economists is concerned, the preoccupation with the short term has obvious drawbacks. It involves a concentration on shifting and uncertain relationships, an immersion in masses of statistics and refined statistical analysis and a preoccupation with macro-economic model building that make heavy intellectual demands on comparative beginners and may work to the detriment of the more historical and philosophical elements in an understanding of the economy.

Economic forecasting leads inevitably into econometrics to which somewhat similar comments apply. Given the vast amount of economic data it is difficult to see how it can be handled satisfactorily without econometric analysis. The danger is that a greater degree of permanence and weight may be attached to the values of the parameters than is justified. As we all know, a variety of explanations, however dressed up in mathematics, may fit the facts almost equally well. Keynes would certainly have wished to warn us against over-investment in techniques more appropriate to the natural sciences especially if this were done in order to make economics more scientific than it really is.

It is when we turn to the gap between the generalizations of theory and the complexities of real life that the major problems arise. Since illustrations of the gap will abound in other papers it is unnecessary to dwell at length on it here. Three important characteristics of theory limit its value to the policy maker.

First of all, theory starts from definite and stated assumptions and follows its own logic to the bitter end. It assumes that we know exactly where we are, free from uncertainty of the kind so familiar to policy makers when, for example, the figures are not available, are inconsistent with one another, or are subject to seasonal and other adjustments that are themselves uncertain. From precise assumptions theory allows us to draw precise conclusions. But the policy maker cannot rest content with hypotheses. He has to take the situation as he finds it, in all its vagueness and uncertainty, and decide what to do about it. Action to deal with a specific problem takes precedence over intellectual speculation that is free to begin and end where it chooses.

There is the further difficulty that theory is content to handle things one at a time that do not arise in this isolated condition in the real world. Where, for example, activities form part of a network or system, the cost or price of each activity cannot be arrived at in abstraction from the way the different activities are interconnected within the network. The young economist who has been taught all about marginal cost is rarely prepared for the complexities that arise in trying to apply the theory to the pricing policy of public utilities and nationalized industries: all the more because he is not warned that there is a multiplicity of margins to be considered, not just a simple margin at the production frontier. The fact that real world decisions are interrelated with one another makes them much harder to take than the one-at-a-time decisions of the textbooks.

Economic theory is also no more than a partial analysis of human behaviour. But those who have to manage an economy or a business have to deal with real men and women whose responses to policy may not be those postulated by theorists. How a policy works depends to some extent upon how it is received; and Ministers who have occasion to consult their economic advisers may show at least as much interest in the likely response as in the case for the policy itself. Economists now show more interest in how expectations are formed. But economic theory has little or nothing to say about other aspects of behaviour upon which economic performance may be critically dependent: for example, the mood of the working man; his attitude to his job, his employers and society at large; his readiness to accept technical and other forms of change; his fits of bloody-mindedness and militancy.

Even if a problem is the subject of some branch of economic theory, we are not necessarily much the wiser in deciding what to do about it. It is only too easy to confuse the economic context of awkward social problems and the ability of economists to solve them. The fact that economic development changes economic magnitudes, for example, does not make economic development respond to the instruments of economic policy. It may respond more readily to quite different things: preservation of law and order; political leadership; contact with abroad. Similarly, while inflation is an economic phenomenon, the causes of inflation do not necessarily lie in some form of economic malfunctioning. There may be very little that economists can contribute to its control.

CONTEMPORARY PROBLEMS

Let us turn next to the problems posed by the expansion of the market and by the sheer scale and complexity of modern policy making.

One of the central problems, if not *the* central problem, is the information explosion. The volume of statistics has grown inordinately and there are whole digests which are hardly ever looked at. An over-abundance of raw material is not, however, a source of great difficulty. What matters is the torrent of comment and analysis at all levels from the purest of pure theory to articles in the daily press. Seventy years ago there was a single economic journal in the United Kingdom and perhaps half a dozen others in the rest of the world. Now there are more journals than any economist could name, much less read, and the number continues to grow. It is said that, on the average, articles published in a learned journal have about five readers each. What is certain is that nobody can hope to read more than a very small fraction of what appears and that the fraction diminishes the further we move from theory to policy. No less massive are the official papers of all kinds: reports of government committees and testimony before them, bulletins, press releases, speeches, answers to parliamentary questions, etc., etc. Then there are the bank reviews, the writings of financial journalists, letters to the editor, press reports and contributed articles. And all this has to be multiplied by the number of countries issuing relevant material, either at the theoretical level or on economic affairs. With such a din going on it is almost a matter of chance what one hears.

A number of consequences follow. One is that books give way to articles and articles to abstracts. Economists read a decreasing number of books annually from the time they embark on their studies and (for a time at least) an increasing number of articles. Policy makers rarely read books on economics although there is one ex-Minister who read three well-known textbooks on a long sea voyage and one ex-permanent secretary who took Marshall's *Principles* with him to Naples to read on holiday.

A second consequence is specialization. It becomes almost inevitable that economists who have to select what they read, as we all do, should come increasingly to limit their field of view. Yet we are all conscious that in an economic system everything interacts and we can only understand the parts by keeping an eye on the whole.

Another consequence is increased dependence on word of mouth. Ideas circulate much faster in personal contact than when one is ploughing almost at random through the 'literature'. In any event Ministers and officials have rarely time to read the 'literature' and would have difficulty in understanding it or in extracting from it new ideas relevant to policy. Even economists in government service can devote very little time to study of the learned journals and tend to draw heavily on intellectual capital accumulated earlier or derived from their own recent experience. Hence they are always at the mercy of obsolescence and of such contacts as they are able to preserve with economists who are still in academic life or at least have enough leisure and incentive to follow current theoretical controversy. Not that government economists fail to develop their own theory: sometimes they do so in advance of other thinkers because the pressure is greater and the material more readily available.

A third consequence is the rise of the conference. If ideas circulate best by word of mouth, conferences are an effective way of spreading them. Some of us who have virtually abandoned reading find conferences an ideal way of catching up or, more commonly, catching a glimpse of changes in progress. But even conferences have their limitations. If the natural sciences are anything to go by, we may yet see conferences of 10,000 or more at which the authors of the main papers are given ten minutes to make their contribution while other authors line the walls of the corridors leading to the lecture room with typed summaries and abstracts for their colleagues to glance at on their way to the next session.

The information explosion is coupled with an enormous expansion in numbers. The universities turn out economists of one kind or another by the thousand every year and some hundreds of them go on to advanced study and a professional career in government, finance or industry. Similarly the business of management in each of these spheres expands the number of consumers, many of them themselves trained economists.

It is a nice question how demand and supply should be married within the policy making machine. Should there be strict segregation within two separate career structures, the economists within an economic service and the administrators and managers within a separate administrative or managerial structure? The answer depends in part on the nature of economic expertise and how easily it can be disengaged from the other forms of expertise and knowledge necessary to administration and management.

The tradition until the 1930s and the later coming of econometrics was that the arguments as well as the conclusions of economists should be capable of being expounded and defended in terms within the comprehension of the intelligent layman. There was very little that mattered in economic theory that could not be mastered by the layman in the course of his career as he came face to face with one economic problem after another. The idea that a short period of study of the subject in late adolescence gave a man an invincible advantage over those who had wrestled for a couple of decades with the matters discussed in the textbooks would have seemed somewhat questionable. There were no doubt some controversial issues of great complexity where it was useful to consult leading economists in some form of Economic Advisory Council or Committee. But until the postwar period, administrators were assumed to be capable of advising on economic, as on other, issues without the assistance of professional colleagues; and the only professional economists in Whitehall were those attached to the Committee on Economic Information.

In the postwar period a different balance was struck and the Economic Section was continued in being first under James Meade and then under Robert Hall. The basic assumption was that a small group of economists would be able to inject economic advice at the point where the key decisions were being formulated and would at the same time help to educate their colleagues in modern economic analysis. Since economists become progressively out of date and the difference between the technical expert and the layman tends to narrow, provision was also made for a circulation of economists between academic life and Whitehall, usually on the basis of a two year spell in the Treasury. This had the double advantage of familiarizing an increasing number of economists with the practical issues of economic policy and bringing fresh minds and fresh ideas to those issues.

Over the past decade all this has changed and it is very doubtful whether it has changed for the better. The circulation of economists between universities and departments has virtually ceased. A growing economic service advises on a diminishing number of decisions alongside administrators who are increasingly sophisticated in economic issues. Is there really scope for a hundred economists in the Bank of England and nearly as many in the Treasury or are they not inevitably steered into research functions better carried on elsewhere or alternatively under-employed and disgruntled as policy advisers? Would it not be preferable to lay more stress on picking qualified economists to fulfil administrative roles and devoting more effort to the training of administrators in economics? Is there not something to be said for limiting the role of economists in government to advising on the major issues and drawing for this purpose on the leading academics, with no more than a quite limited number of economists spending their entire career in Whitehall?

Whether because of the scale and complexity of modern policy making or for other reasons there is a strong tendency toward oversimplification of the issues and their resolution in ideological terms. The public, the government and, from time to time, economists too grasp at fashionable nostrums and give direction to policy by espousing one myth after another. In the postwar period the British have taken as exemplars a succession of countries of whose institutions, attitudes and policies they were grossly ignorant. First came the United States to which productivity teams were despatched soon after the war: efforts were then made to match American achievements in technical development that were out of keeping with the commercial limitations of the British economy. Then came France and the French system of indicative planning. Why the British who had learned all that needed to be known about planning in wartime should have been so fascinated by French planning just when it was about to enter an inevitable decline is a great mystery. Since then, Germany and Japan have been held up to admiration. The one country whose achievements are belittled and largely ignored is the United Kingdom.

The role of myth and fashion is even more apparent in the succession of policies in favour. There are recurrent themes which it is not possible to do more than mention. Planning first of all: often to the neglect of such planning as was really possible or of circumstances that made the plan itself an absurdity; rarely with any recognition of the simple truth that the essence of good planning is re-planning since planning has to be a continuous process and is, at bottom, a way of handling uncertainties. Investment next: as if investment would not occur naturally if other conditions of growth were present. Emphasis on investment was the lazy economist's way of sticking to parameters he could introduce into his models and turning his back on the non-economic factors limiting the return to be expected from new equipment. Then stop-go, blamed for the level of investment which was said to be low but which, seen as a fluctuation around a disappointing trend, was no worse than in other countries: in retrospect, it was not without some advantages as an anti-inflationary device. Devaluation and floating rates, one or other of them regarded as a cure-all and now dismissed just as foolishly as curing nothing at all. Export-led growth, the last survivor from the testament of postwar growth: no doubt a credible doctrine if one believes in the sovereign value of an expanding manufacturing sector but not particularly easy to bring about under British conditions and now regarded as disastrous when the export that makes the running is North Sea oil. Finally, and far more disastrous than any of these, a return to the myths of the past, when governments had not yet learnt to lend an ear to economists, the quantity theory of money and its corollaries.

THE EXTENT OF ECONOMISTS' INFLUENCE

The influence of economists on policy fluctuates and it is never easy to say what that influence is. There are many economists and among them are always some whose views are in keeping with those of the government in office. But coincidence of view is no proof of influence. On the other hand who can say from what source Ministers draw their inspiration? And whatever the source, who can be confident of tracing the impact of Ministers on the march of events? It is all too easy to gain credit by making speeches or taking measures in support of outcomes that are already in the bag. The writings of economists may equally appear to exercise a dominant influence when they are little more than a Greek chorus to events that have a quite different origin. No one could deny the great influence of Keynes: but there are good grounds for doubting whether the acceptance of Keynesian ideas would have done much to accelerate economic recovery in Britain from 1932 onwards and for attributing most of the success of governments in maintaining full employment after World War II to other circumstances.

Yet governments do listen to economists, particularly those who claim to know what should be done. Once they give priority to controlling inflation, governments are inevitably less attracted to theories in which inflation does not figure and are readier to accept, for the time being, doctrines assigning little or no role to governments in relation to other objectives, such as full employment, faster growth, balance of payments equilibrium, etc.

So far as the public is concerned, the standing of economists, at its zenith in the thirty years after the war, is now back again at its pre-war low. But it is not only economists who have lost influence. We live in a society in which all forms of management and leadership, however advised, are under constant challenge. Constructive efforts can be frustrated and brought to a halt with remarkable ease and in a multitude of different ways. The power of the negative is in the ascendant. Consensus and cohesion in the execution of policy are increasingly hard to achieve. In wartime a common effort was possible because there was a predisposition to common sacrifices. Even in peacetime such a predisposition is an essential ingredient in the life of the community if it is to survive as a community. Without a readiness to make sacrifices a country can neither face the burden of change – which imposes sacrifices – nor reach the compromises that allow it to keep in temper.

Where shibboleths and myths do duty for reasoned argument any sacrifices called for are seen out of perspective and the management of the economy is correspondingly more difficult. Debate can descend to the non-professional level with marches, demos, violence and eventually terrorism. Or it can be left at the political level in parliamentary debate and lobbying by pressure groups. There can be no abstracting from the exercise of power in any of these ways. But there is room also for professional debate and economists have a duty to organize such debate so that at least the intellectual merits of different lines of policy are made clear to all concerned. If we are to do battle with the Minotaur in the maze of economic policy we need to be assured of the reliability of the thread that guides us.

There are a number of ways in which, over the past ten years or so, improvements in the organization of debate have been made. For example:

1 The National Institute now runs a series of conferences in conjunction with the ESRC on controversial issues and publishes the proceedings. These conferences have much in common with the panel meetings preceding the publication of Brookings Economic Papers but are more elaborate and less regular.
2 The ESRC also supports a number of specialized study groups bringing together economists from different places with an interest in particular subject areas.
3 Although the London and Cambridge Economic Service is no more, the Clare Group of economists operates in a similar way, issuing a critique of current policy in the *Midland Bank Review* after discussion among themselves.
4 The new system of Select Committees of the House of Commons brings together more frequently than before the views of economists and others on current economic policy.
5 The press devotes much more space to contributions from economists on issues of policy.
6 There are the publications of various bodies studying econom[illegible] policy: the National Institute, the London Business School

Economic Policy Group, the Institute of Fiscal Studies, the Trade Policy Research Centre, the Policy Studies Institute.

In these and other ways there are now ample facilities for debate – far better than at any previous period. It is for economists to make use of these facilities and with the help of the media raise the level of public understanding of policy alternatives. They cannot complain that the remaining market imperfections deny them a hearing.

NOTES

1 M. Abramovitz and V. Eliasberg, *The Growth of Public Employment* (NBER, Princeton, 1957).

2 J. M. Keynes to R. F. Harrod, 1938, in J. M. Keynes, *Collected Writings*, Vol. XIV (Macmillan, London, 1973), pp. 296–297; quoted by Professor B. Corry in A. P. Thirlwall (ed.) *Keynes and Laissez-Faire* (Macmillan, London, 1978).

3

The market and the state

Modern economics can be said to have begun with the discovery of the market. Although the term 'market economy' had yet to be invented its essential features were outlined in the *Wealth of Nations* which provided us with the first coherent model of an economic system and analysed the role of the market within such a system. Since the days of Adam Smith economists have debated the strength and limitations of market forces and have rejoiced in their superior understanding of these forces.

The state, by contrast, needed no such discovery. Its operations were only too visible and were the subject of constant political debate. It was never argued that the state could be wholly replaced by the market and Adam Smith himself laid stress on the positive functions of the state, e.g. in maintaining order, dispensing justice, providing free compulsory education, and abolishing positions of privilege and monopoly. The criteria he suggested for state activity could be used to justify an extensive programme under modern conditions, however slight the programme he approved in his own time. What he reacted against were the ideas he dismissed as 'mercantilist' which took for granted the need to make use of political power in order to achieve economic ends.

The retreat from mercantilism into *laissez-faire* in the course of the nineteenth century did not originate exclusively in the new-found virtues of the market. It was also that the underlying pressures at work were strongly expansionary and needed the full scope that free markets offered in order to yield their potential benefits to society. The genie of technical change was emerging from the bottle and lending a magic to the market that it had never had before. At the same time the forces of democracy

An earlier version of this paper was delivered at the conference at the University of Glasgow in 1976 to celebrate the bicentenary of the publication of *The Wealth of Nations*, and was included in the volume *The Market and the State*, edited by Thomas Wilson and Andrew Skinner and published after the conference by Oxford University Press.

aroused suspicion of the state as the pillar of autocracy and the *status quo*: if not wielding political power tyrannically, then it was at least unprogressive, bureaucratic, insensitive to the opportunities that markets could exploit.

The retreat from state control never led to complete reliance on market forces: the state did not wither away, although it came much nearer to doing so than under subsequent regimes that have set themselves that objective. The market was allowed more scope and freedom but the state still determined the framework of law and regulation under which private initiative could be exercised to meet market requirements.

The pendulum then swung the other way with the emergence of totalitarian governments, planned economies and the virtual suspension of the price mechanism under war-time conditions. Markets were allowed only a restricted scope by all-powerful governments in full control of the economy. Even with the return of peace and the decline of dictatorship, the role of the state remained extensive. Industrial economies were 'managed' or planned by the state, the public sector expanded, and the welfare state developed along lines that made little use of the market. Where at the beginning of the century public expenditure in the United Kingdom was of the order of 10 per cent of GNP and went mainly on defence or paying for past wars, it has come to be of the order of 40–50 per cent and is with difficulty held within these limits.

Economists played an important part in the shift in opinion. They drew attention to various forms of market failure and to undesirable outcomes of the operation of market forces in the absence of government regulation: high unemployment, volatile rates of interest and exchange, rapid inflation, wide differences in income unrelated to economic performance. Their critique rested on models of a market economy that focused on the ways in which it might operate in conflict with broad social objectives. This appeared to establish a presumption that governments should intervene to resolve the conflict. But of course if one starts at the other end, one can construct models of government behaviour that focus equally convincingly on the weaknesses and failures of market intervention. The proclaimed objects of government are by no means the same as the actual outcome of their operations. If one is trying to come to a balanced judgement it has to be based, as every economist knows, on a full assessment of the alternatives, not on an idealized picture of the state or of the market. The pendulum has now swung back again towards greater reliance on the market. In some quarters the cry is to 'roll back the frontiers of the state'. Industries that have been nationalized are being returned to private ownership. Efforts are being made to reduce the weight of public spending and lighten the burden placed on markets by heavy taxation. Earlier goals of policy requiring action by the state are being reassessed. Inequality of incomes is made to sink in significance in comparison with the need for more powerful incentives such as markets can offer. Responsibility for full employment is shrugged off for one reason or another. The most urgent need is now seen as control of inflation, which in turn is identified with control of the money supply – a job for the central bank rather than the central government.

The reaction is most in evidence where the market was formerly most confined. In China in particular the virtues of the market as a decentralizing agent and as a promoter of enterprise have been rediscovered and put on display. In nearly all Communist countries what is sought is a new equilibrium between state planning and the freedom the market confers. In the West the state is also in retreat – at least for the time being.

There is of course never any question of suppressing completely either the market or the state. The antithesis between the two that is now so common should not blind us to their complementarity. In a planned economy dominated by the state it is still necessary to make use of indicators of social priority and, as a first approximation, market prices are difficult to improve upon. Planning without prices and without some kind of price mechanism is bound to be arbitrary, inconsistent and inefficient. To allocate resources without such a mechanism is a complex and wasteful task; and to devise a pricing mechanism that accords with social values and allows citizens to express those values freely is almost impossible without a market that registers their choices. Similarly, an economy without a governmental framework is a prescription for anarchy. Nobody would seriously propose that the state should refrain from all intervention in the market or, if they did, would be able to explain how it could be arranged when the state already *is* the market for a quarter or more of national output.

The only sensible question worth pursuing is the division of labour between the state and the market. For what purposes should market forces be allowed free rein and for what purposes should the state try to regulate or short-circuit them? Are there grounds for expecting that as time moves on, the thrust of market forces will be less powerful or less socially beneficial? Or are there grounds on the other hand for discouraging state intervention because it is increasingly likely to be misdirected, or to cause the market to function less satisfactorily, or to have unfortunate side-effects in the bureaucratic apparatus created, or to transfer or concentrate political power in undesirable ways?

OBJECTIVES THE MARKET MAY NOT SERVE

One reason for the expansion that has taken place in the activities of the state has been the increasing importance attached to objectives of economic policy that the market cannot readily fulfil or cannot fulfil at all.

Equality

One such objective is the promotion of greater economic equality. Historically, the most direct challenge to a system relying on uncontrolled market forces came from those who saw no virtue in the resulting distribution of income. The Marxists in particular pointed out that market forces reflected class structure and that class structure had its own dynamic and would control, and if necessary over-ride, the market in apportioning rewards for economic services. Other economists were bound to agree that, however efficient or indeed indispensable the market in allocating resources to meet consumer demand, the existing pattern of demand was not necessarily in keeping with social justice. Since rich and poor did not compete on equal terms even under so-called 'perfect' competition, the verdict of the market could not be final. Progressive taxation and the welfare state have turned the flank of this line of criticism, although not completely or without cost, since income transfers beyond a certain level react back on the functioning of the market. But once the state is prepared to set aside the verdict of market forces on income distribution it is unlikely to rest content with income transfers. Experience in all countries points to an increasing willingness to operate simultaneously through prices with a view to shielding lower income groups from the consequences of adverse market trends: through control of rents, subsidies on foodstuffs, differential fares, and so on. The consequences of these market entanglements are usually less obvious but almost invariably less happy than those of direct income transfers.

Full Employment

A second macro-economic objective that has brought about an extension of state intervention is full employment. This is not an altogether new objective any more than redistribution of income. To the mercantilists it presented itself as 'setting the poor to work'. Their concern, however, was with a semi-permanent residue of under-employed workers or with the aftermath of war and demobilization. The modern problem is seen more as one of economic stability at a high level. It springs from acceptance of the Keynesian thesis that the market system is not self-regulating and that the price adjustments that keep a commodity market in balance may be powerless to restore full employment in an economy where effective demand fluctuates.

It is of course true that the Keynesian analysis does not by itself require active intervention by the state. If it were possible, for example, to secure continuous full employment by the exercise of monetary policy alone, responsibility for pursuing the appropriate policy could be devolved on an independent central bank armed with all the necessary powers. But this reflection does not take us very far. In the first place, any one objective of public policy, so long as it is not in serious conflict with other objectives and is fairly easy to interpret can be hived off and surrendered to some quasi-independent body. This does not make it any the less an exercise of political power. But, secondly, full employment does not answer to the description given: all the major objectives of economic policy are intertwined and the emphasis and priority to be given to each calls for constant reinterpretation. Any central bank would have to ask itself like any government: how full is full employment? how urgent is it to restore employment to some previous level when demand at home or, still more, abroad weakens? how is employment policy to be reconciled with the danger of inflation or an external deficit? and so on. In any event, how can one separate monetary from fiscal policy? Once the budget becomes so large an element in the economy that the budget surplus or deficit dominates all other sectoral surpluses or deficits, changes in the money supply are either dictated by the budget or can be held within narrower limits only by what may have to be wide fluctuations in interest rates that have disastrous consequences for financial markets. The idea that monetary policy could control the level of employment whatever the fiscal stance adopted by the government is too preposterous to pursue.

It remains true that the use of monetary and fiscal policy to promote economic stability need not involve the state in detailed intervention in the market. But just as distributional considerations lead to various forms of price control, so employment considerations are cited in justification of measures to help this industry or that, to keep particular firms or projects in being, and to continue over-manning in nationalized industries. The more old-fashioned approach of public works, the maintenance of a 'shelf' of projects to be brought down and put into effect in a depression, and the support of specially devised local authority schemes to employ more labour also reflects lack of faith in orthodox reliance on monetary and fiscal policy alone. Governments that disclaim responsibility for the level of employment usually do so from the same lack of faith but continue to search for ways of adding directly to employment. Indeed, they can hardly fail to interest themselves in the level of employment when they employ one-quarter of the working population; and it is natural that the employment they offer in the public sector should be decided directly rather than in response to pressure of their own making through financial channels.

Inflation

A third macro-economic objective that has greatly extended the role of the state is the avoidance of inflation. Here again the objective is not one that can be attained by leaving things to market forces so long at least as the two objectives we have just discussed continue to be pursued. It may be true that there was very little inflation in the nineteenth century except when the government was generating it and that market forces do not necessarily operate so as to give rise to inflation. But in a world in which political power rests with wage- and salary-earners, that power can hardly fail to be used in order to redistribute income and maintain employment. The budgetary struggle over distribution is carried over into the labour market; and full employment, by reinforcing the bargaining power of labour, turns the struggle in the labour market into outright inflation.

Economic systems develop their own defence mechanisms when the pressure put on them rises dangerously. Inflation and external deficits are the defence mechanisms of a market economy when claims are created in excess of what the system can deliver. Unemployment was an earlier and harsher defence mechanism since it ensured that excessive claims would not be made. Even if it were beyond dispute that unemployment would still function to moderate wage claims it is doubtful whether governments that enlist the defence mechanism of unemployment to achieve their aims can hope to continue in power in a fully democratic society. Hence the effort to find some alternative means of regulating wages and prices without altogether superseding market forces. But whereas with distribution of income and economic stabilization there are policy instruments that do not require detailed intervention in the market it is not at all clear that anti-inflationary incomes policies can be devised that avoid the need to intervene extensively.

Balance of Payments

Another objective of policy that has had a powerful influence on the activities of the state is the preservation of external balance. It is not a new objective and Adam Smith for one would have thought it misguided.

He, and still more David Hume, saw no reason why the balance of payments should not look after itself. But countries in deficit or believing themselves to be constrained by their balance of payments have rarely been willing to trust market forces to rid them of the deficit or free them from constraint. Even when they have opted for a floating rate of exchange, or more commonly been obliged to acquiesce in floating, they have continued to justify a wide variety of controls by real or supposed balance of payments difficulties. Sometimes these controls have been primarily over capital movements or have applied to a broad range of imports or exports so as to act as a kind of ersatz depreciation. But very often they have involved outright protection or subsidy to specific industries expected to show large balance of payments gains. The more the state has felt itself obliged by its international commitments to give up overt protection to such industries the more ingenuity it has shown in devising alternative forms of support (including 'non-tariff barriers') that keep to the letter but not the spirit of its undertakings. Such support may be purely protective and have nothing to do with the balance of payments but even when this is so balance of payments' considerations are likely to be urged in extenuation.

Economic Growth

Efforts by the state to accelerate economic growth fall into the same general category. There can be no presumption that market forces 'left to themselves' (if one can give meaning to such a concept) will generate either the maximum or a socially acceptable rate of growth. Once the rate of growth becomes a matter of public concern the state cannot avoid taking an interest in it and trying to bring it more into line either with what it judges to be the economy's true potential or with what the public would find acceptable.

Unfortunately there is simply no way of telling what ought to be done in fulfilment of either of these objectives. We know very little about the forces governing the rate of growth and still less about how to make them operate more powerfully. There is no simple or certain way of establishing the maximum growth rate of which a country is capable or of finding out what rate or rates would be socially acceptable. We cannot be sure that the efforts of the state to accelerate growth will have a significant effect or that they will necessarily be beneficial in the long run. So we are in an area of almost total uncertainty in which economists have expressed themselves for thirty years with unbecoming assurance and have had to unsay in one decade a large proportion of what they said in the previous one.

Nevertheless the stakes are high and the incentive to act correspondingly powerful. Advised or not advised by economists, heedful or not of their advice, governments believe that they can influence growth and have adopted a wide variety of measures in this belief, ranging from increased public investment to tariff protection, university expansion, indicative planning, investment grants or allowances, free trade areas, etc., etc. Whether all of these taken together have been of more than minor importance in comparison with market forces operating in a world of almost continuous full employment is a very open question.

More recently, growth theory and growth programmes have begun to lay more stress on science and technology. But the rate of technical change is very much a matter of the speed of diffusion or what is nowadays called 'technological transfer'; and anyone reared on Marshall or still more on Schumpeter does not need to be told that this is what competition in the market is all about. Once it is taken on board that innovation and growth or development are opposite sides of the same penny the role of the state in promoting growth will need thorough re-examination.

The Growing Importance of the Budget

There are several other macro-economic objectives such as regional policy which it would be possible to enumerate and analyse and which call for some form of intervention by the state. These would be further examples of the emergence in modern times of more ambitious policy goals that can be realized only through collective action. The more importance is attached to such goals the greater is bound to be the emphasis on centralized control over market forces or their supersession by direct action by the state. But is it not *indispensable* to the fulfilment of any of the macro-economic goals (except perhaps incomes policy) that the state should engage in direct intervention in the market: in principle, it would be possible to proceed by way of strengthening or weakening existing incentives and by way of adding to or taking from existing incomes without suspending the freedom of buyers and sellers to react to market forces as thus modified. There is, for example, nothing intrinsic to the objectives that makes them incapable of attainment without a change in the border between the public and private sectors. It is not even beyond dispute that an expansion in the public sector would make any of them more likely to be attained. What logic and experience alike suggest is that all of them give rise to an increase in the importance of the budget and that the main instruments of macro-economic policy are, of necessity, budgetary instruments. Economic management in pursuit of collective goals leads not only to increased centralization but to increased centralization in the

Treasury. Where this is not so it either reflects a disinclination to rely on market forces or an effort to speed up structural changes by long-term planning backed by controls that are not primarily financial.

FAILINGS OF THE MARKET

It is not merely that there are some broad collective purposes that the market cannot be relied upon to serve but that it may fail to function as it should in the allocation of resources.

Market Imperfections

The virtue of free markets lies in the freedom of choice they offer to buyers or consumers, the freedom of enterprise they elicit from sellers or producers and the coordination of economic activity they achieve through the price mechanism. But the enterprise that the market is supposed to harness may not be forthcoming or it may take the form of exercising or acquiring excessive market power. Nobody can be made to compete; and freedom to compete may degenerate into freedom to enter into restrictive agreements or to take over competitors.

Economists have drawn up a long list of market imperfections and failings. There are market imperfections associated with monopoly or monopolistic competition: with ignorance and inadequate knowledge of market options: with externalities of all kinds and consequent divergencies between private and social costs and benefits: with exposure to risk and uncertainty, particularly in relation to innovation: and with decisions between present and future, where the response to current prices may be perverse and calculated to lead to prices in future which, if foreseen, would provoke an opposite response. The implications of each of these would suffice for a lengthy discourse and the success of the state in seeking to correct each limitation could give rise to endless debate. We cannot avoid asking ourselves, however, how seriously to take them and how radically, in their totality, they alter the reliance that should be placed by a modern state on market forces.

War-time Controls

An example will show that they have to be taken very seriously indeed. Suppose that a country is obliged to defend itself against military attack and has to mobilize for war. No juggling with public expenditure and bidding for resources in the market is likely to be as effective or as quick in creating the sinews of war as the use of compulsion and conscription to short-circuit the market and build up the armed forces in the form and on the scale that the government thinks appropriate. Who else but the government can hope to fathom the mind of the government or grasp the necessities that war will impose? Market prices and rates of pay are most unlikely to convey the priorities in governmental strategy or to effect a transfer of men and materials to wartime employment at the rate required. The system of market prices is not designed to promote a comprehensive reallocation of resources from peace to war or vice versa.

Development Plans

The same logic applies to a less developed country where the structural upheavals required may make market prices a poor guide to the adjustments necessary. The indivisibilities, discontinuities, and externalities that are so prominent in such countries make the price mechanism a less satisfactory instrument for regulating economic activity. Where the prime aim of economic effort is the satisfaction of the conflicting wants of a multitude of consumers the market can contribute powerfully to that objective by securing the necessary marginal adjustments. But when the adjustments are no longer marginal and the pattern of supply and demand has to be radically and quickly transformed in pursuit of some over-riding task such as industrialization, it may be difficult to use ordinary market mechanisms in order to reconcile the priorities flowing from such a task with the preferences of consumers. Direct controls, over-riding the price mechanism, may be required to bring outputs promptly into line with the plans of the authorities. The larger the adjustments to be made, the less the time in which they are required, and the lower the elasticities of response to price changes, the greater is the temptation to resort to compulsion in order to avoid violent fluctuations in price. Apart from the abuses to which compulsion lends itself, there is a danger that the state may seek to avoid making any change in price and rely exclusively on administrative measures without the supplementary, and in the long run indispensable, pressure that the market could provide.

Floating Exchange Rates

A further example is provided by fluctuations in exchange rates. Here, obviously enough, professional opinion has moved strongly against administrative control and in favour of allowing market forces free play. But there is the same risk of wide, and eventually perverse, fluctuations in price because of low short-term elasticities. The swing in exchange rates may be so violent that it thwarts the very approach to a new balance between receipts and payments which it is its function to promote. The danger is then of an insistence on exclusive reliance on fluctuating exchange rates without any dampening of the fluctuations out of reserves of foreign exchange or by administrative measures to reinforce market pressure.

In all such cases one can of course pooh-pooh the case for direct action by the state by denigrating all forms of official intervention in the market. Those who run a war economy or make plans for developing countries or intervene to stabilize exchange rates are bound to make major blunders from time to time and when they do their mistakes are likely to be blazoned abroad. But if every argument for state intervention is met by a sweeping attack on ministerial and bureaucratic folly as the *necessary* concomitant of such intervention there is not much point in pursuing the argument. It is just as one-sided to exclude the possibility of improving on the market as it is to think it enough to show that the market is not altogether perfect.

The Problem of Monopoly

Of all forms of market failure more importance has been attached traditionally to monopoly. Where monopoly is rooted in collusion between a group of producers and consumers with a view to exploiting their collective hold on the market the matter is in principle straightforward. Action in restraint of trade can be made illegal. But what if a firm simply grows into a position of monopoly? Or if it straddles the globe so that only part of its activities are within the jurisdiction of any one government? What remedies has the state for abuses of market power in those not uncommon situations? An even more difficult problem is posed by collective bargaining agreements between employers and employed that necessarily reflect the exercise of monopoly power. How can that power be qualified without prejudice to either side? And if it is not qualified how is it possible to avoid an ineradicable inflationary bias that is far more damaging to the economy than any sectional gains levied by the most powerful bargainers in the labour market?

These are not questions to which any short or easy answers can be given. The dilemmas remain. What starts out as the protection of the weak becomes the prop of the strong. Bigness may bring efficiency; but it also brings market power and release from competitive pressure. Monopolies may be broken up; but the parts cannot be made to compete with one another. Freedom to compete can degenerate into freedom to conceal collusion or take over competitors; the enterprise that the market is supposed to harness may take perverse forms. Above all, positions of privilege may rest on political as much as economic power and be as firmly entrenched in the state as in the market.

There may be an even greater danger. There can be no guarantee that the market environment will always make for decentralization in competing units of limited size. A variety of circumstances – modern technology, improved communications, the advantages of marketing in bulk, the greater ease and cheapness of access to finance – may tell in favour of large concerns. The government may have its own reasons for favouring large units over which it can exercise more immediate influence. In those circumstances what is to be done if business becomes increasingly concentrated in a small number of large units? In the United Kingdom the hundred largest firms in manufacturing, which produced 15 per cent of total output before World War I, were producing nearly half by 1960 and may reach two-thirds by 1989. If this is what market forces produce what is the state to do? Suppose, for the sake of argument, that the trend owed nothing to active encouragement by the state and was sufficiently established to persist in the face of strong discouragement. In what sense would it be possible to oppose the state to the market and insist on the superiority of a decentralized system responding to market indicators over a system of direct operation by the state? Is there any reason why manufacturing industry should not go the way of postal services, the railways, and the power stations?

If the question were one to be answered exclusively in terms of economic efficiency the answer must surely be: in principle, no. The scale of operations consistent with efficiency may grow until there is a plain choice between a private and public monopoly and the substitution of a state holding for the stake held by private investors may do little to change the mode of conduct of the business. The mere change of ownership would not by itself limit or transform the role of the market. It would reflect the decay of the market and the fading out of competitive influences. Whatever remained of these influences might be allowed to continue.

The question can be put in those terms, however, only if one abstracts from the characteristic features of public ownership. The state is not simply a new kind of shareholder but a shareholder with very special powers and preoccupations that do not always march with business efficiency. It is to some extent in the same position in relation to public enterprises as any large business is in relation to its subsidiaries. That is, it can leave them to run themselves or furnish them with rules and targets (and, on cause shown, additional finance) or maintain control directly. It can let them be guided by their own judgement of the market or impose its own judgement or it can require them to pursue policies that are essentially non-commercial and do not spring from market considerations. It is this last possibility that, *in principle*, distinguishes the economic activities of government. So long as the growth of business units leaves them as responsive as before to market influences, even if they come to possess more market power, that growth does not detract from the potentialities of the market as a guide to decision making. But if the internalizing of decisions through growth reinforces non-commercial influences on those decisions then the displacement of small firms by large is a vote against the market and in favour of the state. To put the point more concretely: big business is still business when guided by considerations of profit; but public enterprise is likely to have to marry political and commercial considerations. If commercial considerations are diluted by political, the result can hardly be as satisfactory from the limited point of view of economic efficiency; and the question then becomes how far dilution should go? What are the political purposes that are served by state ownership that warrant a sacrifice in efficiency? Could not such purposes be equally well served by the use of state control in order to regulate the functioning of the market?

It may be objected that all this presupposes that there is a market to be regulated. But this seems inconsistent with the initial postulate of growing industrial concentration and a trend towards monopoly. The existence of large firms each able to dominate its own market is quite compatible, however, with the threat of keen competition between them since each may be capable of entering some at least of the markets supplied by other large firms. Potential rivalry can be as powerful a factor as actual in maintaining industrial efficiency. Moreover large private firms show a great deal more flexibility in adapting their structure and activities to changes in market conditions than public enterprises do. If they engage in take-over activities they also sell off or shut down.

As firms grow in size and acquire increasing monopoly power they tend to exhibit more and more of the characteristics of state undertakings. They exert more social and political pressure and are themselves subject increasingly to such pressure. Their objectives of policy become more complex and diluted by considerations of social acceptability so that their pursuit of efficiency is less single-minded. But so long as they are in private hands they can establish their own priorities within the limits of the slack available to them and are simultaneously free to make their own arrangements within the limits set by the state. These limits may be wide and extremely general or they may be narrow and specific to the point that the state exercises more control than if it were the actual owner of the business.

The Market as a Decentralizing Agency

The monopoly case is rather fundamental because it brings us back to the *raison d'être* of the market. The state cannot organize the economy on the basis of simple directions, any more than any army can be successfully controlled by orders of the day. There has to be co-operation based on accepted rules of behaviour, and there have to be incentives that are sufficiently powerful to get the job done. The incentives in turn must either be of the kind that makes an army fight, i.e. calculated to secure co-operation in a common endeavour, or they must take the form of rewards and punishments for individual acts. These cannot be prescribed by the state, just as directions cannot be given, because of the complexity of the economic system. But if they are left to the market in which bargains are struck to the mutual advantage of both sides, the market can graduate the incentives to what is required and provide indicators of action that allow control to be decentralized.

Decentralization, however, is limited by economies of scale. If economic activity is broken down too far and made a matter of individual bargaining it cannot be as efficient as it would be in units large enough to take advantage of those economies. For the sake of efficiency there has to be some submission to central direction. The greater the economies of scale and the economic virtues of size, the more the scope for central direction. Thus arguments about the state and the market are arguments quite as much about centralization and decentralization as about the intrusion or exclusion of political influences.

The International Market

The forces of decentralization are reinforced by the international character of the market as opposed to the national character of the state. So long as the domestic market is open to competitive influences from outside, a limit is set to monopoly powers of all kinds: whether exercised by groups of producers or groups of workers, whole industries or individual firms. It was this aspect of international trade that particularly appealed to Adam Smith. He developed the argument elaborated later by Ricardo that free access to the international market, whether as exporter or importer, was calculated to improve the efficiency of an economy and encourage its growth. The enlargement of the market was doubly advantageous because it made the economy more competitive and at the same time opened up new opportunities of specialization on the basis of comparative advantage.

The mutual benefits that both sides enjoyed from the pursuit of these opportunities were an illustration of his basic thesis of the harmony of opposed interests in all market transactions. The older, mercantilist, view with its emphasis on confrontation and a clash of interests encouraged interference by governments which ran the risk of provoking trade wars while unrestricted trade tended to promote friendly and peaceable relations. Cobden and others in the nineteenth century were so impressed by this argument that they gave priority to free trade even over the abolition of slavery and supported the Southern States in the American Civil War for that reason. Much later is was possible for a major political party to defend simultaneously international free trade and a highly interventionist domestic policy such as the nationalization of all the means of production. Later still it was possible to advocate a Common Market free from tariff barriers in countries dedicated to various forms of *étatisme* and other active industrial policies that inevitably affected, and were usually designed to affect, the competitive position of major industries. Intervention, driven out at the door, came in again at the window.

We need not pursue these apparent inconsistencies or trouble to ask whether the international market is totally different from the domestic. That it is different is evident if only because there is at least one other government involved in every international transaction and the degree of control that can be exercised reflects this fact. There is also the fact that domestic transactions automatically balance while external transactions do not, and that governments may have cause to regret an enlargement of their business with other countries in a way they can have no reason for regretting domestic expansion so long as it is non-inflationary. The international market may encourage the channelling of resources along blind alleys or delay investments necessary to eventual development and encourage investments that are of immediate advantage but involve a high negative yield for the economy at a later stage. The state *may* be more far-sighted or more willing to make the investments that long-term development requires or able to act on a broader front to secure results that a fragmented market would fail to deliver. We have also to recognize that the international market is the domain of the really large firm which may combine a competitive spirit with unmistakable monopoly powers. Like the domestic market the international market tends to favour those already in possession of resources as against those with only limited options, the rich against the poor. Yet on the other hand the international influences which tend to flood in behind trade and investment and to be inseparable from them are likely to be the major factor in successful development.

FAILINGS OF THE STATE

Let us now look at matters the other way round and ask ourselves not what is wrong with the market but what is wrong with the state? We live in a world of increasing centralization in which there is a profound belief in planning and control from the highest motives. This of itself politicizes economic decisions of all kinds and puts pressure on the state to expand its functions, its powers, and its machinery of control without much regard to the cumulative effect of the complex machinery so created. The technostructure of which Galbraith complains is the result of bending the economic system to political demands rather than a means of bending consumers to the will of big business outside and inside government.

Willingness to turn to the state as the agent of social planning and control is reinforced by the change in the balance of political power. Those who exercised political power in the past – the agricultural interest apart – had usually relatively little to fear from the operations of the market and much to resent in the operations of the state. Possessing wealth, they could profit from the cheapness that the market ensured. In safe jobs, they had little reason to fear unemployment. For them, market forces were on the side of peace and prosperity, rewarding the diligent and the enterprising when diligence and enterprise were indispensable to the survival of a hard-pressed economy. But as political power moves from the old to the young, from the capitalist to the manual worker, it is the state not the market that is seen as delivering the goods. The possessors of power are not, as a rule, those whom the market has blessed nor are they content to abide by its verdict. They are willing to use the state, as other social classes have done before them, for the achievement of ever more ambitious targets in furtherance of their own ends. In doing so they are not content merely to see different parameters set for market forces but prefer the creation of fresh organizations under state auspices visibly and directly responding to specific social needs.

Overloading of the State Machine

The net effect of the change in intellectual climate and social pressures is to overload the state machine and to overload it unnecessarily. Additional, often conflicting, responsibilities are thrust on it without enough thought being given to the consequences of the overload: bureaucracy, inefficiency, and waste, frustration and the consequent danger of corruption, disregard for regulations and later for the law, contempt ultimately for the business of politics and for the state itself.

There is a need for devices that allow the state to devolve some of its responsibilities: for agencies that can be made to function to the public advantage without detailed supervision by the state: for ways of securing the broad results desired through voluntary effort with a minimum of state participation: in a word, for reviving the use of the market.

What scope is there for enlarging the use of the market within the general objectives we associate with the welfare state? We have seen one such enlargement in the past few years with the move from fixed to floating rates of exchange. But the international sector (if one could isolate international influences within a single sector) is a law unto itself and requires separate treatment. Confining ourselves for present purposes to the public sector we can detect a limited number of possible openings.

Free Public Services

For example, we have the large range of services provided free by the state and absolved from market tests of priority (on the demand side at least). It is not at all obvious why this range of services should be picked out and why it should be so readily accepted that services should either be provided free or at full cost. (Housing is one of the few exceptions.) The effect is usually to increase demand to the point at which the kind of service offered is diluted in order to keep down the bill. At the same time competitive services that maintain higher standards (or purport to do so) are provided privately but efforts are often made by the state to put obstacles in the way of such provision. This polarization of services between free and full cost and polarization of customers between those content to queue and avoid payment and those willing to pay and avoid queuing seems neither necessary nor efficient. Yet in one direction after another the government in Britain seems determined to put an end to intermediate solutions. Even in the case of housing, where the economic consequences of abolishing rent would be so dramatic that it is hardly necessary to explain why that situation has still not quite been reached, there is a polarization between council tenants and owner-occupiers that is perhaps the most important single line of division in British politics.

The bill for the wide range of services involved is a large one and rather arbitrary judgements have to be made on the size of the bill that can be afforded. One can understand the logic of the situation where the consumer is offered no choice, as with army uniforms, and either is required to take what he is given or, if a charge were levied, would be obliged to make a compulsory purchase. This applies to defence services where the taxpayer has to accept what is voted by his representatives and there is no other way of settling the matter. But what of health, education, pensions, etc.? The state does not deprive consumers of all choice since it permits a parallel market to exist side by side with its own administered supply. But why should the official supply be at zero price when other necessities like bread and butter or housing are not? The combination of zero pricing and a limited allocation of funds means that the free services have to be rationed without ration cards and the rationing process is bound to be arbitrary and difficult. Perhaps some minimum charge to the beneficiaries would still be preferable to present arrangements even if the charge had to be waived for large numbers of consumers with limited means.

Commercial Services

Where services provided by the state or a public undertaking are charged for, as in the nationalized industries, familiar issues of pricing policy arise. There is no need to recapitulate the controversies associated with those issues. But there is another deeper problem arising out of the statutory monopoly that nationalized industries usually enjoy. In a competitive market or even where there is a private monopoly it is possible to improve the services provided by creating a new organization superior to those existing or, after a successful take-over bid, by a reorganization of the resources employed. But a statutory monopoly is beyond such influence. There is no way in which a thrusting and imaginative outsider can back his claim to be able to improve on the *status quo* and every reason why the existing organization should seek the quiet life to which good monopolists traditionally aspire. How is the public sector to devise the counterpart of a take-over bid, or even the threat of one? How can it ensure that public undertakings undergo the drastic surgery that exposure to competition in a free market would undoubtedly call for?

Part of the answer lies in the willingness of the state to qualify the monopoly powers it has assumed through nationalization. The question at issue from this point of view is whether the state is prepared to permit various forms of choice to continue. Does the Ministry of Defence insist on taking over the manufacture of armaments or is it prepared to buy equipment from private firms? Does the state insist on exclusive operation of all coal mines and steel mills or will it permit competition from mines and steel mills in private hands? Does the Post Office prohibit the organization of private postal services? Could new coal mines be sunk with private capital? Are consumers of coal free to place orders for imports from abroad or are they free only to purchase imported oil? Do any of the nationalized industries so organize themselves as to promote competition between the constituent parts? What, in short, is the importance that the state attaches, once it attains a position of monopoly, to the continued exercise of choice and the continual risk of supersession? What does it do to ensure that the range of services between which consumers can choose is at least as great as efficiency requires?

CONCLUSION

The load on the modern state has increased steadily, continues to increase, and in the opinion of many ought to be diminished. But the increased load does not in the main reflect ideological antipathy to reliance on market forces. It is much more the outcome of new and wider ambitions for social control: fear of unemployment on the one hand and inflation on the other, a more egalitarian temper, concern for social justice, for the environment, and for human needs for which the market does not cater, the trend towards industrial concentration and larger business units. These have caused the budget to expand, the relative importance of the private consumer to shrink, the totality of social organization to grow, and far more of this formidable total to devolve on public authorities. All this adds ineluctably to the importance of organizational as opposed to market instruments of economic coordination and inflates the role of the state as the centrepiece of social organization. But in most industrial countries the private sector is still far greater in size than the public sector and the market remains indispensable to the functioning of the economy, whether as an agency for the coordination of activities in the private sector or as the meeting place of private consumers and public authorities. Even as a network of dealings within the public sector itself, the market retains its usefulness and significance although various normal responses to market changes can then no longer appear. What requires thought is how more use could be made of the market in order to relieve the overload on the state, perhaps at the cost of some slight derogation from the prime objectives of state intervention.

This is essentially a question of organization. It is not just a matter of changing the boundary between the public and the private sector or of giving the consumer more freedom of choice. It is also a matter of how the public sector should be organized; how competition within it can be recreated; how the decision-taking units in each part of the public sector can be restructured from time to time without take-overs, bankruptcies, and the machinery for reorganization used in the private sector. It is a matter also of the limits within which the private sector should be asked to operate. These limits could be drawn in such a way by high taxation, government regulation, or administrative order, as to make the line between the private and the public sector an irrelevance and for this reason alone most of the argument about nationalization that continues even today, is itself irrelevant. But the limits could also be drawn in a way that enlarged the scope for private enterprise at the same time as wider social interests were more securely guaranteed. This would be so if restrictive practices by management or workers were effectively outlawed. It would also be so if the state found means to prevent the use of economic power to enforce claims conceived in the interests of limited groups whether of workers or their employers.

The danger of overloading the state is least in a static world since routine and overload rarely go together. If there were no need for concern about growth it might be possible to heap more duties on the state without undesirable consequences. But in a dynamic world it is otherwise. The managerial burden of responding to change readily becomes excessive and the need to use market forces and indicators in order to relieve the burden mounts correspondingly. It is the great virtue of the market that it provides a testing-ground for responses to new influences, for eliciting and trying out alternatives and demonstrating which new ideas have greatest survival value. It can also provide a measure of managerial performance and a test of the survival value of managements. When the market is allowed to decay this selective function is endangered. In the absence of a market, committees have to take its place in the adjudication of known alternatives, in providing a stimulus to the devising of new ideas, and in judging managerial capabilities. Committees have their virtues; but they are usually a poor substitute for a market.

It was the experimental character of market responses that Adam Smith stressed most heavily: the efforts of every man to improve himself by offering the consumer a better deal. It was the shortcomings of the state in its efforts to encourage development and improvement that disposed him to scepticism of its pretensions. No doubt he overstated his case. The focus of the market is too narrow; the choices that consumers and producers make are governed by a far greater number of variables than the state can take into account. What a man buys does not tell us what he wants from life; what he is able to sell is only to a small extent the fruit of his unaided efforts. There is in the background the society in which his wants and his efforts take shape, the facilities and opportunities, the social capital and the social pressures that condition his behaviour. We are more conscious perhaps than Adam Smith of the need to see the market within a social framework and of the ways in which the state can usefully rig the market without destroying its thrust. We are certainly far more willing to concede a larger role for state activities of all kinds. But it is a nice question whether this is because we can lay claim, after two centuries, to any deeper insight into the forces determining the wealth of nations or whether more obvious forces have not played the larger part: the spread of democratic ideals, increasing affluence, the growth of knowledge, and a centralizing technology that delivers us over to the bureaucrat.

4

Keynes and the planned economy

Keynesianism, said Richard Kahn recently, is in danger of becoming a dirty word. The mismanagement of the British economy is laid at Keynes's door long after his death. Was he not the man, in the words of Brendan Bracken, 'who made inflation respectable'? Who but Keynes is to be blamed for the 'mistaken' belief in budget deficits; in fine tuning; in a simplistic approach to demand management? Who turned our attention away from the quantity of money? Who killed the gold standard? Who destroyed belief in the good old automatic regulators and left us at the mercy of political misjudgement and cowardice? Above all, who opened the door to a steady growth of government intervention in economic affairs and with it an increasing invasion of individual rights and liberties?

It is a catechism that must sound curious to any economist brought up between the wars, when things were certainly different. It suggests a consistency and a weight of influence never attributed to Keynes in his lifetime. It overlooks Keynes's horror of inflation, his extensive writings on the subject, his warning (for it was his more than Lenin's) that to debauch the currency would prove the surest path to revolution and the destruction of capitalism. It represents Keynes of all people as an enthusiast for government intervention when almost the only government department for which he ever proposed new duties was the Treasury, a department with an administrative staff numbering just over twenty when he first joined it.

PLANNING AND MANAGEMENT

Similarly when the name of Keynes is associated with the idea of a 'planned economy' it is as well to remember how rarely the word 'plan' actually

Paper delivered at Keynes Seminar on *Keynes and Laissez-Faire* at the University of Kent, Canterbury, 1976 and included in the volume of that title (Macmillan, 1978).

features in Keynes's writings. What he talks about constantly is *management*. The word appears in the heading to nearly every chapter of the *Treatise on Money*, Volume II, Book VII. In *The Means to Prosperity* there is again no reference to planning apart from a casual use of the word 'plan' in the Appendix. Policies, proposals, programmes, but no plans are discussed. The *General Theory* is equally silent on planning. It is only in *How to Pay for the War* that the word 'plan' is used over and over again to describe the proposals put forward. It is as if Keynes judged that economic policy in wartime has to be governed by fixed objectives that have no counterpart in normal peacetime operations and that while it may be appropriate to talk of 'economic management' when at peace, it is more appropriate to talk of 'planning' when at war.

Yet even when he used the term 'plan' Keynes did so in a very special way. The ideal type of plan in his view was the rule of the road. Nobody was the worse for having to conform to a general rule imposed from outside and the convenience of such a rule to all users of the road was conspicuous. Keynes thought the need to limit civilian demand in wartime an 'ideal opportunity for a common plan' satisfying the same criteria. Saving was a way of limiting demand but it was no good one man saving more if his neighbour promptly saved less. If all together saved more under a plan of deferred pay, demand could be kept within the limits required. The compulsions of planning for a predetermined goal became worthwhile because the alternatives – inflation on the one hand or shop shortages on the other – would distribute the same burden of economy between individuals more arbitrarily, less fairly and with more waste and more damage to the war effort. Only when there was an agreed objective beyond the reach of individual effort was there a case for planning.

The objectives of peacetime are less fixed than in wartime and the methods appropriate to their realization have to be correspondingly more flexible. In this sense Keynes was the apostle of economic management rather than of economic planning. But the growth of economic management is largely a function of the more ambitious objectives that we now set for ourselves, partly under Keynes's influence: full employment, faster growth, greater economic equality, and so on.

If we ask what Keynes's contribution was to economic management as practised since the war we have to consider these objectives and how they appeared to Keynes and to those whom he influenced. We have to recognize that up to 1939 Keynes's direct influence on the system of economic management, although real, was limited and he could, of course, have no direct influence on the system as it has evolved since his death. When he re-entered government in the war his energies were heavily concentrated on external finance rather than domestic economic policy. His hopes were set on a better peacetime settlement than in 1919 and he was caught up in the prolonged international negotiations over postwar reconstruction.

THE ROLE OF GOVERNMENT

It seems best to start from what he himself had to say about the role of Government and then go on to review how far postwar developments reflect his ideas.

He was, of course, writing at a time when the state was a decidedly smaller element than now in the economic life of the country. Leaving aside defence expenditure and interest on the national debt, public expenditure had been under 6 per cent of GNP before World War I. It was about 30 per cent in the 1960s and a still higher percentage in the 1970s. If he was urging more action by government it was not overloaded governments for whom he was prescribing.

Except for *The End of Laissez-Faire*, published 60 years ago, none of Keynes's writings provides us with a systematic analysis of the scope for government action. At no time in the last twenty years of his life did he publish a discussion of the economic functions of government. His interest in economic problems was largely a function of their urgency. In the 1930s, when unemployment was at its peak, it was the restoration of full employment that engaged him to the exclusion of lesser problems. In the last few years of his life he was concerned wtih the immediate problems of a war economy and the equally pressing need to prepare for the rebuilding of an international economy after the war. It was these problems that fuelled his imagination and were the starting-point of his theorizing. He developed his theories in order to help him gain the right answers to urgent problems and to assist in persuading his colleagues that he had found the right answers.

Keynes moved from problems to analysis and from analysis to proposals for action without allowing his judgement to be inhibited by some preconceived view of the principles that should govern state intervention. Yet there is a consistent view of the state and its duties that emerges from his work and is given fullest and most coherent expression in *The End of Laissez-Faire*.

There he quotes with approval Burke's dictum that 'one of the finest problems in legislation (is) to determine what the State ought to take upon itself to direct by the public wisdom, and what it ought to leave, with as little interference as possible, to individual exertion'.

'Perhaps', Keynes goes on, 'the chief task of economists at this hour is to distinguish afresh the *Agenda* of government from the *Non-Agenda*;

and the companion task of politics is to devise forms of government within a democracy which shall be capable of accomplishing the *Agenda*.'[1] In resorting to this Benthamite nomenclature Keynes emphasized that there could be no Benthamite presumption that government interference was 'generally needless' and 'generally pernicious'. His own view, which he frequently expressed, was that we were bound to settle for a mixed economy and that it was not possible to decide on abstract grounds what to include in the Agenda of government and what to exclude. He did however provide an important criterion of Agenda by suggesting the separation of those services which are technically social from those that are technically individual. 'The important thing for government', he argued, 'is not to do things which individuals are doing already, and to do them a little better or a little worse, but to do those things which at present are not done at all.'[2]

He did not elaborate upon this important dictum but confined himself to three illustrations of it, covering a single page, and dealing in turn with control of credit, control of investment, and control of population. The first and most important is worth quoting in full:

> Many of the greatest economic evils of our time are the fruits of uncertainty, and ignorance. It is because particular individuals, fortunate in situation or in abilities, are able to take advantage of uncertainty and ignorance, and also because for the same reason big business is often a lottery, that great inequalities of wealth come about; and these same factors are also the cause of the unemployment of labour, or the disappointment of reasonable expectations, and of the impairment of efficiency and production. Yet the cure lies outside the operations of individuals; it may even be to the interest of individuals to aggravate the disease. I believe that the cures for these things is partly to be sought in the deliberate control of the currency and of credit by a central institution, and partly in the collection and dissemination on a great scale of data relating to the business situation, including the full publicity, by law if necessary, of all business facts which it is useful to know. These measures would involve society in exercising directive intelligence through some appropriate organ of action over many of the inner intricacies of private business, yet it would leave private initiative and enterprise unhindered. Even if these measures prove insufficient, nevertheless, they will furnish us with better knowledge than we have now for taking the next step.[3]

This passage is essentially a plea for demand management exercised through a central bank under public control or ownership. It is an idea that Keynes stuck to throughout his life, although his view of the causes of unemployment and business fluctuations changed and developed and he came to lay more weight on fiscal than on monetary policy in the exercise of management. The ingredients of the view are interesting. He starts off with risk, uncertainty and ignorance as the source of inequalities of wealth on the one hand and unemployment and inefficiency on the other. He then finds a remedy for ignorance in improved economic information and a way of neutralizing risk and uncertainty through financial control over the economic conjuncture. He claims that this would permit of a reconciliation between the exercise of private initiative and the collective regulation of economic activity and so purge capitalism of some of its worst defects.

These are all recurrent themes in Keynes. He insisted on the need for improved data on economic aggregates. It was with his encouragement, as a believer in conjectural arithmetic, that Colin Clark and, later, James Meade and Richard Stone laid the basis for national income accounting. Any reader of *How to Pay for the War* must be struck by his efforts to make statistical bricks with very little straw; but in most of his earlier work one can find the same kind of calculations and the same appeal for more comprehensive and reliable statistics. Nothing would have pleased Keynes more than the transformation in economic statistics that has taken place in the past generation even if he might be chastened to find how much in the dark we remain about what is really going on in the economy.

In wanting more statistics did he want more state intervention? Not necessarily. He regarded more and better information as he regarded the rule of the road: something that helped everybody. Business needs better information just as much as government; and it also needs to learn how to use statistical information – a matter to which very little attention is customarily given.

It was also typical of Keynes to insist on the importance of risk and uncertainty. Keynes had given six years to the study of probability and a great many more to the study of the stock market. He was alive to the importance of luck, confidence, animal spirits and the state of mind of the business community. Investment, economic growth and the level of activity in the economy were all at the mercy of the unforeseen and of the confidence, or lack of it, with which the future was approached. Just as ignorance could be reduced by better information, risk and uncertainty could be reduced by better social organization. Appropriate financial policies could moderate economic fluctuations and offer producers steadier and more calculable markets. It would be to the common advantage if the same output were produced with less ups and downs. It was a principle already familiar to pupils of Marshall and elaborated in Pigou's *Industrial Fluctuations*.

THE 'TREASURY MAN'

Then there is the 'appropriate organ of action', the central bank or Treasury, charged with the duty of eliminating fluctuations in activity. Here we have the key element in Keynes's approach to government activity. He was, *par excellence*, the Treasury man, the believer in financial agencies of control, who would regulate the economy by skilful management of demand rather than by interventions operating directly on supply. When the budget was small, as it was before World War I, and when all orthodox opinion insisted that it should be balanced in peacetime, there was little or no scope for effective demand management through fiscal policy. So it was to monetary policy that Keynes looked for a regulator of demand in the 1920s and indeed until after the publication of the *Treatise*. It was only gradually that he came to see that the budget was a more comprehensive, direct and powerful 'organ of action' able to operate over the whole area of spending and saving, not just selectively like credit control. Monetary policy had proved too slow and too weak as a stimulant after 1932 and was likely to prove too expensive on the restrictive tack in wartime in terms of the interest burden it would leave behind. But there is no reason to suppose that Keynes was ever wedded to the one type of instrument rather than the other. What mattered was that control should be exercised over aggregate demand in the interests of full employment, less uncertainty and greater efficiency.

In all Keynes's writings we find the same insistence on monetary management as the prescription for a well-run economy. Throughout the interwar years it was as a monetary reformer that he was known and the proposals he put forward for consideration by government were invariably financial. At the outbreak of war when he came to write *How to Pay for the War* he again opted for a financial device. This time, however, it was not a device of monetary but of fiscal policy: deferred pay or postwar credits. He explained that it would not be possible to limit consumer demand sufficiently by high taxation and that the real choice lay between three possibilities: inflation; a system of postwar credits; and limitation of demand by shop shortages mitigated by rationing. He regarded the latter course, just as he regarded inflation, as wasteful, inefficient and unjust. It would also detract from the war effort since it would involve running down stocks and deflecting supplies from exports and military requirements. But it was what we were heading for in the absence of a scheme of deferred pay.

Anyone who remembers these years will agree that Keynes was right to emphasize the importance of regulating effective demand, first by expanding it before the war and by keeping it within the limits of capacity thereafter. Much of the thinking of the period was hopelessly muddled because it started from supply, not demand, and relied on administrative controls over supply to bring back prosperity when these controls merely improved the position of one group compared with others. These were the days when quotas on Danish butter reduced the quantity imported but sent up the import bill; when unemployment was to be cured through land settlement; and when it seemed more important to some people to get prices up than output.

Even when Keynes felt that market forces were not working satisfactorily and would work better with government intervention, he thought instinctively of redirecting these forces rather than superseding them. For example, he was very much impressed by the instability of the commodity markets and the wide swings in the world price of primary commodities within extremely short periods. All this seemed to him highly inefficient and quite unnecessary. But his proposed remedy lay in a scheme for buffer stocks which would leave the commodity markets discharging their normal functions and allow the buffer stock manager to intervene freely and (if he did improve matters) profitably. Similarly when Keynes proposed limitation of imports in 1931 he suggested *not* the use of import quotas but a revenue tariff: a device less likely to cause disruption of normal market relationships, and similar in principle to the import surcharge introduced in 1964.

Nevertheless Keynes regarded various forms of intervention as indispensable to monetary management. It is difficult to say how far he was prepared to go in exercising control by limiting particular activities or constituents of total demand. He would certainly not have subscribed to the idea that it was sufficient to rely on control over the money supply especially if this meant that the monetary authorities should divest themselves of the whole panoply of monetary weapons that they have developed or contemplated. He was particularly insistent on the need to control investment, domestic and foreign, and was ready to support the use of quite sweeping powers for this purpose. So far as domestic investment was concerned he was conscious of the limitations of monetary weapons and accepted the need to vary public investment contracyclically through public works or in other ways. I doubt whether he would ever have favoured control of private *industrial* investment, but several times he urged the setting up of a National Investment Board to coordinate the larger schemes of capital development. Indeed, he would latterly have preferred limits on domestic investment by administrative action rather than by changes in credit conditions disturbing to accepted notions of the proper long-term rate of interest. Similarly, in face of the difficulty of reconciling full employment and external balance he wanted control over foreign investment and progressed from asking for control over new capital issues to insisting on the need for control over all outward movements of capital through exchange control. The full consequences (as well as the limitations) of such controls over investment were not apparent in Keynes's lifetime.

SEMI-AUTONOMOUS BODIES

In *The End of Laissez-Faire* Keynes outlined a second principle of government–industry relations supplementing the general argument for demand management. 'In many cases', he contended, 'the ideal size for the unit of control and organization lies somewhere between the individual and the modern State.' 'I suggest', he went on, 'that progress lies in the growth and the recognition of semi-autonomous bodies within the State – bodies whose criterion of action within their own field is solely the public good as they understand it.'[4]

This idea by itself does not take us very far. Students of the behaviour of semi-autonomous bodies might want some guidance on the basis of identification of the public good. It is hard enough to lay down rules for the nationalized industries but a great deal harder to prescribe for semi-autonomous bodies that may want to know when and how far to bow to market forces, what customers to cater for or treat preferentially, how to balance the interests of employers, customers, owners, conservationists, minority groups and so on. The examples Keynes chooses – the universities, the Bank of England, and the Port of London Authority – do not bring out the nature of the problem that would be faced in productive industry if the only criterion of action were the public good.

It is also not at once clear what difference he has in mind between such a body and a nationalised industry. The distinction is not made easier to understand when he first hesitates over including the railway companies among semi-autonomous bodies and then argues that it would make very little difference if they were nationalized. 'There is', he says, 'no so-called important political question so really unimportant, so irrelevant to the reorganization of the economic life of Great Britain, as the nationalization of the railways.'[5]

What Keynes is really concerned to argue is that joint stock companies as they grow bigger and older come to behave more and more like public corporations. Writing 50 years ago – and what he says still applies – he pointed out that 'one of the most interesting and unnoticed developments of recent decades has been the tendency of big enterprise to socialize itself.'[6] I had always thought that I was making an original observation when I wrote after the war that British industry was semi-nationalized (especially when 75 per cent of industrial profits were paid in tax) and when I argued more recently that as the business unit grew larger and more monopolistic it became more and more indistinguishable from a public corporation.[7] But the gist of the matter is there already in 1926. Owners and managers grow apart: the making of large profits 'becomes quite secondary' while the stability and reputation of the business takes precedence; and all this is the more likely where its great size or semi-monopolistic position renders it 'conspicuous in the public eye and vulnerable to public attack'. Hence 'the battle of Socialism against unlimited private profit is being won in detail hour by hour'. On the other hand there is bound to be 'a waning of enterprise: the faults as well as the advantages of State Socialism'.

In spite of what he had to say about nationalization of the railways, Keynes wanted public utility and other enterprises with large fixed capital requirements to be turned into public corporations. But he regarded the battle for greater public control of industry as largely phoney. Nineteenth-century individualism and nineteenth-century state socialism sprang from the same intellectual root and were equally misguided: the one by a negative emphasis on avoiding limitations on freedom, the other by a positive stress on destroying monopoly. The task for the future 'must be to decentralize and devolve wherever we can, and in particular to establish semi-independent corporations and organs of administration to which duties of government, new and old, will be entrusted without, however, impairing the democratic princple or the ultimate sovereignty of Parliament'.[8]

Keynes's philosophy was nicely balance between hatred of the love of money and hatred of bureaucracy and the muddle it caused. He was no admirer of unregenerate capitalism but declared that the *class* war would find him 'on the side of the educated *bourgeoisie*'.[9] He wanted more intervention in the interests of greater equality and yet not too much for fear of shackling freedom of private initiative. He would have liked a great redistribution of wealth through taxation, and proposed a capital levy, but recognized that if private enterprise were to function it would renew inequality by rewarding the lucky as well as the farsighted. To a remarkable degree he agonized far more over money than over power although others have felt it more repugnant to human dignity to acquiesce in the concentration of power than in the concentration of wealth. But he might well have echoed the comment of G. M. Young:

> People whose chief object in life is wealth are as a rule less intelligent than people whose object is power, but, on the other hand, are far less disposed to do active wrong to those beneath them or about them. They may from negligence or

selfishness or mere thick-wittedness, do much harm . . . but it is harm of a kind which is largely controllable by public opinion, by legislation, by science.[10]

INTERNATIONAL MANAGEMENT

A third important strand in Keynes's thinking – which, however, does not appear in *The End of Laissez-Faire* – was the need for international management. He was often accused of economic nationalism and in an anarchic world he accepted the need for each country to preserve its freedom of action. He wanted governments to begin by managing their own affairs: the domestic market, which they alone could regulate; the currency which reflected their own credit; the foreign exchanges, foreign lending and investment, and transactions with other countries. Without international management, however, the task of individual governments would become infinitely more difficult. Just as individuals could not develop their full potential without government planning of the level of effective demand and other matters, so individual countries would find it hard to keep in internal and external balance and maintain full employment unless they operated within a framework of international institutions planned and managed for the common good.

When Keynes started to develop this view in the 1920s there were practically no international institutions to build on apart from the League of Nations and occasional international conferences, none of them particularly successful. There was some cooperation between the most important central banks, especially between the Federal Reserve Board and the Bank of England. But the world financial system no longer danced to the tune of the Bank of England as it had done now and again in the nineteenth century. Even with the creation of the Bank for International Settlements in 1930 and the Tripartite Agreement between Britain, France and the United States in 1936 there was very little international management. It was only with the war that the possibility of creating an entirely new monetary system emerged. It was at this point that Keynes's personal influence was most strongly felt. What was finally agreed at Bretton Woods and after was not what he proposed but it did at least reflect much of his thinking.

It is hard for any young economist now to imagine the very different state of the world in, say, 1936. Nowhere is this more true than in the contrast in international institutions. One may lament the profusion of such institutions or their impotence or their philosophies. But they have at least one consequence that is often overlooked. They mean that the leading personalities in the economic life of the main countries know one another, are in frequent touch, and have had an opportunity to argue out their differences and compare notes on their successes and failures. This is true not only of the politicians who have always had opportunities of meeting but of senior administrators, businessmen and labour leaders whose horizons in the past were far more limited by national boundaries. International cooperation and planning may not yet be what Keynes had hoped for. But it is a great deal more real and more effective than in the years when he was trying to call it into being.

It is of course possible to take the view, as many people still do, that international management is a mirage, good for providing futile employment for thousands upon thousands of bureaucrats and diplomats, swelling the self-importance of governments as they stumble along the primrose path in pursuit of will-o'-the-wisps, and pandering to the popular illusion that governments and only governments have it in their power to change things for the better. There are those who sigh for automaticity, for the days of the gold standard, fixed exchange rates, and an inelastic money supply. They would rejoice if more things were taken out of the hands of governments and shaped by recognizable necessities. Those of this pessimistic school of thought distrust discretion in attempts to control what we only half understand. They would rather accept fixed rules to achieve fixed objectives, however harsh the consequences of abiding by the rules.

On this there is no doubt where Keynes stood. He trusted to human intelligence. He hated enslavement by rules. He wanted governments to have discretion and he wanted economists to come to their assistance in the exercise of that discretion. But he certainly held no exalted view of the wisdom of governments or the virtues of economic science. On the contrary he harped on the fallibility of governments and was for ever attacking the decisions they took. He was more charitable to his colleagues, the economists, but left the distinct impression in some quarters that until he came along they had spent much of their time preaching mistaken doctrines. No doubt he expected that in due course cries of '*tu quoque*' would be heard from his successors.

The unwisdom of governments and the errors of their advisers weighed less heavily with Keynes than the need to hold open the door to better management of our affairs. More damage would be done in the end by blind trust in some man-made institution that excluded all discretion than by considered policies which could improve through time as experience accumulated. In any event nearly all institutions did in practice leave room for discretion and those that did not were almost invariably modified so that they did. The gold standard, for example, was increasingly a managed standard. Equally, the rigid requirements of the Bank Charter Act of 1844, to take another example, had to be got round whenever they really began to bite. The choice is very, very rarely between management and some automatic rule dispensing with management; it is essentially between different ways of exercising managerial discretion and accepting or rejecting the need to consider well in advance where and how discretion might most fruitfully be called into play.

But of course Keynes never imagined that one can dispense with rules. Without them life is simply incalculable, arbitrary and chaotic. There has to be a framework of rules and conventions that one can take for granted and it is this framework that is described as a system. Keynes devoted himself in his last years to schemes for international monetary reform designed to create a new system that would harmonize international monetary relationships. The International Monetary Fund and the International Bank for Reconstruction and Development were not built to his specifications. But he recognized the need for institutions along those lines. The discretion that he wished national governments to enjoy had to be tempered by the discipline necessary for international collaboration and international management. What balance between the two he would now favour in the light of postwar experience no one can be sure; but it is certain that he would have wanted a system that would evolve, rules that could be altered as circumstances altered, and as much discretion as could be left to national governments consistently with the preservation of a satisfactory international system.

KEYNES'S INFLUENCE

Given these strands in Keynes's thinking – demand management and control of investment in the interests of full employment; the potential development of public or semi-public corporations; and the need for a satisfactory international monetary system – what has Keynes's influence been on the policies of governments?

It was not very conspicuous before the war. He was listened to but his recommendations were rarely the basis of policy. When he published his *Essays in Persuasion* in 1931 he described them as 'the croakings of a Cassandra'. In the 1930s he gave his blessing to the cheap money policy pursued after the suspension of the gold standard but he was not the originator of the policy. Nor were his proposals for the finance of the war, although widely acclaimed, the cornerstone of budgetary policy. When deferred pay was introduced it was on a very limited scale: a gesture rather than Keynes's 'radical plan'. The capital levy that was to follow after the war never took place: when James Meade put it forward Keynes himself laughed the idea out of court as 'capital levity'. Family allowances, which he suggested in 1939, were introduced only when the war was over. The direction in which his influence was mainly felt before, during and after the war was in monetary policy and debt management. It was an influence exerted on the side of low rates of interest and a low burden of war debt. The consequences of this in the postwar period will be discussed in a moment.

After the war, when he was no longer alive to make his own contribution to policy, Keynes, in a sense, came into his own. His influence was exerted, as he had always expected, through a new generation in sympathy with his ideas. At the end of the *General Theory* he had pointed to the lag that usually attended the acceptance of new doctrines:

> In the field of economic and political philosophy there are not many who are influenced by new theories after they are 25 or 30 years of age, so that the ideas which civil servants and politicians and even agitators apply to current events are not likely to be the newest.[11]

By 1945, and still more by 1950, many of those who had been brought up on Keynes were well into their thirties and climbing into positions of influence in different countries. In the Central Banks and Ministries of Finance Keynesian ideas were sure of a hearing and increasingly accepted as a basis of policy. But in the process of elevation to an established ideology there was inevitably some oversimplification and a substitution of dogma for theoretical insight. Politicians in particular were content to know the endpoint to which Keynes's theories led without wasting time in tracing the path by which his conclusions were reached. There is a revealing passage in Ronald Walker's *From Economic Theory to Policy*, published in 1943, in which he describes how:

> In the library of the Australian Parliament at Canberra there is a copy of the *General Theory*. The first 300 pages, in which the theory is worked out, are of virgin whiteness; the last 80 pages, with the practical applications, are well thumbed and heavily scored.[12]

The idea that weighed most with politicians was that mass unemployment resulted from a deficiency of demand and could be cured by increased spending. This was not in itself a particularly helpful insight into the problems of the postwar world which proved to be very different from the world in which Keynes lived and wrote: a world in which unemployment stayed obstinately at an unprecedented level (never falling in the UK below two million in the 1930s) and in which it seemed inconceivable that prices could rise very much or very long in peacetime. In the postwar world, mass unemployment virtually disappeared and deflation was replaced by inflation. There was no lack of demand and rarely any governmental scruples about spending more for fear of unbalancing the budget.

UNEMPLOYMENT AND INFLATION

One can regard this new situation in two ways. One can argue that the new generation of economic medicine men were equipped by Keynes to cure a disease that had disappeared and that their prescriptions for avoiding unemployment merely made inflation worse. Or one can argue that we owe it to Keynes that the problem of unemployment did not return after the war and that we have ourselves to blame if we have not worked out since his death how to combine full employment and stable prices.

Neither of these views seems to me satisfactory. Both attach far too much importance to the influence on events for good or bad of a particular set of ideas, which were by no means the exclusive basis of policy, if indeed policy had the importance in postwar economic development that both views assume. It seems to me very doubtful whether politicians are 'the slaves of some defunct economist', even if the economist is as powerful a thinker as Keynes; and still more doubtful whether in a democracy policies govern events rather than the other way round.

The universality of full employment in the postwar period, for example, makes it difficult to attribute it to successful economic management in a particular country or to the influence of Keynesian ideas in that country. It seems more likely that the circumstances were propitious for a prolonged investment boom and that the pressure for high government spending, although an important circumstance of this kind, was only vaguely connected with Keynesian ideas.

What was perhaps of more importance was the accommodating and often expansionary monetary policy pursued. Here there is a definite link with Keynes. In the early postwar years the British government in particular went out of its way to keep down the rate of interest. This was in its interest as a borrower and it was in the general interest of the taxpayer since the budget was correspondingly smaller. But it increased the incentive to invest when this was already strong and reinforced the inflationary pressures at work. Keynes might well have approved: the situation was quite unlike that in 1919–20 when he recommended putting the Bank Rate up to 10 per cent to curb a speculative boom. But if inflation was not to be controlled by monetary policy the alternative was to restrict consumption in other ways and continue control over investment. This was the policy which the government adopted.

It implied the use of physical controls of a kind that Keynes did not normally favour and a corresponding extension of government intervention in industry. It was not possible to control investment in the years immediately after the war merely by limiting capital issues, sending letters of guidance from the Bank of England to the commercial banks and similar devices. It was necessary to ration new building by an elaborate system of licensing and starting dates, complicated further by arrangements to allocate steel, timber, etc., and to limit investment in new plant by machinery licensing, including the licensing of individual machines procured from abroad. Some parts of the system were extraordinarily cumbersome and hopelessly inefficient: import licensing of machinery, for example, would have seemed to Keynes the prime example of a control to avoid. Similarly, control of international investment implied exchange control in great detail, often with the maximum inconvenience to businesses trading abroad; and it is not clear how far Keynes would have pressed for such control in face of the anomalies and frustrations it generated. What cannot be denied, however, is that by giving countenance to the idea of controlling investment, domestic and foreign, and insisting on low rates of interest in a potentially inflationary world, Keynes was throwing his weight behind a continuation of tight government control over industry and trade.

Although circumstances may have been favourable to full employment after the war the system of demand management that evolved to preserve it was undoubtedly Keynesian. This was particularly apparent in the technique of short-term economic forecasting that was developed. The whole system of thought underlying the forecasting derived from Keynes: the projection of effective demand by category, the interrelation between the constituent parts, the parameters, lags and mechanisms of adjustment, the emphasis on a limited horizon with more or less fixed resources, even the relegation of monetary influences (as distinct from expenditure influence) to a subordinate place. The Treasury was steeped in Keynes. But this was not true of other departments of government. The problems with which they wrestled did not disappear as soon as a steady pressure of demand was achieved. They were faced with the task of building things up, not of cutting things down to size, and on these positive tasks of organization Keynes had little to say.

KEYNES AND PLANNING

To put the matter concretely: what would Keynes have done in the Department of Economic Affairs or in the preparation of a National Plan?

I think one can assume no enthusiasm for either. It is inconceivable that he could have encouraged the publication of anything called a 'plan' in a country on the verge of devaluation and not yet reconciled to it. But he was in any event strongly against planning in the sense of moulding an entire economy to meet fixed, detailed objectives specified without much regard to consumer demand.

Keynes did not survive the war long enough to take part in the postwar debate on planning. But he would have observed without surprise that the strongest commitment to planning was on the part of those with least experience of it, and that those who had spent the war in the planning of industrial outputs to meet government requirements (such as in the Planning Division of the Ministry of Aircraft Production) were the most sceptical of the pretensions of central planning. The great virtue of financial planning, in which Keynes did believe, was that it *de*centralized organization while central planning did just the opposite. His kind of planning was intended to make possible an enlargement of individual freedom as the rule of the road does. So he found no difficulty in expressing agreement 'morally and philosophically' with 'virtually the whole' of von Hayek's *The Road to Serfdom*, although he had some reservations about the pronouncements on economics.

'I should say', he wrote, 'that what we want is not no planning, or even less planning, indeed I should say that we almost certainly want more. But the planning should take place in a community in which as many people as possible, both leaders and followers, wholly share your own moral position.'[13]

Planning for Keynes meant regulating economic activity by demand management using fiscal and monetary policy. This involved more government intervention of a rather special kind: control over monetary policy, willingness to run budget surpluses and deficits, cooperation with other governments and international bodies like the IMF. But it did not necessarily imply an increase in the size of the budget or an extension of the public sector or intervention in the affairs of individual businesses or industries. It is not possible to regard full employment policy as responsible for any major enlargement of the role of the state or any positive encroachment on the freedom of the individual. On the contrary it was designed to give individuals the wider freedom that comes from the opportunity of employment. For this purpose all that Keynes required of the budget was that it should direct expenditure and raise revenue so as to redress any imbalance between the two in the private sector.

INCREASED STATE ACTIVITY

But if full employment is exonerated what is to blame for the heavier burdens we now put upon the state and for the harassments to which we expose ourselves in consequence? The answer is complex. On the one hand, there is the temper of the times. People have been increasingly predisposed to accept without challenge the need for government control to serve the common good. On the other hand there has been no lack of highly desirable aims for the government to profess. These aims have usually led the government to tax more and spend more and above all to administer more. It is fundamentally because we have set our sights higher and expect more from the state that it intervenes more in our lives.

One example of this is the call for greater economic equality. It is not easy to provide a simple measure of the amount of public expenditure to which this has given rise. But if we aggregate public spending in the United Kingdom on education, health and housing and add pensions and other social security benefits, the total comes to £85,000 million for 1985–86 or over 60 per cent of total public expenditure. How much of this would be incurred if the ideas underlying the welfare state had never been formulated no one can say. But it is not unfair to regard this large total as reflecting an endeavour to ensure some minimum standard of provision for all and the bulk of it as a transfer from the better-off to the less well-off.

The budgetary consequences, however, are only part of the story. In all kinds of ways legislation conceived in the interests of equality, fairness and non-discrimination complicates the life of us all. The National Health Service is a good example. Expenditure has grown steadily because unless it expands it is necessary to deny treatment to some while granting it to others and at the same time the progress of medical science makes the treatment of each progressively more expensive. Once medical services have to be rationed – as a ceiling on expenditure would dictate – queues necessarily form and issues of parity of treatment begin to assume more importance and occupy more time.

Equality, moreover, is only a single strand in government intervention. There is also the effort to promote faster economic growth. With no Keynes to reveal the secret of faster growth, the state is the more determined to take action the less successful its previous efforts. It is ambitious to demonstrate its success in the latest and most expensive products of technology rushing in with unlimited funds where private investors are inevitably and justifiably more cautious. The state becomes increasingly interventionist because it is increasingly fidgety and dissatisfied with the pace set by private industry.

Thus it is not possible to lay at Keynes's door responsibility for the great extension in the part the state plays in our life. As I have explained elsewhere,[14] the origins of this lie in forces more powerful than the vision of even the greatest of social scientists: in the aftermath of two world wars that mobilized the entire population under the banner of the nation state; the transfer of power to the manual worker that this involved; the growing realization of that power under conditions of full employment and the perception that it could be used through the state for economic and social ends; the spread of democratic ideals by which the transfer of power was legitimized; the development of the welfare state and steeply progressive taxation as the outcome of these ideals; and on top of these political trends the steady pressure of a centralizing technology in industry and government and the emergence of a powerful and competent bureaucracy in response to that pressure.

The dominant forces at work making for increased state intervention were not let loose by Keynes nor would they have enjoyed his unqualified approval. Yet in one important way they gained strength from his influence and his ideas. For the centralizing tendencies would have been greatly weakened in the absence of a fuller understanding of economic management such as Keynes helped to supply. It was a sense of improved understanding that emboldened the state to extend its responsibilities: a belief that Keynes had liberated us from ignorance and danger so that economic forces would never again be allowed to get out of hand. Indeed, since regulation by the state was inevitable if full employment was to be secured, the more deeply the state involved itself in the running of the economic system the better.

Against this must be set the really important contribution that Keynes would have claimed he was making to our conception of how an economy should be run. For him 'the commanding heights of the economy' were not this industry or that. He had no use for an extensive programme of nationalization nor for elaborate schemes of licensing and control. What mattered was control of *demand*; and this could be exercised quite simply through existing financial machinery by the Treasury and the Bank of England. He wanted the *minimum* of intervention consistent with the fullest sustainable use of the country's resources. He should be credited with the retreat from the attempt after the war to perpetuate wartime controls by christening them 'planning' rather than charged with the subsequent outbreaks of interventionism, under banners no less misleading. Keynes taught us how to plan through the budget. There *are* other ways of planning. But those who think they understand them would do well to make sure before advocating them that they have first grasped the full significance of Keynes's approach to planning.

Keynes insisted on control over the level of effective demand as a precondition of full employment. But he was well aware that this was not a sufficient condition. His writings in the 1930s are strewn with references to perversities in the behaviour of markets that might thwart the efforts of governments to expand demand: panic reactions based on slogans of the past or distrust of governmental intentions. Deficit financing, for example, might be ineffective in a world in which business retrenched still more in face of what it took to be evidence of unsustainable extravagance by governments. Attempts to create additional liquidity by adding to the money supply might merely generate alarm and an appetite for still more liquidity or lead to an outflow of funds and pressure on the foreign exchanges. Demand management might not be the straightforward business it is so often thought to be.

WAGE INFLATION

But there was also a much bigger reservation to be made. Keynes saw earlier and more clearly than most other economists that curing unemployment would weaken the economy's resistance to the inflationary bug. In the *Economic Journal* in 1943 he referred to the view that:

> a capitalist country is doomed to failure because it will be found impossible in conditions of full employment to prevent a progressive increase of wages. According to this view severe slumps and recurrent periods of unemployment have been hitherto the only effective means of holding efficiency wages within a reasonably stable range. Whether this is so or not remains to be seen. The more conscious we are of this problem, the likelier we are to surmount it.[15]

Writing to Frank Graham at the end of 1943 he asked:

> How much otherwise unavoidable unemployment do you propose to bring about in order to keep the Trade Unions in order? Do you think it will be politically possible when they understand what you are up to?[16]

He went on to argue that 'other, more reasonable, less punitive means must be found'. But he did not claim to have found them. To another correspondent at the end of 1943 he wrote:

> The task of keeping efficiency wages reasonably stable (I am sure they will creep up steadily in spite of our best efforts) is a *political* rather than an economic problem.[17]

And in June 1945 he was writing

One is also, simply because one knows no solution, inclined to turn a blind eye to the wages problem in a full employment economy.[18]

But how can one go on turning a blind eye? One has to decide whether the labour market responds to the money supply or vice versa. If wage inflation is essentially a political problem how can we be sure that the Keynesian prescription for full employment would not call for extensive government intervention? The prescription calls for political action to prevent wages from rising ahead of productivity and we do not know what political action would be required in order to do what unemployment is alleged to have done in the past to temper the bargaining power of labour to the needs of price stability. So long as we do not know we cannot say with assurance how much intervention and what kinds of intervention Keynes would have accepted as the price of full employment.

NOTES

1 *Collected Writings of John Maynard Keynes*, Vol. IX, (Macmillan, London, for Royal Economic Society, 1972), p. 288.
2 Ibid., p. 291.
3 Ibid., pp. 291–2.
4 Ibid., p. 288.
5 Ibid., p. 290.
6 Ibid., p. 289.
7 Above, p. 49.
8 J. M. Keynes, *Collected Writings*, Vol. IX, p. 302.
9 Ibid., p. 297.
10 G. M. Young, *Sunday Times*, 14 January 1940.
11 J. M. Keynes, *General Theory of Employment, Interest and Money*, (Macmillan, London, 1936) pp. 383 - 384.
12 E. R. Walker, *From Economic Theory to Policy*, (University of Chicago Press, Chicago, 1943), p. 72.
13 Cited by R. F. Harrod, *The Life of John Maynard Keynes* (Macmillan, London, 1951), p. 436.
14 Above, p. 38.
15 J. M. Keynes, *Economic Journal*, June - September 1943, pp. 183 and 185, quoted by Lord Kahn in 'On re-reading Keynes', *Proceedings of the British Academy*, Vol. 60 (1974), p. 379.
16 Lord Kahn, 'On re-reading Keynes', p. 380.
17 Ibid., p. 387.
18 Ibid., p. 387.

5

Planning and decision taking under conditions of uncertainty

There are no doubt some plans that are almost wholly free from uncertainty. For example, we can plan how to make the most of our income, knowing in advance what prices we will have to pay for the things we want. The chances are, however, that we will miss a bargain or two because we can't possibly know all the prices at which goods are on offer and even if we knew all today's prices we couldn't possibly know tomorrow's. We also don't know what our income will be, so that we are bound to be uncertain whether to buy today or wait till tomorrow.

Where we are looking to the future – as all planning we need consider does – uncertainty inevitably enters. It is this uncertainty that makes planning so difficult. If we could get rid of uncertainty – if we lived in a very stable and predictable world – it would be much easier – and at the same time less necessary – to plan ahead. On the other hand, if things are changing very rapidly and the uncertainties are multiplying fast, it may be impossible to plan for the future: all that can be done in these circumstances is to improvise – to react to events without any fixed plan – and this is the very opposite of planning. Freedom from uncertainty makes planning simple but almost superfluous; acute uncertainty, multiplying and enduring, makes planning virtually impossible.

Before we go on to consider the intermediate situation in which it is necessary to weigh up a limited number of fairly definite contingencies we need to reflect on the kind of planning we have in mind.

Paper delivered to successive courses on 'Planning under conditions of uncertainty' at the Civil Service College, Sunningdale Park.

PLANNING AS AN ECONOMIC PROCESS

Planning is usually associated with investment, i.e. the commitment of resources in the expectation of a stream of future benefits. Even where plans may make no mention of investment, as in health, educational and military planning there is normally a decision to commit resources in order to achieve some future result.

This raises at once questions as to the degree of commitment and the assessment of benefits. How flexible is the commitment? Can the investment be delayed or advanced, reduced or reinforced? Could the resources be put to different and better uses? How are the benefits to be measured and discounted so as to admit of comparison with the cost of the resources used? Economists have developed techniques for finding an answer to at least the last of these questions through the use of dcf calculations. But where large resources are about to be committed irrevocably all these questions need to be put.

Again, since the world does not stand still, any targets set by the plan must be subject to constant review. The timetable, the commitments, the benefits in relation to costs – all need periodic re-planning. The market may change, resources may become more expensive, or the plans of competitors may nullify the original aim. It is not only in war that the success of one plan lies in thwarting another, the enemy's, plan; or that the truth needs to be grasped that planning is a continuous process so that the essence of all good planning is re-planning.

PLANNING AS AN ORGANIZATIONAL AND SOCIAL PROCESS

When an individual plans his own affairs, how he sets about it is of interest chiefly to himself. But large scale planning involving many people raises organizational problems of a different kind. If their cooperation is required to make a success of the plan then the plan must make provision for that cooperation. This raises a wide range of issues as to how the plan takes shape – who draws it up, who is consulted, who approves it – and as to how it is implemented – by command or instruction or voluntary cooperation or by offering incentives such as payment? Many people attack or approve planning without specifying any antithesis to it so that it is not clear what would happen in the absence of planning. If the issue is one of comprehensive planning of an entire economy then the alternative is to rely on market forces to link together the planning units which we call firms rather than turn them all into subsidiaries of one vast holding company called the state. If the issue is the more limited one of how an individual unit, public or private, should set about planning its activities, then the contrast is between a more deliberate assessment of future prospects and possibilities leading to the preparation of a programme for production and marketing over a longish period and a more casual *ad hoc* response to the movement of prices, the flow of orders or other tangible changes in market conditions.

There are several aspects of the more complex form of organization which we call planning. The most important of these centre on the issue of delegation. If the activities of a large group of people are planned this means that they must try to conform to the plan rather than respond independently to market or other signals.

If we regard planning as essentially coordination ahead of events we can see at once that it raises two central problems. The first of these relates to centralization and delegation. Coordination may make for greater efficiency but it does so by limiting the freedom of action of the units coordinated. When the activities of a large group of people are planned, this implies that they must try to conform to the plan rather than respond independently to market or other signals. From this arises the danger of inflexibility: the individual in immediate contact with the situation has to abide by instructions from above or can exercise his judgement and initiative only within the limits of delegated responsibility allowed for in the plan.

The second problem is that of uncertainty. The plan is formed ahead of events and events may not have been correctly foreseen. It is precisely because of this uncertainty that delegation is necessary and the greater the uncertainty the greater the need for delegation. But the further delegation is carried the more difficult is coordination. Thus the central problem of planning – to find the optimum balance between centralization and decentralization – arises out of uncertainty. If uncertainty can be reduced, for example by improving communication between the centre and the periphery, it will be possible to centralize more. Planning can be carried further, and more reliance put on the plan, if it can be more quickly adapted to the latest information and if the change in plan can simultaneously be communicated more quickly to those affected. Alternatively, if uncertainty can be contained – that is, if authority can be delegated to deal with localized uncertainty while the planning unit confines itself to uncertainties with a wider compass – centralization can be carried further in directions in which it is truly advantageous without running counter to decentralization where it is indispensable. In the first case the system of communication is critical, in the second it is the planned division of responsibility. The conclusion to be drawn is familiar: in face of uncertainty, planning rests fundamentally on efficient communication and careful delegation.

Apart from these two central problems there are others. Do we understand sufficiently what is going on to intervene and seek to control it through a plan? And if we do mean to exercise control do we know for what purposes we intend to do so? We are probably uncertain on both scores. We have usually only an imperfect understanding of how the world works and only limited and unreliable information about what is happening now. At the same time we may well be uncertain who will have the deciding voice in the framing of a plan, whose interests the plan is to serve, what objectives are to be given priority.

Thus in addition to the problem of delegation and communication there are problems as to the validity of the model we use of the world in which we operate, as to the reliability of the data at our disposal and as to who has the last word when a plan is put into operation. Uncertainty attaches to all of these problems and frequently dominates them.

We need also to allow for the way planning decisions are actually taken. Government departments – and business corporations as well – do not usually make important decisions in an atmosphere of calm detachment in which all elements in the situation are carefully weighed. The atmosphere is often one of crisis because nothing less than crisis will elicit a decision. The crisis is not necessarily unforeseen but it comes unexpectedly and has not been prepared for: the injunction to be ready for the unexpected is rarely obeyed. So decisions have to be taken in a hurry, sometimes in conditions of near panic and flap. On top of this are the struggles between the interests affected: within departments, between departments, at meetings of Ministers. Decisions taken in a dogfight can hardly be entirely rational. But those who know what they want and, having thought things through, can explain why, are at an advantage.

Sometimes the decisions to be taken do not admit of analysis in quantitative terms. It may be impossible to advance beyond gut feelings that hardly admit of interrogation, still less of argument. In all commitments to an unknown future there is necessarily an element of sheer animal spirits, as Keynes once pointed out. If things go consistently well it is much easier to plunge than if things have constantly gone wrong for some time; and since things are usually more likely to go well in future if the plunge is taken simultaneously by a number of decision takers, a buoyant mood can be self-sustaining. If one contrasts the situation in England – where repeated efforts to get something going are brought to nothing time after time – with the situation in Japan – where the opposite applies – one can see how a mood may take root and be difficult to alter: and how also such a mood may play as large a part in decision taking under uncertainty as the application of any known technique or procedure.

Leaving these considerations on one side let us return to the sources of uncertainty already listed and go over them one by one: the data, the model, the scale of preference, and communication between all concerned.

The Data

Planning requires a flow of accurate and up-to-date information. But this rarely exists and its absence is the source of much of the uncertainty in planning. It is no use lamenting the lack of data: collecting more does not remove the uncertainty and may indeed add to it. The cry of Ministers, faced with difficult decisions, is invariably for more data. But what they really would like is more certainty. In a world where the big decisions are necessarily taken in ignorance and uncertainty it is no use kicking against the pricks.

What *can* be done, however, is to make the fullest use of available information and try to reduce the area left to pure judgement by carrying measurement and estimation as far as possible. In modern life, information tends to be compressed into statistics. This makes it much easier to handle. There is no escape from relying heavily on statistics, often without an adequate knowledge of the circumstances of their origin, their reliability and completeness. But in the process of compression something is inevitably lost.

The layman needs to handle statistics with great care. Ely Devons used to say that 'statistics are for the statistician', by which he meant that it is rash to take them at face value. One needs to know their family history: where they come from and what they have been through. Any simple set of figures like the unemployment returns or the rates of inflation quoted in the newspapers will illustrate how difficult it is to interpret them correctly. In the 1960s there was hardly a single occasion, if any, on which it was possible to tell from a London evening paper, month by month, whether the level of unemployment had risen or fallen. The seasonally adjusted figures were not printed, still less was one warned that the seasonal adjustments were themselves liable to change. In the 1970s when the figures unmistakably increased it was by no means easy to judge what change was implied in the state of the labour market or whether the figures were any longer a reliable guide to the degree of labour shortage. Similarly, when inflation rates are quoted they are usually measured over a period of twelve months, not in relation to what is happening currently – which may be very different – and they invariably relate to consumer prices when the behaviour of costs may be far more significant.

These difficulties of interpretation – of which examples could be multiplied – come to the surface immediately we try to digest statistical information into a forecast. A forecast is essentially an attempt to resolve uncertainties and prepare the way for a decision. In all planning it is necessary to form a view of the future and for that purpose forecasts digesting the available statistical data are indispensable. Although the forecasts are nominally in terms of the future they are to a large extent statements about the past. That is, they are based on models of how things worked in the past and assume that the same model will continue to operate in the future. Moreover, so far as the recent past is concerned, they require an effort to reconcile the conflicting and incomplete data so as to fit it into a self-consistent picture: so much so that if one asks what is going on now the most satisfactory answer is likely to be the latest forecast rather than last week's conflicting statistics. We never, in fact, start from a known position but have to begin by forecasting the present.

The first source of uncertainty, therefore, lies in the data. How far can we trust the information that we have, knowing that it is incomplete, not internally consistent, subject to revision, and difficult to correct for seasonal or irregular variations? We must do the best we can by giving time to the study of the data, treating figures more like unexploded bombs than like pepper in a pepper pot.

It is also important to keep an eye on the right data. If we are studying population growth, for example, it is more important to examine the movement in age specific fertility rates than simple birth rates. It may also be more significant what is happening to third or fourth births than what is happening to total births. It is necessary to establish what are the most sensitive indicators of change. This takes us to the second source of uncertainty, the model. How confident are we that we have the right model or picture of what lies behind the figures: the inner logic of the relationships influencing their behaviour?

The Model

In planning for the future we need to have a picture of the future. One way of forming such a picture is by preparing a forecast. This fits the available information into the framework of a model which is essentially a theory specifying the key variables in the situation and their relationship to one another. If the theory is mistaken and the variables and their relationships are mis-specified the forecasts will be correspondingly unreliable. The virtue of a systematic forecast is that it obliges the forecaster to consider all the evidence with the help of a carefully framed hypothesis that appears to have worked in the past. Even if the hypothesis is correct this will not make the forecast right but it does make it more likely to be right (i.e. it reduces uncertainty) on that assumption.

There are, of course, ways of trying to dispense with models by simple extrapolation of past trends and these methods may perform just as satisfactorily as the models – for a time at least. All forecasting relies on extrapolation in one form or another since it presupposes the persistence of forces, identified in models or unidentified in trends, that have been at work in the past. The same is true in the natural sciences where, since nature does not take a leap, the whole business of forecasting is a lot easier. But even in the natural world, as we know from weather forecasting and mineral exploration, mistakes can still be made where the information is imperfect and the model inadequate.

Preferences

The third source of uncertainty arises in the weighing up of alternatives and the establishment of preferences. The preparation of a forecast does not by itself imply any particular course of action. What decision is taken in the light of a diagnosis or forecast depends upon who, if anyone, has the last word and what the objective of policy is. In a company the last word may rest with the managing director or the Board and the objective may be profit. In such circumstances decision taking is relatively straightforward since the criterion of action is simple and explicit and any doubts can be quickly resolved. But in government decision taking matters are much more complicated. There may be no identifiable agreed objective except in war time or it may be too vague – 'the national interest' – to be of much good. The planners – official or ministerial – may be in disagreement in their assessment of the situation or in their scale of preferences and the general public may be at least as divided, but less well informed. Whose preferences is the plan to express? In a democracy there can be no authoritarian elimination of dissent: there has to be some way of reconciling differences. In a so-called 'unplanned' economic system, the reconciliation is effected through the market without debate, each participant deciding for himself how he will spend his income and in what job he will earn it. But where there is a conscious effort to plan economic activity it is necessary either to proceed on the basis of *ex cathedra* pronouncements on the desirability of particular outputs or by votes or surveys that register what people say they want. The same antithesis arises in one form or another in all planning: those for whom the plan is designed have either to accept it without more ado because the planners 'know best', or they may be consulted through surveys of opinion or consumer behaviour, or in the last resort they may use their votes, if they have any, to assert their preferences.

It might seem that in government planning the weighing up of alternatives and deciding between them was a matter for Ministers. As everyone familiar with *Yes Minister* knows, this is a great over-simplification. In principle no doubt a Minister is 'in charge' of his department, takes responsibility for it, and on all important issues either formally registers his decision or takes the matter to Cabinet for decision there. But in practice he is faced with the simple fact that time is short and decisions almost endless so that there is no escape from delegation. This may limit the discretion of officials but still allows their preferences (or biases) considerable play. The Minister is constrained in what he decides by the limitations of his briefs and by the need to leave a great deal to his officials. He is even more constrained by the need to carry public opinion with him. His word is law only so long as he remains in office and his decisions are bound to be coloured by his natural desire to stay there. Thus there is nearly always a question whether the preferences expressed in a ministerial decision are those of his officials, of the Minister himself, of the Cabinet, or of the public (as perceived by the Minister or the Cabinet).

All this introduces a fresh aspect of uncertainty. The officials may be uncertain of the Minister's own views and he of theirs. There is, after all, no guarantee that the Minister will seek their views on every issue nor that they will be given the necessary opportunity to establish his in the limited period for which he is with them. The Minister may be uncertain how far he is speaking for his colleages and although this can readily be put to the test, there is a limit to the number of issues he can hope to raise in Cabinet as well as some disposition to have his own way without running that gauntlet. As for the public, it is by no means easy to judge, in the absence of votes or other means of counting heads, what it is thinking. The public may be content that the Cabinet should manage the nation's affairs without constantly sounding out opinion on every issue and that it should present itself at election time on its general record. Management does not usually imply waiting to be told what to do. But there are many issues – especially those involving public expenditure – where it is not the competence or incompetence of the government that is in question but whether the collective preferences of the public have been correctly assessed. If the matter is one of simple fact it should be possible to establish the truth by enquiry: for example, by an opinion survey. Such surveys are usually left to the media or academic bodies to conduct and are still viewed with great suspicion because many surveys are clumsily conducted and carelessly interpreted. Nevertheless the use of surveys as a means of eliminating uncertainty as to public preferences is now an established procedure.

There is uncertainty therefore as to whose preferences are decisive and sometimes also as to what the preferences that are thought to be decisive really are. There is also uncertainty as to how strongly other people's preferences are held. A Minister may learn this only when summoned before the Prime Minister and the Cabinet may learn it only when they are thrown out at an election.

The fact that there are these uncertainties complicates the business of decision taking. It means that the Minister may have his eye on one set of uncertainties while his official advisers have their eye on a quite different set. They may be seeking to impress on him uncertainties as to the outcome of a decision while he is reflecting on his officials' motives in seeking a decision or on how the decision will affect his political future. The problem of communicating uncertainty from one level to the next which we discuss below is compounded by uncertainty as to the level at which decisions will be taken.

Where this form of uncertainty is narrowed or removed (as in a dictatorship) and the power of decision is highly concentrated it is not uncommon to find an appearance of greater efficiency. Uncertainty does not usually make for efficiency. But where it arises our of freedom of choice the appearance of greater efficiency after that freedom has been removed may be deceptive and mean no more than that the wishes of the decision takers have been more effectively carried out whether they accord or not with what others want.

Communication

Decisions usually involve several people, not all of whom are aware that they are taking part. This point is often overlooked in current decision theory. Very often a decision is prejudged or prejudiced by failure to take action early enough; and this failure may occur well down in the hierarchy because a junior official, with limited discretion, was not aware of what was happening, or did not grasp its significance, or did not report it, or had not imagined that action of a kind unfamiliar to him could be taken at a higher level. It is not true, therefore, that only Ministers take decisions: it is nearer the truth to say that they expect to take the decisions referred to them for decision. But how they take decisions depends upon how matters are presented to them. It is highly important how the element of uncertainty is conveyed from one level to the next.

In a government department dealing with highly technical issues, there is a problem of assessing uncertainty and communicating the uncertainty from one set of officials to another and from officials to Ministers. Even if the very latest techniques have been used by the experts, they may have to express the outcomes, as they see them, in terms not readily understood by the ordinary administrator and quite baffling to Ministers. The engineers, economists and administrators may all talk different languages, none of them the language of the politician.

This situation is not unlike that in a large business corporation where expert and commercial opinion have to be married at Board level usually after the preparation and submission of memoranda and previous discussion in committee. In a one-man or family business, and in others dominated by a single individual, the procedure may be less elaborate and the final decision depend more on instinct and flair. In business, too, there is less need to ensure that the grounds for decision are carefully set out since decisions are less public and less open to public challenge. In government the very fact that decisions may be called in question in Parliament or the press tilts the scale against boldness. Where the immediate costs are high and the pay-off distant and doubtful, Ministers tend to 'play safe' in the sense of avoiding unpopular decisions. But they do not 'play safe' in the quite different sense of minimizing uncertainty. On the contrary, they tend to prefer large and expensive projects, with which their name will be associated, that have caught the public imagination. There will always, so to speak, be a Concorde.

With public projects, the uncertainties may appear differently to those who take the decisions and those who foot the bill. The benefits, too, that sway an official or a Minister may seem less striking to the electorate. Even when the benefits are tested exclusively from the point of view of the public good, there may be a wide difference between the expectations of the public and those who act on its behalf. It is not easy for the public to weigh the probabilities and they have obstinate preconceptions that are often ill founded. In a democracy, however, the presentation of expert assessments and Ministerial judgements for popular approval may be inescapable and add a further stage to the business of communicating uncertainty from one level to the next.

Forecasts provide a good illustration of the problems involved. In government, unlike business, the forecaster and the decision taker are rarely identical. A forecast represents the best judgement of those who prepared it but it does not, if expressed simply in figures, tell the whole story to a decision taker or convey all that the forecaster thinks. If it is intended to help a Minister decide how to run his risks, it may in fact mislead him if he trusts the forecast and does not enquire into the risks of error. The forecast may express the most probable outcome but as Voltaire remarked, 'the probable seldom happens'. What has to be conveyed along with the forecast is some indication from the forecaster of the confidence he has in it, the chances that there may be very different outcomes, the loss or damage that is likely to result if there is a divergence from the forecast and no allowance has been made for such a divergence in the action taken.

We come back in the end to the necessity of delegation: the impossibility that everything can be decided by one man and the consequent need to devolve responsibility to others. Whether one is looking at the chain of responsibility vertically in an administrative hierarchy or horizontally at the various clusters of expert advisers there has to be trust in the other man's judgement. It is not possible to take in all the evidence at each stage in decision taking whether the evidence is technical and offered by experts or non-technical and offered by administrators. Successive filterings limit what has to be decided at the top to the decision taking capacity of the man at the top. But for him the biggest decisions have to do not with what is filtered but with who should do the filtering. Good judgement is the most powerful weapon for handling uncertainty and good judgement of other men's judgement is the most powerful weapon of all.

This conclusion runs counter to the idea that it should be left to the expert to decide. Boards of Directors, it is often argued, should have more scientists on them when the decisions to be taken may have a large scientific component. This is doubly mistaken. First it is usually technology not science that dominates technical decisions and scientists are not necessarily good technologists. In any event there is far more to science than any one man can know. Second, decision taking is itself a craft and those who practise it have to learn when to trust an expert and which experts to trust. Some experts are also good decision takers but it is not, as a rule, their expertise that makes them so. So while scientists may be very useful members of Boards it is not their scientific knowledge that should be decisive but their good judgement and in particular their good judgement of other experts.

SOCIAL ASPECTS OF PLANNING

Once the social aspects of planning are fully grasped its complexity is immediately apparent. Planning decisions are not, in the nature of the case, taken by single individuals who are perfectly informed, know for certain what is going on and what to expect, and are free from the need to persuade, explain and defend their decision. The implementation and monitoring of planning decisions are also not carried out in isolation by individuals possessed of full knowledge and able to do the whole job by themselves. A great many people are usually involved at all stages. Moreover the decisions themselves are by no means discrete Yes/No affairs, so that each can be isolated from the next and treated separately.

They have often to be taken in the context of other decisions, either simultaneously or sequentially. They may be recurrent, so that what is done now sets the stage for later decisions or delimits what can be done next time. They may relate to part of a whole system so that every other part of the system is affected. Within the economic system, for example, to commit resources in one direction may be to deny resources in another, not necessarily deliberately but because prices or interest rates or exchange rates are affected and react on other decisions. Again the decision may require the agreement of many different parties so that it is essentially conditional and the main uncertainty may attach to the best strategy for achieving agreement. There is then a risk that agreement for its own sake is exalted above the merits of the plan agreed upon. Similarly where a decision presupposes a successful negotiation it has to take account of a possible failure to agree.

All these complications limit the scope for a precise and uniform approach to decision analysis. But they suggest the need for a flexible strategy that takes full account of the various eventualities.

COPING WITH UNCERTAINTY: PROBLEMS AND PROCEDURES

It is easy to recognize the existence of uncertainty and the difficulties it creates. But it is not so easy to find ways of reducing it or learning how to handle it.

The most important thing is to be conscious where the main uncertainties lie, review the likelihood of the various contingencies and decide how much they matter. The more it is possible to attach magnitudes to the chances that things will go wrong in the ways envisaged and to the damage that would result in each case, the better. It is then possible at least to form some judgement of the cost of the uncertainty. In some kinds of decision it is also possible to go on and decide what contingency margins should be used, what reserves should be held against the contingencies and what provision should be made in the form of stocks or standby plant or other emergency equipment. There may also be ways of using some form of insurance that sets one man's uncertainty alongside another's and so achieves the greater certainty of the average outcome. An obvious example is the use of futures markets where it is possible to buy or sell for delivery at some future date at a price known today.

In coping with uncertainty one can turn either to maxims or mathematics. Both have their uses but both are liable to encourage dangerous illusions – maxims because they don't always apply and mathematics because it can make for false exactitude. What follows makes use of neither but tries to single out some common problems.

The Short Run and the Long

One of the major problems in dealing with uncertainty is to strike a balance between the long term and the short. To a planner who is under the necessity of making long term commitments it is a constant source of worry and frustration that the current situation is changing all the time, sometimes quite radically, and not only diverting attention from the long term but deflecting resources as well and casting doubt on the wisdom of long term plans. Most administrators (and the general public) kick against short run fluctuations and long for greater stability. But the fluctuations are real and cannot be ignored. If one could be sure that they were nothing more than fluctuations, and left the trend completely unaffected it would be quite reasonable to concentrate exclusively on the trend and hence on the long term. But it is never possible to be sure that this is so. The deviation from trend may be the signal of a change in trend to which a response must be made eventually and a much bigger and more awkward response if it is unduly delayed. On the other hand, if every change is construed as a change in trend the end result is a series of sweeping changes of plan that may prove to be entirely misguided because the underlying trend reasserts itself. We are all familiar with the danger of over-reaction that turns a shortage into a sure harbinger of surplus and the surplus in turn into the certain prelude to a shortage. The Stock Exchange, where one can observe from day to day the operation of uncertainty on bargaining, provides ample illustration of these propositions in the fluctuations that occur in market prices.

How then is one to reconcile the short run and the long when one cannot distinguish with confidence a wobble from a bend? The answer must depend on circumstances.

First, if the wobble is upwards there will be increased pressure on capacity and the issue is then whether to enlarge capacity. A decision can be delayed, pending more evidence of a persisting change in trend, if it is possible to use existing capacity more intensively. For example, a few years ago when it was doubtful what the future demand would be for higher education, one possible course of action was labelled 'tunnelling through the peak', implying that standards would be reduced for the peak years by reducing staff–student ratios and in other ways that avoided increased investment in staff and buildings. As it happens, the expected peak was removed by government cuts and there was no need for 'tunnelling through'. But the debate did make subsequent adjustment to these cuts easier than it would have been by preventing the substantial investment that might otherwise have been put in hand.

Secondly, if the wobble is downwards so that there is surplus capacity, the problem is one of keeping in being capacity that would become redundant unless demand revived. The excess capacity may be physical, and take the form of surplus buildings or plant, or human and take the form of a specialized staff, or it may consist simply of the goodwill represented by established connections that have to be maintained. Whatever the form, excess capacity is costly and it is only possible to maintain it in being by drawing on reserves. So if an adjustment in capacity is to be delayed in the interests of leaving long term plans intact until there is greater certainty of the need for change, reserves have to be built up in advance. Reserves constitute a form of insurance and are one of the standard devices for coping with uncertainty. Others are discussed later.

A simple example of the difficulty of reconciling the long term and the short is provided by the rate of exchange. There is a great deal to be said for holding to a fixed rate but short term pressures may make this very difficult. The reserves necessary to keep the rate from falling may be very large because the financial markets of the world dispose of enormous resources which a single government cannot match; and if they become convinced that the currency is overvalued, governments are unlikely to make a contrary view prevail unless they take all the measures that market operators (rightly or wrongly) believe to be required. The same can also be true in the opposite direction because there is a limit to the amount of foreign currency a government will be ready to acquire in exchange for equivalent amounts of its own currency. In one direction the government runs out of foreign exchange; in the other it has to inflate the currency to an extent that it judges to be dangerous. So in the end governments have been forced to allow the value of their currencies to float even when they were anxious to maintain external stability. They may think that fixed rates provide greater certainty: but this is so only if there is certainty that the rates will remain fixed.

The exchange rate does, however, serve as an example of how short term and long term uncertainties can be balanced against one another. The higher the rate goes, the greater the likelihood that it may have risen too high and the lower it falls, the more likely it is that it has fallen too far. So in normal circumstances there is a self-limiting element in the fluctuations that occur. By letting the rate reflect expectations, the government can bring in market forces to lend it some stability – within wide limits, however – and these forces are bound to take some cognisance of long term influences on the rate. There remains a question whether the market or the government is the better judge of a sustainable rate and whether some of the uncertainties that cause the fluctuations are really unavoidable or are either of the government's own making or the fruit of misconceptions and misunderstandings in the market.

Timing

A second problem is the timing of action. In any situation it is possible to decide either to do nothing, to act or to delay action.

The case for doing nothing at all is not always developed as a logical alternative because it tends to be taken for granted, particularly by Ministers under public pressure, that something *should* be done. If in the end nothing is done, this is more commonly because of failure to agree on what it would be best to do than because inaction is judged to be the most satisfactory outcome. But wherever it is proposed that resources be committed there should be a base case in which *no* further resources are committed. When British Rail submitted its modernization plans to the Treasury in the mid-1950s they showed a satisfactory return on the investment but did not make clear that if no investment took place there would be a very heavy loss so that all that the investment proposed would do was to convert the heavy loss into a smaller loss and leave in operation lines that had no chance of ever showing a profit.

Delaying action is a way of buying time either because delay will enhance the return on the eventual investment or because it is hoped that uncertainty will diminish or be resolved by some expected event. If cross-channel traffic is increasing rapidly it may pay to delay building a tunnel because the chances that it will show a profit when it comes into operation are enhanced. Similarly it may be wise not to build a tunnel at once if it is thought that a submerged tube would be preferable but there is some uncertainty about the technical feasibility of laying a submerged tube across the Channel and there are grounds for expecting an early resolution of this uncertainty.

In a far more general way, the *timing* of action is a decision of great importance in its own right. The question when to act may not be seen in the same light as the question whether to delay action but it is surrounded by the same uncertainties. The Chancellor has very little choice as to the time of year for his Budget but as soon as the Budget has been launched and before the Finance Bill has been passed he is quite likely to be asking himself whether he should take further action and if so, when. He is then faced with the difficulty that he does not know with any certainty what his Budget has done to the economy and that it may take quite a long time before he can weigh up whether it is working in the way he expected. Indeed, he can never know this with any certainty for he can neither be sure that he fully understands how the economy works nor know for sure whether what is happening can be attributed to his Budget or to quite different factors. He may feel obliged to act simply because he is uncertain, especially if there are circumstances such as holidays, or Christmas shopping, or by-elections that would make it difficult to act if he waited any longer.

The problem of timing arises most obviously with what one may call 'divisible' decisions: that is, decisions that can be taken in bits. In most decisions there is an element of flexibility of this kind since some part of the decision can be deferred while the rest goes ahead. For example, in the Channel Tunnel case it would be possible to build one tunnel and leave until later the decision whether to build the second. In all uncertain situations we have to ask how easy it would be to change our minds. If we dislike uncertainty we may be prepared to decide only on part of a project and defer the rest even although the total cost, if the whole project eventually goes ahead, is thereby increased.

There is of course some danger in approaching all decisions in terms of possible delay. To most people it spells indecisiveness and if carried too far can certainly breed it. It is better to regard deferment as merely a special case of the need to decide on the timing of any action proposed.

Alternative Plans

Any analysis of possible courses of action should be in terms of alternatives. What has to be settled is the most attractive alternative in relation to whatever turns out to be second best (including the possibility of doing nothing). In comparing the alternatives we must follow some well-known rules: (a) bygones are for ever bygones (for example, the fact that we have spent heavily on, say, a new railway line should not have any influence on our decision to use that line rather than send goods by road); and (b) only increments count. Any costs that would continue to be incurred, and any benefits that would continue to be enjoyed, whichever way we decide should be left out of account when we come to decide.

Forecasting

What crystallizes uncertainty is generally the forecast that provides the basis for action. It is therefore very important that the forecaster should be brought into the discussion. He may know nothing of the alternative plans under discussion and be unable therefore to relate his forecast to those alternatives. However expressed, the forecast conveys very little of the forecaster's assessment of contingencies and will be affected to some extent by his understanding of the use to which it is likely to be put. There are always people who automatically accept a set of figures when it is put in front of them, including programmes and forecasts that are already out of date and known to be wrong but not yet superseded, or that were prepared for some special purpose so that they are deliberately high or low. Some forecasts, moreover, are 'catching' in the sense that they set a fashion and other forecasters are unduly influenced by them. If decision takers want to use a forecast, therefore, they should try to establish what elements in it are 'hard' and what 'soft' and interrogate the forecaster so as to get his guidance on the underlying uncertainties.

There is a school of thought which hankers after embodying these uncertainties in the forecast by making it bifurcate, with an upper and lower limit rather than a single series of figures. Such a treatment no doubt allows forecasters to convey a little more of what is in their mind. But it is an illusion to suppose that Ministers will pay much regard to the spread between the figures rather than to a straight average between them; and in any event, doubling the number of figures submitted is no substitute for bringing in the forecaster. Nobody else can adequately convey the uncertainties as he sees them.

Experts

Finally, we come back to what is perhaps the cardinal issue. Forecasters may help to assess some uncertainties, especially if these lie in the statistics. But what of the technical uncertainties: the kind of problem posed by nuclear power stations, large aircraft, microchips, and so on? Techniques change over time and these are the changes that revolutionize our lives. But how can one become aware of the technical risks and judge what will work or be a commercial success? What experts can one turn to and how can one possibly trust any of them?

If there were a simple answer to this question, commercial success would be easy. It is precisely the expert who knows what can be made to work and what can't that any successful firm is anxious to recruit. Government departments have plenty of experts but they are not always selected because they have this flair and if they do have it, they may find a more lucrative career open to them elsewhere. But whether one takes advice inside or outside Government there are only two ways of picking an expert. One is to decide who knows what he or she is talking about and knows too the limits of his or her knowledge. The other is to go by a person's track record. There is no guarantee that either will yield the right results. The first person may be more plausible than sound and the second may have been lucky and run out of luck. But it is at least a help, in defending a decision, to be furnished with arguments by someone who carries conviction or by somebody who can be shown to have been in the right in the past.

But here again we are dealing with human judgement. It may need some practice to judge between one expert and another; and it is not necessarily the experts who are to be blamed if the advice accepted turns out to be wrong. It may be a comment on the inexperience or poor judgement of those who took the advice.

6

The limitations of shadow rates

There is widespread agreement among economists that market prices, including exchange rates and interest rates, are not reliable measures of social costs and benefits.

This conclusion is based partly on an enumeration of the various circumstances that cause the market to depart from a fully competitive model and partly on an appreciation of the limitations of competition itself. In an imperfect market, or one in which the number of competitors is limited, prices may be expected to diverge from marginal cost or this in turn from social opportunity cost. The theory is part of accepted doctrine. How to apply it is another matter: what importance to attach to the divergences between market price and social cost, which factors play the biggest part in causing them, how far and in what ways state intervention could improve the situation – these are questions on which reasonable men may differ and the answers are likely to be different in different countries and at different stages of economic development.

Even if competition were perfect, there would still be reasons for viewing market prices as unreliable guides to social valuations. The rate of exchange, for example, however freely it is allowed to respond to competitive pressures to buy or sell on current or capital account, does not register the 'true' scarcity of purchasing power over imports. The social return to additional imports might well differ from the social cost of the additional resources required to produce an equivalent value of exports. The rate of interest is an equally imperfect measure of the social importance of jam today compared with jam tomorrow. The appropriateness of a particular degree of capital intensity may also be wrongly indicated by the use of existing measures of the cost of labour and capital even when

From *Employment, Income Distribution and Development Strategy, Essays in Honour of H. W. Singer*, ed. A. Cairncross and M. Puri (Macmillan, London, 1976).

labour and capital markets are as competitive as they are ever likely to be.

It is consideration of these *general* sources of unreliability that has made economists advocate the use by planning agencies of 'shadow' prices in preference to the prices established by market forces. There is no need to present the case in detail since it has been expounded by a series of eminent economists from Tinbergen to Little and Mirrlees. What I should like to concentrate on are the limitations of shadow prices and the reasons why in practice it is difficult to make use of them.

In case of misunderstanding, however, let me say right away that there is usually no great difficulty about selling the idea of shadow prices to planning agencies and that many agencies do engage in calculations using shadow prices. The World Bank has done so for at least thirty years; the British Treasury introduced its 'test rate of discount' decades ago in the appraisal of public investment projects; and there must be many countries or departments of government where, for example, public procurement from abroad is based on shadow prices exceeding market prices by an administratively determined margin. What is less clear is whether the use of the test rate of discount has had more than a very slight effect on the level and composition of public investment, or whether those in charge of government procurement policy would act differently if the words 'shadow prices' had never been uttered.

I start by drawing attention to the analogy between shadow prices and the theory of socialist pricing that found favour with Oscar Lange in the 1930s. Lange wanted to draw on welfare economics for a rule (price to be equated with marginal cost) that would introduce 'rationality' into socialist planning. What he ended up with was a prescription for the establishment of market prices that had much in common with shadow prices since they were to be administered without regard to profit or loss and were intended to reproduce the price effects of perfect competition under conditions of absolute monopoly.

There was a certain intellectual fascination about this prescription and the debate which it started still continues. But there always seemed a curious unreality about it. One was struck, for example, by the incongruity between a socialist theory that implied the maximum decentralization and a world in which the USSR was practising the maximum centralization. The problems of economic organization seemed to be dissolved in those of price fixing. As in most socialist theory of the time, management was taken for granted; but unlike most socialist theory, Lange's prescription reduced central planning almost to vanishing point and assigned to managers the job of fixing prices, not of carrying out some predetermined plan. It simply disregarded the basic problem of marrying centralized and decentralized decision taking.

The idea of shadow prices in its *postwar* form is a great deal more realistic since it confines the use of these prices to a limited number of centrally taken decisions. The suggestion is not that each price fixer should be told what price to charge, or provided with a formula for price fixing, but that the decisions taken by 'the authorities' in managing or controlling the economy should be governed by a set of shadow prices instead of by actual market prices. The presupposition is that the government is already intervening extensively, but is operating a substantial public sector and is seeking to control much of what is left to the private sector. Shadow prices provide a means of coordinating the various forms of control on a consistent basis of social valuation. In that sense they lend rationality to existing controls and are designed to correct some of the sources of distortion in the allocation of resources. If one is starting from a highly centralized economy (and side-stepping the arguments pro and con centralization), it is always much easier to make a case for over-riding market forces and market prices than it is if one is starting at the other end with a fully decentralized economy and trying to make a case for a new principle of pricing that seems to throw doubt on decentralization itself.

Let me now catalogue some of the difficulties that one encounters in using shadow prices.

Arbitrariness

If an administrator does his sums in market prices he can usually establish what figures to use. He may get confused or the market may be very thin and the significance of current price quotations obscure. But at least he should know what information he is after.

With shadow prices it is otherwise. There is usually no objective test of the 'right' figure. Many administrators get no further than registering that the market price is too high or too low. They may not know where to go for a ruling on the alternative figure to use as a shadow price. There may also be reluctance to publicize it. If there is a shadow rate of exchange higher (for foreign currency) than the existing parity, governments may wish to keep it secret for fear of letting it be thought that it conforms to their private views and hidden intentions *in relation to the parity*. Much the same reasoning still applies when the currency is floating. But of course secrecy runs counter to widespread use of shadow rates and is bound to introduce some element of inconsistency between decisions where secrecy can be preserved and those where it cannot.

Suppose that these inhibitions can be removed and that there is some authoritative source of shadow rates, e.g. the Planning Office. How is it to answer requests to be told how they were arrived at? It is too much to suppose that other departments and outside critics will find no reason to challenge a rate departing widely from the market price. If the calculation is a complicated one, as it inevitably is, will everyone take it on trust?

I remember attending the final session of a course for administrators from less developed countries which had dealt extensively with the use of discounted cash flow techniques. Since the purpose of the session was to establish the value of the course, I took the opportunity, when invited to ask a question, to enquire what rate of discount each administrator would use in the various dcf calculations he would make on his return home. For a full minute there was dead silence. Eventually the Mexican member of the course offered to reply: he said he would use bank rate. I don't recall that anyone else saw anything odd in this reply, or that he could explain why bank rate should be used or what the current rate was. No other participant volunteered an answer.

This was not, I believe, an exceptional incident. I suspect that a number of countries have toyed with the idea of using shadow rates and given up because they didn't know *what* rates to use. The appropriate shadow exchange rate, for example, is not easily established. The question is not one of overvaluation or undervaluation (where there are objective, if imperfect, tests). It is a highly complex matter, couched partly in terms of elasticities of demand, but ranging over hypothetical capital flows and some rather vague judgement as to the restraint imposed on development by shortage of foreign exchange.

Variability

Next there is the problem of variability. Whatever rate is promulgated in one set of circumstances may be quite the wrong rate in another set of circumstances. Market prices are usually fairly sensitive to changing circumstances and expectations, but administered prices are much less so and hypothetical prices even less so. If shadow prices are to be used, there ought to be provision for review and revision from time to time but in practice revision seems to be infrequent and rarely automatic.

Ineffectiveness

Shadow rates are normally intended for government use and do not apply to transactions in the private sector involving either private firms or households or individual income earners or spenders. This means a double standard of value; rightly so, since shadow rates are intended to reflect social valuations while transactions in the private sector naturally reflect private valuations. But the line between the private and public sectors is sometimes blurred; and within the public sector there are a large number of subordinate authorities that may be reluctant to apply shadow rates without compensation or incentive.

Local authorities, for example, engage in extensive building operations. If they are to apply a shadow rate of interest half as high again as the rate at which they can borrow how is it possible to ensure that they refrain from borrowing for purposes that they consider necessary and socially advantageous at the going rate? At the higher (shadow) rate, they might prefer to postpone construction or reduce the volume of work carried out: but unless they are *obliged* to pay the higher rate it may play no part in their decision making. Much the same applies to nationalized industries, especially if they are adjured to abide by commercial criteria and have a financial target to meet. So long as they can raise the money at the market rate why should they behave freely as if they could not? On the other hand, if they can be compelled to use shadow rates would it not be simpler to require them to borrow from the central government at rates *actually charged* on their borrowings and diverging from market rates to the same extent as shadow rates? How in other words can shadow rates be applied 'down the line' without becoming market rates?

This is a bigger difficulty than it may seem. Economists may find it convenient to think idealistically of government as a unified centre of decision, interpreting the public interest in a definitive, consistent, unchallenged and comprehensive set of rulings. But this is of course plain nonsense. In wartime or under a powerful dictatorship there may be some approximation to such a state of affairs. But in ordinary circumstances in a plural society members of the public go their several ways within the law and have different conceptions of the public interest to which they expect an elected government to respond. So government is as much a matter of reconciling, placating and cajoling as of enunciating and instructing. In a managed economy the arts of management take priority over legislation and among the arts of management must be included that of affording initiative and responsibility to subordinates. If the management lays down rules it can make some of them absolute but only at the cost of limiting initiative, unless the rules are fully and clearly explained in a way that carries conviction. This is true even *within* the central government but is even more true of relations between the central government and subordinate authorities.

The danger is, therefore, that the central government may seek to make use of shadow rates when the rationale of these rates is not easy to convey and when those who are expected to use them may have a strong incentive not to do so.

Inconsistency

From this danger arises the likelihood of inconsistency in the application of shadow rates. Where the central government can apply them directly it will apply a test differing from the market test which, however, may continue to be used in other parts of the public sector and throughout the private sector. Hence the use of scarce resources may be distorted by the duality of standards and the end result may be less satisfactory than the uniform application of market prices, however great the objections may be to doing this.

Inflexibility

The use of shadow rates usually implies the application of a single, standard corrective to market prices: for example, a single rate of discount different from the market rate, a single rate of exchange expressing the shortage of foreign exchange, a single adjustment to market-determined wage rates. But strictly speaking there is a multiplicity of rates, differing from one transaction to another, that should be used to measure social costs and benefits. Labour, for example, is not a homogeneous commodity and is scarcer in one region, or one occupation than another. The divergence between market and shadow rates appropriate to men may not be appropriate when applied to female labour nor the divergence for one age group accord with that applicable to another. Similarly it may be easier to improve the balance of trade with one country than another; the same considerations that lead countries from time to time to make use of multiple exchange rates would justify the use of multiple shadow rates for transactions with different countries. Even with shadow rates of interest it is not clear that one should discount all future benefits near and far at the same rate (although no doubt it would be possible to meet part of this difficulty by varying the margin between spot and forward prices for the benefits concerned).

This criticism may appear to amount to no more than a suggestion for greater sophistication in the use of shadow rates. But in fact it goes further than that. It is a criticism of general correctives as such and an assertion of the need to look at each government decision in detail without trying to short-circuit it by some quasi-automatic rule. Of course it is literally impossible to engage in sophisticated analysis of each decision so that the criticism can be taken only to apply to a limited range of major decisions, leaving the minor ones to flat rate modifications of the shadow rate variety.

ALTERNATIVE PROCEDURES

This brings us to consideration of the alternative ways in which governments can take cognisance of divergences between private and social valuations. Let us take, by way of example, three types of intervention: tariffs, subsidies and rationing.

Tariffs

It is not self-evident that a government would be wiser to use a shadow rate of exchange ten per cent above the market than to impose a uniform ten per cent tariff. It is true that a tariff bites only on imports whereas in principle rates of exchange affect all transactions. But in practice shadow rates are almost certain to function exclusively as a protective device discriminating against public procurement of goods and services from abroad. So if there is already a tariff on imports what more can a shadow rate do?

As far as I can understand the reasoning behind shadow rates of exchange it rests either on the supposed advantages of an undervalued exchange rate or on the hostility and possible retaliation that tariff changes would provoke. Tariffs are the subject of treaty obligations and commitments to international bodies like GATT, while shadow rates can be presented as a purely domestic affair. Where purchases are made by the government itself the use of tariffs would seem a clumsy and unnecessary way of proceeding. But in general the use of shadow rates is a kind of *pis aller*, to be recommended if direct action on prices is ruled out on other grounds.

Subsidies

Subsidies also seem a more effective way of operating on prices than recommending the use of shadow prices. Indeed, if shadow prices are used by public authorities in such a way as to give rise to deficits it may be necessary to introduce subsidies simultaneously. In that event shadow prices are a kind of rationalization of the subsidy and a device for focusing attention on the need for a subsidy.

Rationing

When there is a need to limit demand quickly governments do not usually resort to shadow pricing. They introduce controls in the form of quotas, licensing or allocation arrangements. If shadow prices are arbitrary, these arrangements can be still more arbitrary. But they do offer the government greater certainty in the level of demand to be met since it is possible to limit what is sanctioned to the supply that is expected to be in prospect.

Take, for example, capital rationing. A government, like a large industrial concern, may operate two methods of limiting its capital expenditure without ensuring consistency between them. It may use preselected cut-off rates of return and approve only those investments one by one that are expected to yield a higher rate; at the same time it may adopt a capital budget and try to confine total capital spending within predetermined limits that vary with access to additional funds. The size of the capital budget may or may not be consistent with the cut-off rate of return in use. If the budget shrinks, it may be possible to proceed by investigating the rank order of projects in the vicinity of the cut-off point and move up to a sufficiently high cut-off rate of return to eliminate projects with capital requirements equal to the economies required. But when changes have to be made quickly and immediate economies are called for, the eventual rate of return over the life of each investment ceases to be the relevant basis of decision, especially where deferment is possible. The over-riding need is to make cuts that take effect quickly; and although in principle this could be done through a high short term shadow rate, in practice there is no alternative to pruning by inspection.

Or suppose that foreign exchange is inadequate to meet the demands on it. The government may either let the rate of exchange depreciate or impose an import surcharge, or it may instruct officials to treat the existing rate as too low by, say, ten or twenty per cent in any calculations of relative cost, or it may try to short-circuit the whole process of adjustment by quantitative restrictions linked with an import budget. In the latter event officials have to decide which imports to cut without waiting to see how the sums would work out at a different level of import prices.

Now it is easy to denounce arbitrary cuts by officials and point to the superiority of delegated response. If the issue abstracted from time so that the technique used could continue in use indefinitely I should agree that other methods were much to be preferred as a way of limiting imports. But one can rarely abstract from time. Very often the question is how to make emergency cuts; and for this purpose not only are rationing arrangements often more effective but they may also do less harm if they are quickly imposed and quickly removed.

The rate of discount The main use of shadow prices is in project appraisal. This is a difficult enough operation if market prices are used.

The question is whether the substitution of shadow prices, and in particular a shadow rate of interest, improves matters.

Experience in Britain justifies some scepticism, however powerful the reasoning in favour. For many years the Treasury has made use of a test rate of discount, intended to represent the social opportunity cost of capital, for the purpose of separating projects yielding an adequate return from those unlikely to do so. The basis of calculation of the test rate was clearly set out: it was intended to equal the return that large concerns in the private sector used in similar calculations and at the same time the recorded yield on equity capital over a long run of years. Whatever objections may be taken to the conceptual basis of calculation or to the actual rate emerging from it, it was not these objections that limited the applicability of the test rate. The real difficulties lay elsewhere.

First of all there was the fact of accelerating inflation combined with efforts on the part of the government to hold down prices. This meant on the one hand a distortion of the price structure that made it difficult to know what price relationships to project into the future, whether as market or even as shadow prices; and on the other a distortion of the financial return to capital assets because of price control. The government showed no interest in basing its decisions explicitly on *any* set of price relationships rather than on its own untutored view of social priorities; and an equal lack of interest in the financial outcome of past investments. The nationalized industries were allowed to run up losses at an annual rate of well over £1000 million a year and pressed simultaneously to maintain or expand new investment. In short the atmosphere was hardly congenial to a refining of pricing principles.

At an early stage it was proposed to use the test rate of discount as a means of checking the growth of public investment. The rate was in fact increased in 1968 from eight per cent to ten per cent. But there is no evidence that any major investment project was affected. The most likely candidates were nuclear power stations and houses. But it was generally agreed that a variation between eight per cent and ten per cent would not tip the balance between nuclear and other less capital-intensive forms of power generation. The local authorities were not specifically asked to put their housing programmes through the hoop of the TDR, and would certainly have jibbed at recovering in rent the full addition to the yield on new housing that the higher rate of discount would have required. After long discussion it seemed clear that it was only on a limited assortment of smaller new works (but not repair) that the higher rate would bite.

If this is so, it is not very encouraging to the use of shadow rates. But there are other difficulties. Some kinds of public investment, such as roads, yield no revenue and cannot therefore be self-financing. Those who have to make a case for road investment have no recourse if required to justify their proposals using the test rate of discount. Other forms of public investment may be able to generate all or most of the capital they require out of profit and it is rare to find the ploughing back of profit examined as searchingly as the use of borrowed funds.

Then there were some government departments that had difficulty in seeing where uncertainty entered into the calculations and were suspicious of them for this reason. It is true that decisions as to capital intensity are in principle distinct from decisions as to risk and uncertainty. But the fact is that very few major investment decisions turn on capital intensity. In industrial countries the one outstanding exception is in the supply of energy where there are widely different capital coefficients in alternative ways of adding to the supply of fuels and of generating electric power. In less developed countries the major exception is probably in the construction of dams. The importance that economists attach to factor proportions in the decisions of *producers* (consumption raises quite different issues but for some reason is rarely considered) does not accord with everyday business experience or with the choices normally arising in public investment decisions. Hence it is quite reasonable to be suspicious of methods of project appraisal that attach prime importance to the rate of discount used rather than to the risk that the return will be less than expected.

Now every economist knows that so far as it is possible to deal with uncertainty at all, it can be done by adjusting the series of expected quasi-rents so that there is nothing incompatible between using a standard test rate of discount and treating uncertain investments differently from safe ones. But if one finds that the test rate of discount derives from experience in making investments financed largely with equity capital while almost all public investment is financed with loan capital the suspicion must linger that there is something fishy in the whole procedure.

Thus there are frequently many important administrative obstacles to the use of shadow prices. But can there be any real harm in trying to use them? Surely it is impossible to pretend, most of all in the less developed countries with their discontinuities, indivisibilities, and immobilities, that one can take existing market prices as a firm basis for the appraisal of investment projects? In a world of inflation it is already necessary to think in terms of prices other than current market prices. For many other purposes countries have no option but to think in terms of resource costs, not market prices. Once one gets away from market tests, why not try to establish what prices would conform to the true requirements of the economy?

This reasoning is strongly reinforced if there is already a multiplicity of controls which *inter alia* distort market prices. Each control, in correcting one supposed distortion, changes the context within which the others are operating and may cause them to generate fresh distortions. If exports of metal scrap are prohibited and the price kept down, the steel industry may fail to build blast furnaces on the scale that dearer scrap would make profitable. If different bodies fix different exchange rates for poultry, eggs, and feathers (as happened in Yugoslavia in the fifties) how does one decide what effort to put into chicken-farming? It becomes almost indispensable to work out a set of shadow prices as a touchstone of the utility of expanding or contracting different activities. Without shadow prices, it is easy in such circumstances to lose all sense of social cost.

On this I would comment that before putting up signposts in a maze one ought first to ask how one got there in the first place. When controls threaten to destroy all the familiar landmarks it may be better to remove some of the controls than try to rationalize them. From this point of view it is useful to look at the three key features of less developed countries that give rise to most of their controls: shortage of foreign exchange; shortage of capital; surplus of unskilled labour. These features are not always present; but it is usually easy to demonstrate when and why they are present.

Take, for example, the shortage of foreign exchange. If devaluation were used as a remedy it might have to be at once frequent and severe: frequent in order to offset a relatively low secular rate of expansion in demand for the main exports of most of the developing countries; and severe because of price inelasticities of demand on the side both of exports and imports. Variations in the exchange rate would not, in these circumstances, be very effective in keeping the balance of payments in equilibrium and might even be perverse in their effects. More direct methods of enforcing economy in the use of foreign exchange might be preferable and the measures adopted might well be based on shadow rates.

Much the same can be said of the shortage of capital and the surplus of labour. Neither the shortage nor the surplus is likely to be satisfactorily disposed of – although both might be reduced – by price adjustments under the conditions obtaining in developing countries.

While these are not circumstances altogether peculiar to the developing countries they apply to them with special force and need to be taken into account by them in all major decisions of policy. What is open to dispute is how extensively this should be done and with what degree of refinement. These are matters that can only be settled on the basis of experience. But my own bias would be in the direction of relatively simple adjustments to market prices for purposes of estimation and for limiting the range of issues to those where it was demonstrable that it really mattered to the economy (*not* just to the outcome of individual projects) which basis of calculation was employed.

If I had to account for this bias I should lay emphasis on three factors which I forbear to elaborate:

1 Scepticism about making controls scientific. Governments introduce and operate controls for all kind of reasons, many of which would not stand examination by a professional economist or are patently non-economic. I doubt whether the substitution of carefully estimated shadow prices would be allowed to determine the operation of the controls and prevail over political and other factors.
2 Doubts about precise methods of estimating shadow prices. It seems to me doubtful whether the more elaborate methods of working out shadow prices (e.g. for exchange rates) have any real claim to be used in preference to far more rough and ready calculations.
3 The need to measure the significance of shadow rates. It any government is being urged to make use of shadow prices it ought to have some idea how much it matters, and what the social return would be on the substitution of shadow for market prices. For this purpose it would be helpful to have a ranking of the decisions or types of decision most likely to be overturned in terms of the expected gain to the economy as a whole. Perhaps this is asking too much. But one wants to start from some indication of the changes that a thoroughgoing use of shadow prices would make. One ought also to take account of controls that are already operating (as is not unusual) on a basis that weights decisions against the use of imports and capital and in favour of labour.

I come back in the end to my starting point. The theory of shadow prices is well established. What we know less about is the scope for their use in different kinds of economy and the directions in which it matters most whether market prices are superseded by shadow prices.

7

Innovation, imitation and growth

It is a great honour to be invited to deliver the first in what I hope will be a long series of lectures at Imperial College intended to be of common interest to economists and engineers. The need for both to join forces and understand one another's approach to common problems is particularly great in a country so beset as Britain by economic problems and so dependent on engineering for its livelihood. No doubt we all need to make sure that we have first mastered our own discipline before getting to grips with another. But economics would become a very arid and unfruitful subject if it limited itself to purely conceptual relationships without regard to the light that other disciplines can throw on business behaviour; and engineers might find that economic theory helped them to examine the choices open to them in a different and better perspective.

I have chosen innovation as my theme, confining myself to innovation in technique, because it has both economic and engineering aspects. It is part of my argument that success in innovation depends on the skill with which these two aspects are combined. My second reason for choosing to speak about technical innovation is that it is the principal source of improvements in the standard of living. This is not always apparent from textbooks on economics which devote much more space to investment and capital accumulation as influences on economic growth. It is true that a lag in capital accumulation may hold back economic growth; but there is not much evidence that it can be accelerated by an increase in capital intensity – i.e. by using more capital per unit of output. Economists have also laid stress, from Adam Smith onwards, on the importance of wider markets and the greater efficiency that comes from increasing the scale

An earlier version of this lecture was delivered in Oxford as the final contribution to a series on innovation and reprinted in *Inflation, Development and Integration: Essays in Honour of A. J. Brown* ed. J. K. Bowers (Leeds University Press, Leeds, 1979). The version reproduced here was delivered at Imperial College of Science and Technology in February 1981.

of operations. This certainly plays a part but one that is usually subordinate to technical change, and itself involves technical change.

If technical innovation is the main source of economic growth one might expect it to form the starting point of theoretical treatment of economic growth. But economists, while regarding the *consequences* of technical change as within their domain, have tended to think otherwise of its *origins*. Normally when they come to discuss changes in technique these appear ready made, sporadically, exogenously. This seems to me to misconceive the way in which technical change takes place and is incorporated in commercial practice. There is no hard and fast line between the successive stages lying between an original concept, its development for commercial use, and its subsequent spread over a variety of applications. At each stage new ideas may be injected possessing the same element of novelty as the original concept, though perhaps not to the same extent, and a succession of modifications will result. But from start to finish the whole process is suffused and surrounded by commercial pressures. Technical innovation is not something that obeys a different logic from other business operations: it is an integral and endogenous part of modern business.

THE CONCEPT OF INNOVATION

But this is to anticipate. Let me turn to the development of my argument starting with the concept of innovation. I take this to include any element of novelty introduced into the established order of things. The novelty may be in ideas or attitudes or customs or institutions or methods of doing things or in things themselves. It is an innovation in any country if a new law is passed and in some countries it is an innovation if the laws are strictly enforced. There are countries where it would be an innovation if cows ceased to be sacred, and there have been others where it was an innovation if a man could make more money than his neighbours without having his house burnt down or suffering other mischief.

I need hardly dwell on the infinity of problems we should have to consider if innovation were so broadly defined that it covered all forms of change: intellectual, social and economic as well as technical. We have quite enough to discuss if we limit ourselves to technical change provided we recognize that innovations in technique interact with other types of innovation and are themselves influenced by the cultural environment in which they occur. Indeed, the main problems posed by technical innovation are precisely those that derive from this interaction. If we ask why technical change is faster in one country than another or even in one industry than another the chances are that we shall find ourselves obliged to look beyond technology and beyond economics to cultural factors and the restraints imposed on the process of innovation by such factors. Attitudes may be more hostile to new techniques or less responsive to financial incentives in one place than another and the commercial pursuits that give rise to innovation may be viewed with favour in one place and positive disfavour in another.

INNOVATION, INVENTION AND IMITATION

If, for the moment, we do not pursue these interactions but confine ourselves to the essentially technical forms of innovation, we have next to ask whether innovation should be taken to include every step in the process by which some new product reaches the market place or some new process comes to be adopted commercially. Some writers have sought to distinguish innovation from invention on the one hand and imitation or diffusion on the other. But is there a clear line of division between these three things? There is certainly an intellectual distinction between them, but in practice they run into one another.

When invention takes place, for example, it may take the form of a new idea for some mechanical contrivance of which there is not even a working model, much less a carefully engineered product ready to be marketed at a known cost. An obvious example is the Gillette razor blade which was conceived by Gillette in a kind of vision while he was shaving and which required for its eventual production some years later several major additional inventions. Here at least 'the' invention can be segregated from its subsequent commercial exploitation. But the later inventions, e.g. those necessary to roll steel to the thinness necessary for the production of razor blades, cannot be segregated in this way. They involved expenditure to exploit Gillette's idea in much the same way as expenditure on advertising the blades after they were in production. So even if we contrast the first invention with the commercial innovation of the safety razor we can hardly avoid regarding the later, additional inventions as part of it.

The fact is that there are various stages in the introduction of a new product or process, from the original concept if there was one to the construction of a working model, the erection of a pilot plant, the design and re-design of the finished product and its marketing on a commercial scale; and the distinction between invention and innovation has very little to do with the number of stages or their allocation between the one and the other. The true distinction is between the technical and commercial aspects of the whole operation. On the one hand there are problems of design and satisfactory performance; on the other, there are commercial problems that need enterprise and business ability. It is possible but unlikely that the two kinds of problem present themselves in sequence so that the invention takes place before innovation begins. The more common situation is one in which the two sets of problems are present throughout. Although some inventions are not prompted in any way by commercial considerations and may even be largely fortuitous, most inventions take place as a response to a known requirement in the market place and all are of economic significance only if a commercial application can be seen to exist. At the same time, the innovation, or introduction to the market place, is founded on calculations of profit that generally lead to modifications in the original design or process and these share the characteristics of invention. There are, so to speak, mini inventions up to the point of actual manufacture.

It is not inevitable, therefore, as some earlier writers on innovation were inclined to suppose, that the different roles are performed by different agents: that an inventor comes on the stage looking for an innovator or entrepreneur who may or may not present himself. But that does happen quite frequently and many private persons who have hit on a good idea offer it for sale to a going concern. Or a small business incapable of meeting the financial and other costs of developing an invention may sell it to a larger business with the necessary resources. Most inventions covered by patents are probably handled in some such way. Professor Jewkes has shown in his *The Sources of Invention*[1] the continuing importance of the individual inventor and the small business in some of the most important inventions of the twentieth century. It has also been pointed out that about two-thirds of the 'basic innovations' made by engineering companies come from outside the company and that, even inside the company, 'the technical solution to a minor innovation problem' usually comes from personal know-how. Nothing I have said is inconsistent with these contentions. On the contrary, the very use of the term 'basic innovations' where most people would say 'major inventions' and 'the technical solution to a minor innovation problem' where others would say 'mini invention' shows the difficulty of distinguishing between invention and innovation except as different aspects, technical and commercial respectively, of a single process of introducing new products and processes to the market place. Each aspect may be dominated by a single individual, one an inventor and one a businessman, because new ideas and bold decisions are most likely to come from individuals. But they may also involve a great deal of discussion and experimentation by teams engaged in technical development or boards of management pursuing a corporate strategy. We should not try to settle which is the typical case by mere terminology.

What applies to invention and innovation applies also to invention and imitation. The process by which an invention comes into general use can again be broken up into stages, the pioneering work of the innovator being followed by its diffusion as the original invention is more and more widely copied. This sequence of events is often so depicted that the whole process of diffusion can be represented as one of imitation, devoid alike of the originality of the inventor and the enterprise of the innovator. But in practice this is rarely how things fall out. The work of the pioneer is normally incomplete and capable of further improvement; and the improvements are likely to be made by the so-called imitators in an effort to compete with the pioneer. The process of diffusion, in other words, is likely to involve fresh invention and fresh enterprise as successive modifications are made to the original design, usually by competing businesses. Once the first step has been taken, it may be followed by others just as big. In any event, if the original invention is taken up in a different country, to meet the requirements of a different market, it is likely to have to undergo quite substantial changes because of differences in the cost of materials, labour and capital, different climatic and cultural conditions, different scales of manufacture, different consumer preferences, a different balance between home and export requirements, and so on. Adaptation by imitators to meet these differences may require fresh acts of invention on the one hand and will certainly require acts of enterprise, which is the essential feature of innovation, on the other. So the imitators can claim to be, in some sort, innovators, too. Just as there are likely to be mini inventions once an innovator gets to work on an invention so there are likely to be minor innovations once an imitator starts to copy an innovation.

SOME ILLUSTRATIONS

It may make these propositions more concrete if I take some examples familiar to you all. Take, first, the motor industry. Who invented the modern motor car? Nobody did. The idea of powering a road vehicle with a steam engine was obvious enough in the railway age and must have occurred to many people. But that is a far cry from the mass market for petrol-driven private cars that exists today. Along the way one can point to a whole succession of inventors who gave us the various engine components, introduced rubber tyres, improved the suspension, and so on. One can also recall major innovators like Henry Ford who invented none of these things but were just as important to the evolution of car design. Each car company may have imitated the others in manufacturing something called a motor car; but no two companies made exactly the same car and each claimed to offer the public better value for their money than its competitors. Innovation was a competitive process in which the ideas of inventors provided one of the motive forces and in which those ideas were themselves a response to competitive pressures.

If we turn from motor cars to locomotives and aircraft we find much the same state of affairs. One may be able to point to the first occasion on which a powered vehicle operated on railway tracks or took off in flight. But it is, broadly speaking, true to say that nobody invented the locomotive or the aircraft. A succession of men contributed to their conception and development. Their contributions were hardly ever made in isolation from commercial pressures. Each new invention was developed and brought into use where it was thought to serve some commercial purpose and not otherwise, except in the case of military aircraft where non-commercial influences predominated. Once the state becomes directly involved, as in the Advanced Passenger Train and Concorde, other factors enter, for good or ill. But the historical experience in the days when these things were left to private enterprise was one of a response by inventors and innovators alike to the requirements of consumers as registered or at least tested in the market.

Another example is provided by the steam engine itself. Most people seem to think that it was invented by James Watt. In fact, Watt did no such thing. He made an improvement of great importance to the economic use of steampower by introducing the condenser. But the steam engine had been in course of development for a long time before Watt and continued to be developed by others long after Watt until the thrust for a given input of fuel was several times greater than in the early Watt engines. Nothing so clearly brings out the incremental character of the innovative process or the combination of technical and commercial skill that it involves as the history of the steam engine.

INNOVATION IS INCREMENTAL

Let me dwell for a moment on this incremental aspect of innovation. Those who were brought up on the history of the industrial revolution will remember this as a familiar theme in the development of the cotton industry. Each invention created new needs and opportunities and generated fresh inventions in response to those needs and opportunities. One invention brought forth another. But there is a less familiar aspect of the matter. One major invention – the kind that nobody can overlook and that sticks in the memory – takes a long time to digest. As it is absorbed a succession of mini inventions takes place: either minor improvements or consequential changes elsewhere in the economy. Just as a stone cast in a pool sets up ripples along the surface, so an invention has effects that go on spreading out as more and more businesses get to work to improve or take advantage of the invention and in doing so make fresh inventions that are less dramatic but may be of even greater importance.

When attention is drawn to the importance of 'cumulative progressions of small scale technological improvements' it is presumably this technical aftermath of major inventions that is principally in mind. Some years ago the National Institute for Social and Economic Research examined the rate at which a number of important new innovations such as the floatglass process, the LD steelmaking process, and so on, were adopted in each of the main industrial countries. They found that the British record in those instances was no worse than that of other countries. But if the issue was whether innovation was as rapid in Britain as elsewhere this evidence was not, in my view, decisive. As I pointed out:

> Where there is a dramatic change in technique of which everyone is well aware, and where there is a large saving to be made by adopting it, there are good reasons for expecting one country to show the same alacrity in innovation as its neighbours . . . But it cannot be assumed that for the myriad of small improvements in industrial products and practice that make up the main stream of technological advance the same laws hold good as apply to the conspicuous leaps forward that seize the public imagination.[2]

I went on to suggest that it might be because this flow of steady small improvements was comparatively sluggish in Britain that the country was lagging behind industrially.

INNOVATION AND GROWTH

This brings me to the practical significance of my argument so far. We can take it for granted that the transformation in material standards of living over the past two centuries is largely the result of innovations in the techniques in use. These innovations have allowed us to produce a wider variety of goods at steadily diminishing real costs. Innovations of the kind we have been discussing are simply one aspect – probably the most important aspect – of rising productivity. Productivity in turn is the main source of economic growth. All economic growth that cannot be attributed to larger inputs of labour and capital must be due to larger outputs per unit of input, i.e. to higher productivity and to the innovations yielding that high productivity. The obstacles to growth about which we hear so much are likely therefore to take the form of obstacles to innovation. Any worthwhile theory of economic growth is likely to have as its principal component a theory of innovation.

If we want to understand economic growth, therefore, we would do well to begin by studying innovation. Similarly, if we want to see our material standard of living rise faster we should consider what might be done to encourage innovation.

So far so good. But what has this to do with the rather semantic analysis with which I began? If there were a sharp line of division between invention and the commercial adoption of the invention by an innovator and invention were exogenous and unrelated to commercial needs, it would be natural for a government to concentrate on innovation and let invention look after itself. No doubt it would still offer the inventor patent protection with a view to encouraging more invention (but, historically speaking, patents were in fact introduced for the benefit of Elizabethan innovators who were not inventors). An individual government might also be expected to reason that since, in the nature of things, most inventions of any importance are bound to be made abroad it would be wise to reconcile itself to this presumption and devote its energies to promoting the adoption and diffusion of inventions of foreign origin. But for some obscure reason governments of industrial countries rarely act this way.

LINKING TECHNICAL FLAIR AND BUSINESS JUDGEMENT

Now what difference does it make if invention and innovation are bound up with one another so that invention is soaked in market influences and innovation is almost impossible without extensive mini invention? If the normal situation is not one of technical certainty and commercial uncertainty but of *general* uncertainty then the link between the men who understand technique and the men who understand business becomes of crucial importance. Technical flair has to be married to good business judgement. A successful business has to have at its disposal the necessary *technical* expertise to re-design a new product in the light of market possibilities and engineer it into production; and it has also to have strong commercial management that can form an accurate judgement of market trends and at the same time communicate the significance of these trends to its technical staff.

It is this union of two different kind of expertise that is the most intractable element in innovation. It is not at all clear what governments can do, if anything, to strengthen the link between the two. They can do much to improve the supply and availability of engineers and chemists;

they can try to improve the financial rewards to enterprise; and they can help to make funds more freely available for investment in new products and processes. But to the extent that innovation is *more* than taking a commercial risk through new investment, financial assistance is of limited value.

It is at this point that more radical voices are raised and a much wider role for the state is claimed. There will be those who point out that I have not so far made any reference to the growth of R & D, the new importance of so-called science-based industries, the possibility of restructuring industry to allow the state to put its full weight behind promising new knowledge. I have indeed carefully refrained from using the words 'research and development', 'science' or 'science-based', 'restructuring' and 'knowledge'. I have also made no reference so far to 'technology'. These are all words calculated to give rise to confusion in any discussion of innovations in technique.

THE ROLE OF SCIENCE

Let me look first at the part played in innovation by science. There is a large literature that gives great prominence to the influence of science and there have been occasions on which politicians have promised to revitalize British industry in a white-hot scientific revolution. I have never myself found much historical evidence of the direct influence of science before the twentieth century and I confess also to some distrust of science when it becomes white hot. Most inventions until comparatively recently have been the work of men with a quite limited background in science and those responsible for the commercial application of inventions have usually had still less familiarity with modern science. The traditional sequence, contrary to the common belief, is that the scientist tries to understand the invention *after* it has been made. Even today many important inventions make no great demand on scientific knowledge. The invention of the jet engine, we have been reminded, required no more than a cadet's knowledge of engineering.

This may seem puzzling to those who are dazzled by computers and Concorde, moon rockets and nuclear reactors. There is obviously a growing range of activities in which further progress calls for a thorough and expert knowledge of the latest scientific thinking. This makes science a very important input into those activities, just as familiarity with the properties of various paints has always been a very important input into the activity of painting. The innovator, like the painter, has to know enough to judge what materials to use and what knowledge to draw on. In the activities where science counts for much he must himself be enough of a scientist to coordinate the work of scientists with the work of other specialists and build the indispensable bridge between the technical experts and the commercial and financial experts.

The interests of the scientist are fundamentally different from those of the innovator. The one asks 'what is the truth of the matter?' the other, 'how shall we set about it?'. The one is concerned to understand, the other to produce. The two face quite different sets of problems and the difference tends to be blurred when people add, almost absentmindedly 'and technology' after 'science', as if subscribing to a takeover bid by science for technology. Whatever technology is, it is not science and usually it is rather messy and unscientific. It is much more akin to innovation since the technologist too is concerned with production and with how to set about producing. The technologist has to equip himself with all that modern science can usefully teach him but he has also to learn on the job what works and what does not work. It is this know-how and personal skill, acquired by experience, and often incommunicable except by example, that is the hallmark of a good technologist. The scientist, on the other hand, deals in a different kind of knowledge that can be made public in communications to *Nature*, written down and transmitted without his personal intervention, living a life of its own independent of its discoverer.

Turning out more scientists is not, therefore, the high road to more rapid innovation and economic growth. It may be helpful in a limited range of activities that make great use of scientific discovery but even this is far from certain. The main 'science-based' activities relate to chemical processes and various aeronautical and electrical engineering products. The contribution of scientists to these activities, so far as it takes the form of new scientific knowledge, is usually freely available or available, if patented, at a price. It is the engineering side of the business, the design of the finished equipment or process plant that is the more difficult to copy. Indeed, if innovation in science-based activities had all the rigour and calculability of pure science it is hard to see why the postwar record of Britain in those very activities should have been so disappointing. It is precisely because innovation is an encounter with the unknown – with the difficulties of getting things to work satisfactorily and on competitive terms, of judging market trends and assessing alternative techniques under conditions of great uncertainty – that science cannot guarantee success. The fact that scientists have played so important a part in putting a man on the moon should not blind us to their limitations in less ambitious projects where cost is a first consideration and the list of established alternatives already on the market may be a long one. Nor should we overlook the contention that it was not science as such but 'engineering know-how, skills and organization that brought about jet propulsion, nuclear power generation, communication satellites and space travel'.

THE ROLE OF R & D

Just as there is a mistaken belief that science holds the key to innovation so it seems to me there is an almost equally mistaken belief that innovation can be reduced to something like routine, thanks to R & D. Michael Fores has pointed out that there is a good deal of hocus pocus in R & D since in engineering at least it is nearly all development and practically none of it is research. Development is a way of taking some of the uncertainty out of innovation by trying things out on a smaller scale or in prototype before going into production. It is obviously a useful method of procedure where large capital funds are about to be committed and it is of growing importance because of the increasing frequency with which innovation requires large indivisible investments. But in many industries quite modest expenditures on development are adequate. The necessary design work can be carried out with a staff to which no one thinks of applying the R & D label. In the motor-car industry, for example – and not just the British motor-car industry – R & D is negligible. The same is true of the building industry, shipbuilding and a host of industries making consumer goods.

Of course one cannot take for granted that these industries have nothing to gain from research and development undertaken by themselves, or that they gain nothing from research and development in other industries. It is entirely possible that, just as most of the major inventions used in one country originate in some other country so most of the major advances in technique affecting one industry are made in another industry. The use of steam power in the nineteenth century had perhaps more effect on manufacturing industry than any other single invention; but the steam engine was not pioneered in any of the manufacturing industries that used it. Similarly, in more recent times the use of plastics or container transport or computers has had major effects on industrial practice and productivity in a wide range of industries. The textile industries, for example, have been revolutionized by the introduction of synthetic fibres, to the original development of which they contributed nothing. The industries in which innovation raises productivity, as recorded in the statistics, may be quite different from those that originate the innovation. So if one is looking at the source of major advances in technique and not at their subsequent influence or at the long process of trial and error and mini invention by which industry after industry profits from these advances, it is conceivable that research and development plays a very important role.

There is no doubt of the significance of this role in a limited group of industries. The development of a new synthetic fibre by the chemical industry may cost up to £1000 million. The development of a new aeroplane or a new computer can also be extremely expensive. This is so even though the aeroplane and the computer have already been invented so that development means no more than the introduction of a new model.

Designing a new aircraft may not appear to offer much scope for invention; but the various modifications required do add up to a series of mini inventions and are likely to involve large-scale investment. The process of trial and error by which development takes place is far removed from an exact science. We have yet to find a way of reducing major technical changes to routine. All we can say is that technical change, in the nature of things, is highly dependent on engineers and chemists and hence on the engineering and chemical industries, which already account for half the manufacturing labour force in all the leading industrial countries. What proportion of that half is or should be engaged in R & D is partly a semantic question and partly a matter of the kind of development work likely to be worthwhile.

To imagine that heavier expenditure on R & D will by itself speed up industrial innovation is, to say the least, highly optimistic. It has been pointed out that there is something like an inverse correlation between national R & D expenditure and the rate of economic growth. But I should not want to draw any conclusions from that since a great deal of development work is simply excluded from the statistics because of the way the figures are compiled; and in any event a great deal of the R & D in the United Kingdom, in the United States and the USSR has very little to do with advancing productivity in civil industry and is expenditure incurred at government expense to meet military and semi-military requirements. Similarly when Sony is instanced as a firm which 'became rich without any R & D and now that they are rich . . . have a hell of a big R & D department' I should hesitate to conclude that Sony were wrong before or after they became rich. That was not worth-while when they were quite small may be well worthwhile now that their capital commitments are much larger. The growth of an individual firm's R & D budget may be an interesting phenomenon to study in its own right. But we should beware of concluding that larger R & D budgets all round would give a corresponding fillip to industrial innovation.

THE ROLE OF INDUSTRIAL STRUCTURE

In addition to science and R & D there is a third recipe for more rapid innovation that is sometimes suggested and this takes the form of making changes in the structure of industry. Some people point to the inventiveness of small companies and would like to see industry made more competitive. New divisions within existing large companies might reproduce the conditions favourable to innovation in smaller companies. On the other hand, some people would like to see a more monopolistic structure because monopolies may hope for larger rewards from innovation if there is no danger of a swarm of imitators cutting into their profits. On this view, the state with its wider interests and more secure monopoly powers might be thought to be a more enthusiastic innovator than any private company. All of these contradictory views have been urged at one time or another with some show of reason.

The issue may not superficially appear a particularly important or interesting one. But if innovation is the key to economic growth and the form of industrial organization has a major influence on it, there is a great deal at stake in finding the most propitious industrial structure. If the state is likely to foster innovation more successfully than private industry the case for widespread nationalization is enormously strengthened; and conversely if the state is likely to slow down innovation or make a mess of it the case for relying on private industry becomes much more attractive. Similarly it is important to know how far competition promotes or discourages innovation or at least under what conditions and with what degree of competition innovation is most likely to prosper.

It is generally agreed that there is no simple connection between market structure and innovation. Empirical studies yield conflicting conclusions and are often based on doubtful indicators of innovative input (such as R & D) or output (such as patents). Most writers lay emphasis on the importance of profits as a spur to innovation, on the need for competent management and on willingness to take risks. But when the more specific question is asked: ‘what forms of competition are likely to favour innovation?’ there is no clear answer. It goes without saying that where innovation involves very large capital outlays the firms concerned must be correspondingly large and there may not therefore be room in the market for more than two or three – perhaps only for one. In the chemical industry, for example, the investment necessary to develop a new fibre may be beyond the means of firms smaller in size than ICI. In nuclear power engineering where an equally heavy outlay on development is necessary the scope for competition is just as narrow.

But it would be a mistake to assume that the only choice, even in such cases, was between a purely monopolistic form of organization and a highly competitive one. Industrial organization is highly flexible and there are all kinds of devices for preserving some element of competition and some scope for private enterprise. A state-run or state-controlled monopoly like the Atomic Energy Authority may take responsibility for some of the more uncertain stages in development or for development costs beyond the means of private firms leaving subsequent production to competing firms. Use can be made of the familiar institution of the holding company, so common in the private sector and so rare in the public sector. Or a division of function may be worked out on the model of the Admiralty's arrangements for placing orders for warships before World War I when shipyards competed in design and subsequent orders for a ship to the winning design were placed with several of the competing yards.

THE ROLE OF THE STATE

This brings me to the role of the state in innovation, which was the subject of my Presidential Address to the British Association some years ago. I have not changed my view that governments are usually overconfident, clumsy and wasteful in their approach to industrial innovation and have little understanding of what is required. The experience of Communist countries amply confirms this view but it is not necessary to go outside this country for evidence. However, in a mixed economy, there is simply no escape from direct state involvement in innovation in these industries which are already nationalized as well as in those that sell to the government or buy from the government or receive government support in one way or another; and this adds up to a large slice of the total economy.

The state's contribution to innovation is too vast a subject to discuss at the tail end of a lecture and the same is true of innovation in Britain and the circumstances limiting it. But perhaps I might venture one concluding reflection on this theme before I sum up.

REWARDING INNOVATION

It seems to me that the most important single influence on innovation is the reward which it brings. Without an adequate reward, managements will be inclined to refrain from changes that carry the risk of loss and that might stir up opposition or discontent. In order to face the costs of change they need the prospect of some additional gain. Of course they may be insensitive to such a prospect because they are already making large profits; but as a rule they have an eye to the future and will not want to see competitors steal a march on them. What every management knows, however, is that the full gains from innovation are unlikely to come to the innovator. Some will be taken by the state in extra taxation; some will go to the consumer either because of the need to lower prices in order to extend the market or because competition brings the price down; some will also go to the wage earner if the routine of his work is disturbed and he makes a successful claim for higher wages; and only the residue comes to the innovator and his company.

If one wants to understand why innovation is inhibited in the United Kingdom it is this four way split from which one ought to start. I have yet to see a systematic comparison between Britain and other countries or between one type of investment and another. But there are certainly big differences, not least in the extent to which wage earners can insist on a share in the prospective gains. If a businessman does not innovate but sinks more capital in exactly the same plant and produces by exactly the same methods as before, he forfeits no part of the return on his capital in higher wages. But the moment he innovates he finds himself engaged in a dispute over manning ratios or piece rates or in some other tug-of-war with his employees over the share they feel entitled to claim from the higher profit to be expected from the innovation. I am told that this tussle is peculiar to the United Kingdom. I would argue only that it is a good deal more common in the United Kingdom than in other countries and that it helps to account for the slower rate of innovation and growth.

CONCLUSIONS

I can now sum up my arguments: first of all innovation is not something different from trying to become more efficient: it is simply one aspect of it. Even new products can be regarded as ways of helping the consumer to satisfy his wants more efficiently.

Next, just as one tries harder to improve efficiency if there is money in it and if one has an idea how to set about it, so innovation is a *commercial* response to available ideas and markets.

Thirdly, innovation calls for enterprise and for adequate rewards to encourage enterprise.

Fourthly, at the heart of successful innovation lies good management, coordinating the activities of technical, commercial and financial staff and ensuring the right personal contacts and communication. There are several linkages that are of crucial importance, e.g. between research and development and production, between development engineers and marketing and financial experts, and so on.

Fifthly, the social system and environment must be propitious to new ideas and their adoption. At the most elementary level there must be easy communication between different people and different groups: freedom to exchange ideas, to talk and read and experiment. The spread of technical ideas rests more heavily on personal contacts over wide areas than on any single factor. At a higher level there must be the necessary expertise to draw upon: engineers, well trained and open to new ideas, and managers with the experience required. Those who have the drive and persistence indispensable to innovation (who may not be the most attractive personalities) should be able to count, if not on public recognition and support, at least on acquiescence and freedom from being penalized. If we want golden eggs we should not persecute geese.

Next, in a highly centralized system there is more power to enforce innovation but less likelihood of spontaneous innovation. There is a need in any form of organization to mobilize initiative behind innovation and to decentralize those functions that are either charged with responsibility for innovation or offer most scope for it.

Seventh, if we want faster innovation we should not neglect to reward it. It is not easy to do so directly but a great deal of legislation, including tax legislation, reduces the reward to the innovator. Wage bargaining also tends to remove part of the profit from innovation.

Finally we should always recollect that it is far easier to copy than to create and that the rate of diffusion is far more important than the rate of generation of new developments. We should never be afraid to borrow since in the end that is what everybody but the pioneer has to do.

NOTES

1 John Jewkes, David Sawers and Richard Stillerman, *The Sources of Invention* (Macmillan, London, 1958).

2 Alec Cairncross, *Inflation, Growth and International Finance,* (Allen and Unwin, London, 1976), p. 63.

8

The role of technology and natural resources in the development process

Economists have no generally accepted theory of economic growth. They have laid emphasis on many different factors contributing to it but recognize that the relative importance of these factors must vary from one country to another and at different times in the history of the same country. Heroic attempts have been made, for example by Denison, to assign a value to the various contributions to growth over the recent past in the main industrial countries. But these attempts rarely go beyond an analysis of the changes over time in factor inputs (including employment, working hours, capital stock, and so on), coupled with an attribution of what cannot be accounted for in this way to a limited group of other influences on growth such as economics of scale, education, and advances in knowledge. What is attributed to advances in knowledge is usually more than all the rest put together. Unfortunately 'advances in knowledge' is a synonym for 'unexplained' or 'residual', in the absence of 'further knowledge' so we are not much further on. However we catalogue the sources of economic growth, we do not know enough to impute to each source its contribution to the observed rate of growth.

It is hardly surprising that this should be so. Some elements in economic growth, notably changes in factor inputs, are measurable while others are not. Economists, particularly those who are given to constructing models of economic growth, inevitably give prominence to the measurable elements. But it is not possible to leave the non-measurable elements out of account since they may well dominate the whole process of development. It is obvious, for example, that the values, attitudes, motivations and institutions of any society, the level of education, prevailing religious

From *Reflections on Economic Development and Social Change, Essays in Honour of V. K. R. V. Rao*, ed. C. H. Hanumantha Rao and P. C. Joshi (Allied Publishers Private, Ltd., New Delhi, 1979). The paper was also delivered in Brazil and Korea.

beliefs, standards of conduct in business and government, freedom from civil commotion and strife, competence and dedication of those in authority, and so on, are bound to exercise a major influence on growth. Economic development is not a purely economic phenomenon but interacts with social, political, and cultural development at all stages.

When one singles out natural resources and technology as two elements in the development process, therefore, one has to recognize at the beginning that what matters may not be their direct influence on the creation of wealth but their interaction with other elements, including the social and political environment. This kind of interaction may be difficult to demonstrate and economists may be reluctant to pursue it. Where the economist gives up, the economic historian or the anthropologist may have to come to our rescue and provide the necessary clues to the interactions governing economic development.

Let us for the time being ignore these interactions and concentrate on the direct impact of natural resources on the one hand and technology on the other. Then we must ask: impact on what? What is it that we are trying to explain? It makes a considerable difference, for example, whether we are thinking simply of the movement of GNP, however it arises, or whether it is the movement in productivity rather than production that we have in mind. Economic expansion can take place without any change in productivity by an enlargement of existing resources, or the use made of existing resources, involving quantitative changes only; or it can take place with no change in the quantity of resources, through better use of them involving new methods, new products, or a switch from less productive to more productive uses. The first kind of change would increase GNP but would reflect an expansion in resources and factor inputs, not an advance in productive efficiency. The second kind of change would be qualitative and correspond to innovations in the use of resources raising the level of efficiency.

Anyone starting out from this broad distinction will recognize the second kind of change as the more enduring and the more significant. It is rising productivity that we need for genuine economic development; and it does not require much argument to show that technical progress is the source of most of the innovations that make for a steady rise in productivity. If we all went round with the same view of the world as that of the primitive man, we should be lucky if we even survived, much less attained, whatever standards primitive man may be said to have established. It is technology that has made man what he is. As Bronowski has put it: it was the unprecedented step 'from using rudimentary tools . . . to making them and keeping them for future use that . . . sent man off breakneck at a speed unmatched in three billion years of terrestrial life'. Development as an ongoing process rests on the constant injection of new technology and on the capacity to generate and absorb technical change.

What role is there then for natural resources? At first sight, their influence might seem to be purely quantitative and once and for all opening up the possibility of an expansion in output without any continuing momentum behind the expansion. New natural resources, such as mineral or oil deposits, make a country richer; but they do not automatically involve development, and if they are used up, as technology can never be used up, they may leave the country more or less where it was before. Richness in natural resources carries with it no guarantee of rapid development or eventual prosperity.

This line of thought might seem to dispose of any argument about the relative importance of technology and natural resources. But one could reach quite the opposite conclusion along a different line of thought. Technology, some people might suggest, is universal and, within limits, freely accessible to all countries. If they do not all develop at the same rate there must be some other explanation: it can hardly be explained exclusively in terms of technology but must involve some analysis of the impediments to technology transfer. On the other hand, the endowment of natural resources does vary between countries and must make development easier especially if it is difficult to engage in trade or pay for supplies from abroad. In a country where a chronic shortage of foreign exchange prevents ready access to foreign equipment and foreign technical assistance, the discovery of additional resources may play a decisive part in starting off the process of development.

Or again, what if a country shows no capacity to draw on modern technology and relies entirely on foreigners to supply imports of goods that do make use of it or to establish branches or new businesses within its borders as a way of taking advantage of it? Changes of that kind, unless resulting in an overspill into current domestic practice, may do little to accelerate growth although they may increase GNP.

These contradictory arguments suggest that there may be some confusion in the common use of the terms 'natural resources' and 'technology' and I should like to interrupt my argument for a moment in order to clear up this confusion. The word 'technology' in particular means different things to different people. Sometimes it is used to mean 'knowledge relative to the industrial arts' and sometimes to mean 'the practice of the industrial arts'. Technological progress can then be either an advance in knowledge or it can take the form of some new piece of machinery or equipment such as a jet engine or a nuclear power station. If instead of talking about technology we use the older English word 'engineering', we are more likely to be aware that technology is a messy unscientific business involving action, not just drawing up prescriptions for action. The action is of course guided by knowledge; but a great deal of that knowledge is knowledge about practice, very often with little theoretical content. It is not primarily public knowledge, available in written form and easily transmissible from one country to another, but know-how, learned in the doing by trial and error, the practitioner's skill rather than the scientist's theory.

It is a mistake therefore to confuse technology with science and it is probably also a mistake to link technological advance with what is nowadays called R & D, research and development. Most of what has been written about R & D is highly misleading because it concentrates on a few dramatic changes in limited sectors of industry, and ignores the myriad of small improvements in industrial products and practice that make up the main stream of technological advance. Far too much emphasis is placed on research or on the construction of prototypes and pilot plants and far too little on the central phenomenon of continuous technical development; improvements in *design*. If research is the key function in science, design is the key function in engineering, providing the indispensable link between prescription and product.[1]

While 'technology' is a term calculated to make economists talk nonsense, natural resources may seem explicit enough. But here too confusion is possible. Some natural resources are inherently exhaustible while others are in principle inexhaustible. Mineral deposits can be used once only and have to be treated as a kind of liquid capital while agricultural land is, with improvement, a permanent asset that can contribute indefinitely to growth even if in the process of improvement it becomes less and less a natural resource and more and more a capital investment.

HISTORICAL EXPERIENCE: THE JAPANESE CASE

If, therefore, we want to form a judgement about the role of natural resources and technology in the development process we have to think the matter out more carefully and take account of historical experience. Let us, for example, look at the case of Japan. No one supposes that Japan is particularly rich in natural resources and it is obvious that Japan now ranks very high in technological prowess. But did natural resources play a negligible role in her development?

It is obvious that before economic growth began to accelerate a century ago Japan, like other pre-industrial societies, was highly dependent on her agriculture in which about 75% of the population was employed. Under Tokugawa rule the 'closing of the country' had cut Japan off from the technology developing elsewhere and this applied as much to agriculture as to other activities. The economic backwardness of the country was not paralleled, however, by a similar backwardness in education, urban culture, managerial experience, and social and political institutions. If there was a technological gap there was also a capability of taking advantage of new technology by borrowing more advanced methods from abroad once contact was re-established. This was as true in 1868 as it was in different circumstances after World War II. But the process of modernization hinged on the development of surpluses of various kinds and these surpluses were largely generated by agriculture.

It was found possible to expand agricultural output by traditional methods without any large scale investment of capital. Partly this was done by the diffusion of new techniques such as improved seed selection and the wider use of fertilizer. Where there had been wide regional differences the spread of useful knowledge helped simultaneously to bring the more backward parts of the country to a level of productivity nearer to the average. The peasant was also given a stronger incentive in the shape of a fixed land tax based on the value of land in place of a fluctuating harvest tax.

In the period following the restoration of the Meiji, therefore, the peasantry were able to provide increased food supplies and so make it possible to dispense in large measure with heavy expenditure on imported food and a diversion of funds from productive investment for that purpose. The contribution of agriculture to other surpluses has been sketched by Okhawa and Rosovsky as follows:

> . . . The new government required a rising flow of revenues for social overhead and other investment purposes as well as for administrative modernization. Again the traditional economy played a key role here through land tax revenue and as a source of indirect taxation. . . . Foreign exchange was a vital need for importing modern producer durables and to acquire the services of foreign experts. The Meiji economy secured this exchange largely through the export of tea and silk, both products linked to traditional agriculture. Finally, the Japanese economy needed to effect a labour transfer so as to provide the workers for the expanding modern sectors. These workers came almost entirely from rural areas, and this transfer did not adversely affect the rate of growth of agricultural output.[2]

Thus at least in the early stages of development, natural resources in the form of traditional agriculture played a key part in the process. It was agriculture that released private investment funds and provided government revenue, foreign exchange, and manpower. All these were indispensable to the development of a modern sector making use of modern technology. But equally indispensable was the capability of Japan to borrow and apply modern technology.

The fact is that the development process is fundamentally and inevitably one of absorbing new technology and that the significance of natural resources is that they may facilitate or conceivably thwart this process. If one looks not at Japan but at the oil-producing countries with their abundance of at least one natural resource, their concern is to transform that resource into industrial hardware of modern design and exchange part of their natural endowment for the infrastructure of an industrial society. They do not regard their oil resources as a token of development but as a springboard to development; and development for them means the application of modern techniques to existing industries and the establishment of new industries using these techniques.

The example of the Middle East is a reminder how rarely any country enjoys an endowment of wide variety of natural resources and how often a single resource dominates the early stages of development. If there is plenty of oil there may be little or no water, if there is fertile land it may be subject to flooding or drought; if there are minerals they may be almost inaccessible or far apart from sources of fuel and power. World demand for any one natural resource may decline. Even for natural resources in general, whatever the Club of Rome may suggest, there is no infallible law of increasing scarcity. The tendency has been for man-made materials of all kinds, from steel to plastics, to take over an increasing share of the market, and even in agriculture more and more of what is produced reflects manufacturing activity in fertilizer plants, tractor factories, etc., rather than what is done on the farm. To be rich in natural resources is of advantage only so long as the resources are in demand and one can never be sure how long this will be or at least how long demand will continue to grow.

Let us now go back to the example of Japan and see whether in addition to bringing out the role of agriculture and of natural resources in general as a springboard it also throws light on some aspects of the role of technology.

We can start from the common observation that economic backwardness goes with dualism: the simultaneous existence of a modern and a traditional sector of the economy. Development takes the form of a gradual expansion of the modern sector at the expense of the traditional sector through either the growth of new industries or the establishment of modern units in existing industries or the introduction of new methods throughout the economy in such a way as to modernize the traditional sector. The process is a protracted one and one reason why it takes time is that modernization usually involves heavy capital expenditure. Modern and traditional units go on existing side by side. The modern units although more efficient and more profitable cannot expand faster than their resources permit and need time to engage in additional investment. The traditional units, which usually pay lower wages, are able to survive so long as market requirements exceed the capacity of the modern units.

As usually presented, the process is dominated by the limitations imposed by a shortage of capital, and up to a point this is right. But it is also affected by other limitations which may in the end be of greater importance. We have to ask how modern the modern sector is as reflected for example in its power to compete in world markets. Has it taken full advantage of modern technology or have those advantages been watered down in some way or simply overlooked? If the modern sector is not abreast of current practice elsewhere, then the gap between the two sectors will be less wide and the rate of transfer to the modern sector from the traditional one will be slowed down.

We have also to take account of the behaviour of the consumer who may be influenced by modern ideas just as much as the producer. He may be quicker to take advantage of imported goods than the producer is to take advantage of foreign technology. If the wider range of goods induces him to spend more heavily then savings will fall and the capital that might otherwise flow into industry will become scarcer. This by itself would tend to slow down development. If in addition the goods he buys have to be imported, the supply of foreign exchange will contract and the difficulty of financing imports of foreign machinery and equipment will be aggravated.

Japan has scored under both headings: her modern sector is very modern and her consumers have been remarkably conservative. To take the second point first. It is well known that the savings ratio in Japan has been very high and that the contribution of personal savings has been unusually large. In 1961, for example, personal savings averaged 18.4 per cent of disposable income and 63.2 per cent of the personal sector's savings flowed to other sectors, notably to corporate enterprise.[3] If we ask why personal savings are so high, one major reason is that 'the Japanese consumer has exhibited an innate conservatism as shown by slow changes in a traditional consumption pattern. Diet, clothes, furniture, entertainment – and other activities connected with daily life – have altered at rates far below those of income growth.'[4] Similarly, the Japanese consumer has spent relatively little on imports. As recently as 1961 imports of foodstuffs were less than 14 per cent of total imports and imports of consumption goods were no more than 1.5 per cent.[5] In the same year spending on consumer durables, which feature prominently in some discussions of consumer reactions to imported technology, was no more than 3.2 per cent of GNP. The Japanese consumer put no obstacle in the way of rapid development.

The Japanese producer – to go back to the first point – has an equally remarkable record. He has established a modern sector that is ultramodern and is now capable of generating its own technical improvements. This sector is highly competitive in international markets and maintains a level of productivity well above the level in the traditional sector. But what accounts for Japan's success? Why does modern technology not transform other economies just as rapidly?

The first answer to this question is that technology is not easily transferred. Know-how as we have seen is very different from scientific knowledge that can be set down in textbooks and communicated readily to students. It is essentially informal and personal, more akin to skill, and inseparable from the act of investment. To speak of a technological gap is to make the problem seem simpler than it is. There is no easily identifiable 'pool of technology' that one can visit and borrow from as one enters and borrows from a public library. There is instead a vast accumulation of experience in the handling of new techniques that is constantly being added to, and that is related to the circumstances in which the experience has been acquired. It is never easy to draw on somebody else's experience, least of all if one is very differently circumstanced and has very little experience of one's own.

In the Japanese case there was from the outset a deliberate effort to acquire experience abroad. Many Japanese went overseas to study industrial practice and the government set out to build new industries using foreign equipment and methods. There was an outlook congenial to the importation of technology and continuous search for those areas where technological transfer had most to offer or would encounter least difficulty.

The textile industry which accounted for over 40 per cent of Japanese manufacturing until the 1930s was ideal for technological borrowing for several reasons. It was one of the least capital intensive, particularly with double shifting, so that it was well adapted to a labour abundant economy. It had a large domestic market with its own local requirements. The techniques were easily acquired once the necessary machinery was installed. Moreover, textile production could be readily detached from other industries unlike many branches of engineering and the technology was so to speak relatively self-contained. For the same reasons other countries have usually found it easier to build up a textile industry on modern lines than to embark on heavier and more complex types of industry.

Although textiles may be typical of nineteenth century technological transfer, they are very unrepresentative of the process today. It is partly that technical progress has itself changed and accelerated out of recognition. The innovations that sprang from the ingenuity of artisans and tinketers a century ago have been replaced by the work of a highly educated group of specialists using research laboratories, computers, technical journals, pilot plants, and other expensive paraphernalia. As

David Felix has put it, 'today's LDC trying to cop a ride on the technology train is confronted by a quite different and more rapidly moving vehicle than its nineteenth century counterpart'.[6]

This change is particularly evident in the engineering and chemical industries; but it is precisely these industries that increasingly dominate modern industry and account for about half of the world trade in manufactures compared with about one-eighth in 1900. The simultaneous fall in the importance of trade in textiles from a third to about one-tenth is the other side of the medal.

The Japanese miracle is as much as anything the development of a capacity to absorb the technology of those industries, to expand them, and to generate her own advanced technology. She has imported technology on a massive scale. Since 1958 in the modern sector of Japanese industry 25–30 per cent is dependent on foreign technology. But borrowing, as we have seen, requires an effort of search and must find an echo in prior experience. The Japanese have been able to borrow because they have organized their industry for that purpose. They have probably more trained engineers per head than any other country and this is perhaps the most important single fact about Japan. The technical staff of Japanese undertakings has been strengthened so as to scrutinize foreign technical achievements, select what was most readily adapted to Japanese requirements, and carry out any necessary modifications in design or production planning to suit Japanese conditions.

Until 50 years or so ago there was little to distinguish Japan from other less developed countries in Latin America and elsewhere. At the beginning of this century, for example, Japan's output of steel was lower than India's. At least half of her exports took the form of tea and silk. Wherein, then, did Japan's advantages lie? Some economists have laid stress on the shocks felt by the Japanese ruling class, when the political consequences of their inferiority in technology were brought home to them. It was this, so it is argued, that created the special pressure from above to modernize the economy and permit the absorption of foreign technology. No such shock as a rule accompanies the discovery of additional natural resources. If this brings in new foreign technology, it probably does so by attracting foreign enterprise and foreign capital at the same time leading to the creation of an enclave that may do very little to promote the introduction of new techniques into other parts of the economy.

While Commander Perry's arrival, and the shocks that this created, may help to account for the early growth of Japan, it throws little light on her later development although the whole process was, of course, continuous. Japan's advantages seem to have lain in her initial isolation, combined with her subsequent openness to foreign ideas. Even before the restoration of the Meiji about half the population was in receipt of some form of public education; and Japan continued to rely heavily on education and training in order to develop the talent of her artisan population. In the process she suffered neither from an extensive 'brain drain' to other countries (perhaps because of linguistic difficulties) nor from an equally large scale immigration of unskilled workers such as made economic development rather lopsided in many other countries. There was throughout a determination to follow a do-it-yourself policy, taking full advantage of the technological lag of Japan behind other industrial countries.

TRANSFER OF TECHNOLOGY

When any of the less developed countries looks at Japan or, still more, at the United States, it cannot escape awareness of the importance of technology as a factor promoting rapid economic development. The danger is that technology comes to be thought of as a kind of magic instead of as the fruit of extensive investment, just like the opening up of new natural resources. If it is to add to the productive power of a country, and not just to its resources, it must involve extensive efforts to improve absorptive capacity, including a transformation of the educational system, to inculcate the necessary skills. Just as, in the transference of medical technology, one needs doctors, so in the transfer of industrial technology one needs engineers. There have also to be channels through which discoveries made abroad can be made known and spread and utilized.

The development of technological potential calls for much more than study since it comes, like so many other skills, from practice, and much of the learning has to be by doing, not just by reading. There have to be personal international contacts, which are usually much more productive in the transmission of new ideas and practices, and there has to be scope for the exercise of what has been learnt.

The possession of extensive natural resources may help the transfer of technology or may serve as a deterrent. The exploitation of the resources may be possible without the use of any elaborate new techniques or the creation of new engineering and other skills from which cumulative benefits might grow. If riches come easily there may be no incentive to make long term investments in the building up of new technology or meet the extensive costs of training, research, and development with all the risks that are involved. If affluence generates complacency and neglect of modern technology, the effect of extensive natural resources may be to serve as a *cul-de-sac* which it is attractive to enter but from which, in the end, there is no simple way out.

The major problem in establishing modern technology is that it is very difficult to do it by bits. There are extensive linkages between one form of skill and another, just as there are also extensive linkages between the different elements of investment involved in building up modern industry. The problem can be viewed as very much one of scale on the one hand, and detachability on the other. The domestic market may be too restricted to make it easy to introduce modern techniques unless there are compensating advantages in cost that hold out the prospect of extensive exports. At the same time the capital requirements of establishing a large block of interconnected developments may be prohibitive in relation to the available savings of the country. It is necessary, therefore, to advance stage by stage, minimizing the disadvantages of indivisibility.

These disadvantages are least where it is possible to make use of what economists call 'embodied technology'. Where the technical advances made elsewhere are embodied in machines, or in new raw materials, or in new designs that are easily copied, the problem of transfer is confined to that of paying for what is imported from abroad. It may be also that the machines or materials or designs present no great difficulties in use and there is no additional know-how that has to come with them. Riding a bicycle or driving a car or a railway train is comparatively easy to learn. There are, therefore, large chunks of foreign technology that can be absorbed with comparative ease. They can be detached from the complex of foreign practice and swallowed whole.

This applies, as has been suggested above, to most of the textile industry, to light electronics, and to a great many other industries that make only limited demands on foreign know-how.

There is a second range of industries where detachability is easy, provided it is left to the foreigner to do it. By setting up branch factories, multinational firms may be able to transfer, with little modification, the equipment and processes used by the parent company; but their monopoly of the know-how involved, either in production or, more commonly, in marketing, may make it difficult to establish the technology under local auspices. When this happens there is a sense in which the technology has not really been transferred since it is not fully at the service of the importing country and does not add to its domestic technological potential.

In other industries again – particularly the more advanced branches of engineering and of the chemical industry – know-how is not only a much larger element in the total input but it is usually changing more rapidly. The changes in technology are of a character that make it very hard to detach specific applications with any hope of transplanting them successfully in the absence of many other ancillary facilities that only the more developed countries are able to provide.

Finally, technology does not move under the same impulses that make scientific knowledge flow from one country to another. Since it is embedded in productive investment the process of transfer is essentially a commercial one. Somebody has to believe that in the end it will pay and will have to back that judgement by making the necessary investment. No one doubts that natural resources do not open up by themselves but have to be opened up by human effort. It is equally important with technology that there should be the drive, commercial knowledge, and entrepreneurship to start the process off and give it a chance of succeeding.

CONCLUSIONS

1 The main feature of a modern economy is not its physical resources but its command of technology.
2 Development as an ongoing process rests on the constant injection of new technology and on the capacity to generate and absorb technical change.
3 The injection of new technology is a commercial operation that may owe little or nothing to science or to R & D but a great deal to borrowing and adapting what is already known.
4 Borrowing means profiting from other people's experience and is not easy: it usually requires some prior experience and the tendency towards greater sophistication complicates the learning process.
5 Natural resources are important in the early stages of development but are unlikely by themselves to start off a cumulative process of development.

NOTES

1 I have profited in writing the two preceding paragraphs from the work of Michael Fores.
2 K. Okhawa and H. Rosovsky, *Japanese Economic Growth* (Oxford University Press, Oxford, 1973), pp. 14–15. The discussion of Japanese growth in the text is based largely on this work.
3 Ibid., p. 169.
4 Ibid., p. 171. See also the quotation from Uyeda on p. 159.
5 Ibid., p. 305.
6 David Felix, 'On the diffusion of technology in Latin America' (unpublished paper to the Conference on Diffusion of Technology and Economic Development, Bellagio, April 1973), p. 16.

9

Is there a general theory of economic development?

The question: 'Is there a general theory of economic development?' is one that I have been asking myself ever since I was asked by the World Bank in 1955 to launch the Economic Development Institute in Washington D.C. This was conceived of as a kind of staff college for senior administrators from developing countries and the early courses took the form of seminars extending over six months on different aspects of development. It was natural to ask at the outset what place theory should occupy in the curriculum and whether there was something sufficiently distinct from conventional economic theory to be designated 'the general theory of economic development'. These are questions to which I am still seeking an answer.

At that time it seemed to me that if there was a theory, that was what we should make the centrepiece of our teaching. If there was no general theory, we should have to fall back on the lessons to be learned from the Bank's own experience and make use of case studies, most of them relating to single large projects rather than to macro-economic policy. Such case studies would at least communicate a sense of how large projects should be handled and provide a training in project evaluation. The emphasis would be on what was liable to go wrong rather than on dcf calculations, shadow prices and the other components of project analysis as usually taught. Unfortunately this prescription did not allow for the possibility that case studies might be far scarcer than theory. The Bank had no case studies in a form capable of use as teaching materials and was in any event inclined to dwell on its successes without much reference to perils narrowly

This essay is an expansion of talks given at Queen Elizabeth House, Oxford, the Institute of Social and Economic Change, Bangalore, the World Bank, and the School for Advanced International Studies, Washington, D.C.

escaped and to draw a veil over mishaps, oversights and failures from which there might be far more to learn.

Although we struggled manfully to produce case studies that pointed up typical difficulties in the way of development, we were obliged, willy-nilly, to fill out the course with current theory – more theory, to tell the truth, than we really believed in. We included talks on 'the take-off' by Walt Rostow and on vicious and virtuous circles by Ragnar Nurkse. We expounded Rosenstein Rodan's theory of 'the big push' and Arthur Lewis' theory of the critical importance of moving from a 5 per cent to a 10 per cent savings ratio. We worked in references to Harrod–Domar models and incremental capital–output ratios. We got Simon Kuznets to talk to us about changes in the distribution of income in developing countries and Wallace Notestein to explain the trends in population. We ranged over the special problems of agriculture, industry, public utilities, trade, the capital market, and much else.

What the participants absorbed out of it all remained obscure. The effect on me personally was to make me more distrustful of prevailing *general* theories, more alive to the gap between theory and practice and more conscious of the value of a little experience of government planning and control. So far as general theory was concerned, a great deal of it seemed bogus, either because it asked the wrong questions or formulated them wrongly or because it rested on very limited and doubtful evidence. Even if one accepted the theory it was usually not very operational and did not point the finger at lines of action calculated to help on economic development. Those who, like Peter Bauer, put their money on market forces and urged the importance of leaving trade to expand freely had no need to marry their theories with a programme of governmental action. But with other theories it was necessary to ask what the governmental corollaries were and whether they were consistent with the observed capabilities of the government machine. Here experience might take precedence over theory.

PRIME CAUSES AND ACCELERATORS

From the point of view of the administrator (and of his political master, too) there were two fundamental questions. Of these the first related to prime causes. What are the springs of development? What causes it to speed up or slow down? Why does one country show a faster rate of growth than another? The second question was the operational corollary of the first. What can be done to make development proceed faster or more smoothly? What can governments do to assist the process of development?

These are questions that cannot be answered within the customary limits of economics. The economist may have made a takeover bid for the study of development by viewing the whole process in terms of investment. But this simply will not do. Development in the broad sense can amount to the replacement of one civilization by another; and since the days of Adam Smith and Karl Marx economists have been a little hesitant about addressing themselves to such large issues. Anthropology, politics, technology and, above all, history have a part to play in finding answers to the questions I have posed. It is no surprise to me that much of the best work on economic development has been done by economists who have steeped themselves in these allied disciplines – above all, in economic history.

The two questions that I have put could be raised at any stage of economic development. A theory addressing itself to these questions must therefore be applicable at all stages: both to so-called 'developed' and 'developing' countries. This leaves open the possibility that there are such major differences in the application of a general theory to the two kinds of society that separate theories are required to throw light on the forces at work and the scope for action within each of them. Any general theory needs supplementation to deal with the peculiarities of a particular society. But in what follows I shall be concerned first and principally with the factors likely to be common to all societies.

Let me next make clear what I mean by 'theory' and by 'development'.

WHAT IS THEORY?

By 'theory' I mean essentially a *model* of the process of development coupled with a *dictionary* that translates the variables in the model into real, observable elements. The question is therefore whether there is any single model or group of models of the development process exhibiting the interaction of the main variables in a way that tallies with observations of the process as it occurs in the real world. Similarly, the allied question is whether there is a model capable of tracing the reactions on development either directly or indirectly of the use of any given instrument of policy. Do we understand why development occurs and do we know what to do to promote it?

From this point of view what matters is not whether it is possible to develop a theory in the sense of a set of logically interrelated propositions but whether any theory of this kind can be put to use. Are there models that help us to ask the right questions, alert us to the significant issues, improve our intuitive grasp of what is going on?

WHAT IS DEVELOPMENT?

By 'development' I mean not just the growth of GNP but a transformation of the economy that is likely to include changes in attitudes, habits and values and, above all, in knowledge and skills. The essence of development is some element of novelty. More of the same may be growth but it is not development. Growth can occur when the only change is in magnitudes – in the number of workers or the stock of assets – without any real development, technical or human, such as would necessarily affect living standards and methods of work.

Different economists have very different conceptions of development. Lauchlin Currie, for example, argues that the characteristic of a 'developed' country is not a matter of the standard of living but of:

> the possession of a more or less common degree of control or dominance over [its] economic, social, political, demographic and physical environment that enables [it] to adopt more or less appropriate responses to problems as they arise.[1]

In his view, differences in development are evidenced by the extent and pervasiveness in all spheres of life of this domination of the environment. 'It is not just a matter', he says, 'of monetary policy, or trade policy, or rate of growth, or government organization and level of administration, but of all of these *and many more*' [author's italics]. . . . 'The solution of one difficulty rests on the solution of another, which requires the solution of a third, and so on'.[2]

To my mind, Currie is right to associate development with the ideas of control and of cultural change: the example of Iran is a forcible reminder of the way in which development can be set back if rapid environmental change is not accompanied by parallel changes in the prevailing culture. But there is something to be said for thinking of development in somewhat narrower terms and taking as a criterion the shortfall in performance below long term potential.

OPPORTUNITIES AND CONSTRAINTS

When I looked at the literature in 1955 I was inclined to proceed in terms of a theory of opportunities and constraints: demand and supply. Development represents a response to opportunity under various constraints so that the question to be resolved is whether opportunities arise in any systematic way and how constraints come to be relaxed.

Starting from the side of opportunities, one could emphasize at least three different possibilities:

First, perception of opportunities. One could, like Schumpeter, stress the role of the entrepreneur: the businessman who sees the possibility of a new departure capable of yielding him a profit and takes his chance with advantage to the public.

Secondly, opportunities arising out of an extension of the market. These might arise from the opening up or enlargement of foreign markets external to the system. Or they might, as in the world of Allyn Young and Lord Kaldor, arise out of an enlargement of the domestic market that made possible economies of scale: the introduction of more efficient methods that in a narrower market were not worthwhile.

Thirdly, opportunities generated by new knowledge: either new scientific knowledge, publicly available in written form, or the knowledge more commonly involved in technical change that is acquired through experimentation with new products and processes, and is accompanied by a build-up of skill and know-how.

In reviewing these possibilities I came increasingly to the conclusion that the third group was by far the most important. Where technical change was not present, the entrepreneur had little scope: as Sol Tax demonstrated in his *Penny Capitalism*,[3] in villages where even the wheel had yet to be introduced a lively response to market forces did not suffice to set the process of development in motion. It was true on the other hand that technical change might be thwarted or suppressed when no one sought to profit from it: it might simply not occur. Moreover, a group of 'improving landlords' (as in the 1720s in Scotland) or of influential figures conscious of technological backwardness (as in Japan after the Meiji Restoration in 1868) could play a major role in bringing about technical innovation. The entrepreneur undoubtedly had an important role. But the root of the development that occurred was the opportunity of technical change which the entrepreneur seized and without which nothing would have happened.

The alternative starting point would be constraints; and in 1955 it looked to me as if the literature laid the emphasis far too much on these whether it related to 'developed' or 'developing' countries. In the case of the latter a much wider variety of constraints was given prominence. There were, first, the various social constraints: taboos, customs, and disdains, apart from ignorance and lack of education – all tending to narrow opportunities and reduce responsiveness to what opportunities existed. Changes in attitudes and institutions might be necessary so that in their absence development was held up or delayed. Then there were specific bottlenecks: for example, in food, energy, or skilled labour. Backwardness in agriculture, absence of raw materials and sources of energy, lack of workers with the necessary experience and training could all slow down development. Finally there were financial constraints arising either out of balance of payments difficulties or inadequate savings or an initial lack of infrastructure.

Most economists seemed to hurry past the first set, treat agricultural development as a lost cause or as something that could be left to respond to development at more hopeful points in the economy, and go on to make financial constraints the centrepiece of their exposition. A development programme was almost invariably an investment programme; and this directed attention to the supply of savings and the flow of funds into productive investment as the main strategic factor. But while investment is obviously at the heart of the development process this does not mean that capital accumulation as such is a recipe for successful development. It seemed to me that economists were so used to assigning a central role to capital in economic theory and building models that focussed on capital investment that they assumed too readily its critical importance in development. While investment might be the medium through which change took place this did not make it the mainspring of change and development. Just as the monetarists have been mesmerized by an apparent constancy in the long-run relation between the money supply and the price level and have in consequence assigned pride of place to the money supply in their explanation of the inflationary process, so development economists have been led by the apparent steadiness of capital–output ratios into assigning to investment pride of place in their explanation of the development process.

There is no reason to doubt that financial constraints do have an influence, particularly in countries at an early stage of development. Even in those cases, however, experience suggests that they yield to the pressure of opportunity, much as structural change is eased by expanding demand. They are not the major constraint: growth tends to provide its own finance once it gets under way. In industrial countries access to finance would seem to play a relatively subordinate role: there it is the emergence or perception of fresh opportunities that sets the pace.

MARKET EXPANSION, CAPITAL ACCUMULATION AND TECHNICAL CHANGE

Thus if one sets aside social and political constraints such as are of major importance in pre-industrial societies (but have a larger influence in industrial societies than is commonly admitted) we are left with three key elements, all of them familiar to economists from at least as far back as Adam Smith. On the one side, we have market expansion and technical change and on the other, capital accumulation. The significance of these three elements is much more obvious in industrial countries. They operate under different circumstances in pre-industrial countries and much is made of these differences in the literature, which is full of references to population pressure, labour surpluses, monocultures, balance of payments' problems, bottlenecks and discontinuities. I do not propose in what follows to take much account of these differences, many of which find at least some echo in many of the industrial countries, too. I will start from development in the more advanced countries without implying that what is said applies only to them.

Of the three key elements technical change differs from the other two in that there are no set limits to it. Capital accumulation, for example, may, in a given state of technique, be carried to the point at which it is of no further advantage. Market expansion in similar circumstances would also reach a point at which it ceased to feed on itself. But every advance in technical development opens up fresh possibilities of further advance. The exploitation to the full of a major innovation such as steam or electric power may stretch out over a century or more because it leads on to a succession of changes in technique. Technical development is the one inexhaustible element in the whole process.

It may be objected that this is to treat the three elements asymmetrically. Would technical development be inexhaustible in the absence of capital accumulation or market expansion? It would certainly slow down and might very well take a different direction. But there is no reason to suppose that it would cease. What is true is that the three elements interact with one another so that it is not possible to measure the contribution made by each separately. Capital accumulation facilitates innovation which in turn encourages capital investment. Investment also responds to market expansion and some forms of investment (e.g. in transport and communications) react powerfully on the size of the market. As the market becomes larger it permits of more efficient methods of production which still further enlarge it: division of labour, as Adam Smith put it, is limited by the size of the market. This self-reinforcing characteristic of market expansion would presumably soon bump against limits if it took the form exclusively of the exploitation of known techniques that were unprofitable on a smaller scale. But once the market starts to expand there is a response both in investment and in new technical development which add to the stock of productive assets and to the stock of technical knowledge out of which comes fresh development. Thus an expanding market can be – and very often is – the source of technical change. When this happens, market expansion may share some of the inexhaustibility of technical change.

Granted all these interactions and the consequent impossibility of regarding any one of the three elements as exogenous to the whole process of development, technical change has claims to be regarded as the dominant factor. It is obvious enough that in the absence of technical change capital accumulation would be unlikely to add much to GNP per head once the frontiers of available technique were reached. It would be only a matter of time before the rate of growth began to run down *whatever* the level of capital accumulation. Similarly if no improvements in technique lay to hand that could be introduced once the market was extended, there would not be much to be gained from an increase in the size of the market. All that this could do would be to bring into use techniques held in abeyance by the factor of scale.

While it is not legitimate to isolate any of the three key elements and credit it with the total impact to be expected when all three are free to react to one another, there are good grounds for treating capital accumulation as primarily a response to growth rather than a cause of it and for thinking that *dynamic* economies of scale are better treated as a variant of technical change than as an independent factor.

THE NEGLECT OF TECHNICAL CHANGE

But if technical change is the dominant factor why is it that the theory of economic development has not concentrated more wholeheartedly on the phenomenon of technical change: on its causes and how it operates, not just on its consequences for the distribution of income or the rate of growth? Three reasons may be suggested for this neglect.

First, technical change is exogenous and the economist can have nothing useful to say about it. Alternatively, if it is the fruit of research and development, i.e. of capital investment, it should be regarded as a form of investment and analysed as such.

The fact is, however, that technical change, far from being exogenous, is a commercial operation, on a par with other action taken to increase business efficiency and its origins are at least as important to economic theory as the origins of capital accumulation. The economic historians took this point long ago but economists continue to regard technology as none of their business when in fact it should be something they cannot afford to neglect.

The alternative idea that technical change is the fruit of research and development is a piece of mystification. R & D is in fact almost entirely

D, and D is something nearly every businessman does since every change in design involves development and nearly everybody engages in redesign. Some of the expenditure in launching a new or redesigned product or introducing a new process or new method of production can be regarded as an investment and can be related to the resulting gain in profit. But there may also be very little prior expenditure, particularly where the changes are not of the dramatic kind that receive wide publicity but take the form of small, incremental adjustments such as appear to make up the main stream of technical development. Moreover the *total* return on either kind of innovation may far exceed that part of the return that is retained by the innovator and regarded by him as compensation for the expenditure and risk incurred.

The second way of excluding technical change from economics is the one adopted by Marshall. He quite rightly links technical change with competitive efficiency and relies on competition as an agency – *the* agency – of growth and development. The man who makes a better mousetrap drives out the man whose design is less efficient. Marshall's theory of technical change is thus a theory of the way in which competition operates. But he takes for granted that competition is the best way of promoting technical change and that the environment within which competition operates cannot be altered in ways that facilitate and accelerate technical change. This is not self-evident. Competition and technical change, like investment and technical change, need to be treated as two different things.

The third way of handling technical change is to wrap it up in investment and argue that the two are inseparable. Most models of economic growth, so far as they take account of technical change at all, proceed in this way. But there is very little justification for doing so. In modern economic communities, about three-quarters of capital accumulation is in housing, power, transport and inventories. A great deal of this investment is necessary because the community is richer or more numerous and does not give effect to technical change. Much of it is investment in consumers' durables, not producer capital. This is even more true if the figures are taken net of depreciation as they ought to be. In manufacturing industry, if net investment fell to zero, a high proportion of the really important technical changes could still be made when existing capital assets were replaced. In addition, many important changes may either economize capital or may not be embodied in physical assets.

A theory of economic development couched in terms of the three factors discussed above, but giving pride of place to technical change, is not what one finds in the textbooks. Much of the theory for 'developed' countries is in terms of growth models that take growth for granted and make no attempt to account for it. For 'developing' countries most writers concentrate on other features of those countries such as the labour surplus, dependency, and the role of foreign investment. There has, however, been a growing interest in the problems of technological transfer that goes back to President Truman's Point 4 programme of technical assistance in 1950. This interest is largely confined to transfers from 'developed' to 'developing' countries without systematic treatment of the more general problem of diffusion of technical change.

Since the developing countries are unlikely to be at the frontiers of modern technique, technical change in those countries necessarily takes the form of diffusion of working practices or capital equipment already in use elsewhere. In a sense, this means copying and imitating and might seem relatively straightforward. In practice it is rarely so. The equipment has to be adapted to local conditions: modifications are called for by climate, market limitations, the habits and capabilities of the labour force, and so on. Similarly, new products and processes have to be replanned and redesigned to suit a different economic environment. There has to be a staff able to spot and assess technical advances that are taking place elsewhere and would be suitable for introduction under different circumstances. Thus even the borrowing of someone else's technique may demand a high level of skill and experience: immersion in the technical literature, an educational background that makes the literature intelligible, personal contacts, capacity to undertake the necessary work of development. It can be just as difficult to innovate by imitating successfully what has been invented elsewhere as to make and adopt the original invention. The process of diffusion, whether within one country or from country to country, is steeped in mini inventions called for by the adaptations required. It makes heavy demands on the capacity to absorb technical change – a capacity which, like the capacity to absorb other kinds of change, may be low in the less developed countries.

The conclusion to be drawn is that, not surprisingly, economic development is largely a process of diffusion. Just as anthropologists see social development in terms of diffusion of ideas and practices, so economists would do well to look at economic development in the same terms. The theories evolved in each discipline should have something of interest to offer to the other.

CULTURAL AND POLITICAL FACTORS

So far the argument has run exclusively in terms of economics. As an explanation of development this makes it necessarily incomplete and unsatisfactory. The interaction of the three economic factors cited above may be a highly important ingredient in development but the interaction takes place within a political and cultural environment that in turn reacts with economic forces. These wider reactions may be the most powerful element in the whole process. This is particularly true of the social and economic transformation that occurs in the earlier stages of development.

We have to take account of the cultural aspects of development: the changes in values, attitudes, habits and ideas that accompany it; the fresh inputs that such changes may lend to the process; or the powerful drag that may delay or even arrest it if the changes in attitude are slow or perverse. There are innumerable examples of the quickening of development with the spread of a passion for innovation, a strengthening of economic incentives, the emergence of habits of thrift and a growing appetite for material prosperity. These things may be there all along and merely unfold as development proceeds; or they may lie at the root of development and be cultivated and instilled by an elite that sets the fashion. A country like Japan may take the road to economic development in response to fears in high places for its autonomy; a country like Scotland may take the first steps when its landlords abandon dogmatic theology for economic improvement. However it begins, economic development generates cultural responses and is itself the fruit of those responses. Where the responses are hostile, as in Iran, development is limited or may cease altogether. The anthropologist rather than the economist is the expert on situations of that kind.

But of course it is not only at the early stages that cultural factors enter. Anyone studying the vast literature on comparative rates of growth is as likely to find explanations of growth at much later stages of development couched in terms of sociology rather than economics. Britain's disappointing economic performance, for example, is widely attributed to educational and social factors: the disdain of the brighter university graduates for a career in manufacturing industry; failure to attract able young people to the study of engineering; inadequate training arrangements; class divisions affecting industrial relations; and so on. Similarly, it is often suggested that the more rapid growth of countries occupied or defeated in the last war is directly related to the resulting shock to national pride or to the stresses of postwar disorganization that made strong individual efforts indispensable to survival. It is not easy to see how such explanations can be submitted to objective tests. But that does not rule them out or reduce them to mere footnotes to explanations in economic terms.

Then there are the political pressures. Development means change and change can breed resistance. There are, of course, gainers but there are likely also to be losers. Change in the labour market that means better jobs for some may threaten the jobs of others. Some property owners, some consumers, some workers, some communities are better off while of others the reverse may be true. Changes in wealth and in the balance of economic power carry with them changes in status, prestige and political power. These changes may not be minor affairs and the resistances they set up may spill over into strikes, violent opposition, even civil war. On the other hand, change at one point may disturb complacency, routine and inertia at another and open the way to development. To get things moving in some sectors may require the pressure generated by movement elsewhere.

Starting from that proposition one can develop a theory of economic development such as that of Albert Hirschman, in which traditional economic factors – competitive pressures – play a subordinate part. The problem is seen in terms of successive imbalances generating fresh pressures and fresh imbalances, arousing one sector after another to the need for action. The mechanism by which one sector impinges on another through backward or forward linkages may be economic; but the pressures that set the mechanism in motion can be contrived and directed, i.e. they may be essentially political. The scope for applying pressure depends on the existence of organizational slack or the higher pitch of human capacity when pressure is applied. Thus the theory is really one of unused human resources: of shock treatment deliberately fostered so as to put pressure on the economy and jolt it into a different orbit. Unlike the pressure of market opportunities, the pressures envisaged in theories of this kind are largely political and can take the form of threats rather than inducements.

HOW THEORIES DIFFER

In this respect most theories of economic development have one thing in common: they are theories of unutilized potential.[4] They may concentrate on the existence of underemployed labour resources either in the rural areas or, at the going wage, in the towns; or they may focus on some form of slack that can be drawn upon by better organization or greater exertion or better education; or they may point to natural resources that can be put to use (or to more fruitful use) only when markets are opened up in other areas or countries; or they may envisage large gains from structural changes that substitute outputs of higher value for outputs of lower value; or, finally, they may run in terms of technical change and the introduction of new and more productive processes and products. If development occurs, there has to be something capable of being developed and scope for its development. Different theories differ largely in the emphasis they put on the different sources of potential development.

A second difference relates to the extent to which, and the ways in which, the process is thought capable of being accelerated. Some examine the contribution of market forces to the process in order to establish that what is important is to allow the market freedom to exercise its benificent influence and extend that influence by improving transport facilities, communications, education, etc. Others take for granted the need for action by the State and put forward various strategies for fuller utilization of available resources that the State may adopt. These strategies often amount to little more than old fashioned protection and nearly all of them are dominated by a view of the way in which international influences operate on development. So far as this is not so, the debate is usually about the relative significance of agricultural and industrial development and (less prominently) the way in which the State can possess itself of the resources necessary for either of these. In the past, industrialization was pushed ahead only too often on an insecure base in order to meet limited and inelastic domestic market requirements while the opportunities for agricultural and rural development were neglected or discouraged (e.g. by high export taxes).

Over the last fifteen years or so, strategies of development have tended to focus on 'basic needs'. That is, questions of distribution have come to the fore and taken precedence over questions of production. How far this reflected the more rapid growth of production in the 1950s and 1960s this is not the place to enquire. It represents an alternative aim of development but whether it can also serve as a *measure* of development must be very doubtful; and theories of how development *occurs* can hardly be converted into theories limited to a discussion of basic needs.

A third – and in some ways the most important – point of difference between different theories is their treatment of international influences. Some economists see these as healthy or even indispensable: the inflow of ideas, practices and technologies, the opening up of markets abroad, the availability of foreign capital, borrowed or invested, may all bring large benefits and accelerate development. On the other hand, the very fact that these influences are international and come from abroad may be resented or cause uneasiness and opposition. They have to run the gauntlet of nationalism, of antipathy to dependence on foreigners, and of a threat to the sovereign powers of government. There are obvious victims among producing units; the losers and laggards have an obvious scapegoat; those who dislike change can readily identify its source; and above all, two feelings frequently take root – one of loss of control, the other of unequal partnership. Much of existing development theory comes down to analysis of these twin dangers. Opening the door to foreign influences may mean opening the door to foreign control. Trade becomes the means by which foreign enterprises (or governments) come to dominate the development of countries lacking strong government. At the same time the fuller utilization of resources as a result of development accrues largely or almost entirely to the benefit of foreign enterprises and consumers.

Once one has got so far, development theory broadens out into a theory of international relations in which economic relationships are treated as the offspring of power relationships. We can choose between a Marxist approach which sees these relationships in terms of exploitation, colonialism and imperialism; or a more qualified version that sees the advanced countries as taking an undue share of the gains through a steady slide in the terms of trade against the less developed countries; or a neo-classical view that starts out from the mutual benefit that must underlie voluntary exchange and finds evidence of such mutual benefit from international trade irrespective of the stage of development of the trading countries.

ONE THEORY OR TWO?

Whether one takes the broader view that encompasses social and political factors or confines the analysis to economic factors, it is hard to see why we should end up with a theory of growth for the developed, and a theory of development for the developing, countries. There is little in the one that is without some application to the other. There are of course features more or less common to the one group and absent in the other. It is necessary, therefore, to supplement any general theory applicable to all economies by concepts and hypotheses appropriate only to one or other of the groups. But the same applies *within* each group once one takes account of the wide differences between developed *or* developing countries. No one imagines that the resources of economic theory have been exhausted once a few universal truths have been brought to bear on the problems of any country. Every country is a special case and those features that distinguish it from others require separate analysis. If several countries share important features of which economic theory takes no cognizance then theory needs to be extended and supplemented without losing sight of the possibility that similar features may be present to a lesser extent in other economies.

Thus if the question is: 'can the general apparatus of thought which we call economic theory throw light on the phenomena of economic development?', the answer is undoubtedly 'Yes'. That does not mean that all theorists see eye to eye on development, prompt the same questions or draw the same conclusions about what should be done. Nor is it inconsistent with the effort to develop a separate branch of theory to deal with the phenomena of development in the same way as monetary theory deals with monetary problems or industrial economics with industrial problems. But it does seem to me unfortunate and misguided that theories of development should be framed as if only one set of countries was in question; as if development in those countries obeyed different laws from development in more advanced countries; and as if nothing could be learned from an analysis of the process in advanced countries that would contribute to understanding of the process at an earlier stage of development.

NOTES

1 L. Currie, *The Role of Economic Advisers in Developing Countries* (Greenwood Press, Westport and London, 1981), p. 235.
2 Ibid., p. 236.
3 Sol Tax, *Penny Capitalism* (Smithsonian Institution, Washington D.C., 1953).
4 A. O. Hirschman, 'The rise and decline of development economics', in *Essays in Trespassing* (Cambridge University Press, Cambridge, 1981), pp. 7--9.

10

The relationship between monetary and fiscal policy

The relationship between fiscal and monetary policy is one of great theoretical complexity, acute controversy, and major practical importance. Within the limits of a short lecture it is not possible to do more than indicate some of the issues involved and offer tentative judgements on them without penetrating the world of theory very deeply and avoiding altogether the lush undergrowth of econometrics that now surrounds it. It may be more helpful, on an occasion of this kind, to start with an account of the way thinking has developed on the matter before turning to some of the more obvious theoretical considerations governing the mix of fiscal and monetary policy and the limitations to which each of them is subject.

The idea of using fiscal and monetary policy to procure greater stability in output and employment – indeed the very idea of having a fiscal *policy* or a monetary *policy* – is a comparatively recent one. Before the First World War it was taken for granted that a prudent government would try to maintain a balanced budget in good times and bad, although some departure from the rules of financial orthodoxy might be inevitable in time of war. Similarly, in the days of the gold standard, monetary arrangements were designed to maintain convertibility of the currency into gold at a fixed price, an aim that paid no regard to the possibility that either inflation or unemployment might result.

THE INSTABILITY OF INVESTMENT

This possibility, when economic fluctuations first began to be studied, was associated with the behaviour of investment which was seen as highly unstable and liable, therefore, to change abruptly in relation to the thriftiness of the public and their willingness to make the necessary finance

Keynes Lecture to the British Academy, 6 May 1981.

available. The instability of investment might communicate itself to the rest of the economy: there could be no guarantee that the capital market would function in such a way as to preserve an unchanged pressure of demand on available resources. The rate of interest, seen hitherto as fulfilling this function, might not be propelled, quickly and automatically, to the level at which balance was restored between the flow of savings and the flow of capital expenditure and in the process inflationary pressure on the one hand, or a deficiency of demand on the other, might develop and continue. Capital markets, to use the modern jargon, might not 'clear' at an unchanged level of activity.

This failure of interest rates to adjust was explained initially in terms of credit creation. Bank credit might add to the flow of loanable funds when capital expenditure was expanding strongly and this would hold down the market rate of interest below its equilibrium or 'natural' rate. Conversely, a drop in the expected return from new capital investment might not be accompanied by a fall in market rates of interest on the scale necessary to offset the change in expectations.

At that stage in the development of thinking, two practical conclusions were drawn. One was that monetary policy was central to the problem of economic stability: there could be either inflation, if the banks created more credit than was needed to keep investment and savings in balance, or industrial depression, if there was an insufficiency of bank credit, the excess or shortage of bank credit corresponding to a gap between the market rate of interest and the more volatile 'natural' rate at which investment would be held within the limits of savings. The second practical conclusion was that if the source of instability lay primarily in the behaviour of investment, the state might secure greater stability by supplementing private investment in bad times through public works of various kinds. In due course this second remedy was elaborated as a scheme for advancing or retarding public investment so as to counterbalance fluctuations in private investment in the opposite direction.

These two lines of thought – one essentially monetary, the other essentially fiscal – were not necessarily consistent with one another. The rates of interest directly affected by banking policy were short term rates which might have little or no immediate effect on long term rates. They might, as Hawtrey argued, be of crucial importance for investment in stocks, and stockbuilding might be the most volatile element in investment. But if the more enduring difficulty lay in preserving stability in fixed investment, how much reliance could be put on banking policy? On the other hand, could the role of the banks be left entirely aside, as it appeared to be by those who put their faith in public works? Was it right to assume that if public investment took the place of private investment, the rate of interest would be left unaffected?

MARKET FAILURE

When Keynes came to consider the matter, he took a more radical line. The fundamental question to be answered was: what determined the level of output? It was not enough to consider fluctuations if these were assumed to be around a trend that represented a sustainable optimum identified with full employment or economic potential. It was necessary also to consider the possibility of persistent underutilization of available resources because of a deficiency of demand. That deficiency would only persist if there was some defect in the system preventing the kind of response in price that would extinguish the deficiency. In Keynes's view there were two such defects, one relating to the rate of interest and one relating to the behaviour of wages. Neither the capital market nor the labour market 'cleared' through price adjustments; and this failure to 'clear' was not just periodic, so that essentially intermittent departures from full employment resulted, but might be persistent and give rise to a chronic underutilization of resources. If savers became more thrifty there was no guarantee that their access of thrift would be translated via the capital market into additional investment: on the contrary, it was entirely possible that investment might not respond, or respond perversely, and that greater thrift would serve only to impoverish the community by depressing the level of income as the only available means of keeping savings in check. Equally, if unemployed wage earners were willing to accept lower pay, and money wages were reduced in times of depression, there was no guarantee that this would add appreciably to the number of jobs on offer since the reduction in wages could be expected to lead to a corresponding reduction in prices and this might do little or nothing to generate additional demand. Neither the real rate of interest nor the real rate of wages was determined in the way assumed in classical economic theory; and the money rate of interest and the money rate of wages did not adjust so as to allow an excess of thrift or of labour to be absorbed in the same way as a reduction in price allows an excess of some staple commodity to be absorbed in an auction market.

DEMAND MANAGEMENT

Keynes's ideas formed the basis of demand management in the postwar years. If a deficiency of demand may be the outcome of leaving things to market forces, policies are necessary in order to regulate demand. It also came to be accepted that there need be no presumption that these policies should bear exclusively on the level of investment rather than on other elements in aggregate demand such as consumer spending. Given the much greater weight that consumer spending has in GNP, it was obviously easier, in trying to effect a given change in total demand, to operate on consumer spending than to make an adjustment of equal magnitude in investment. The speed with which tax changes affect spending compared with the long lead times characteristic of fixed investment pointed in the same direction.

It was also a corollary of Keynesian theory that the horizon of demand management should be short term. The preservation and prolongation of short term stability was a natural approach to long term stability unless there was some fundamental incompatibility between the two. Any conflict between them implied some form of instability at intervals, i.e. recurrent *departures* from a steady rate of growth. To have no concern with the size of these departures was to regard short term stability as a matter of little importance and to express an unwarranted faith in the self-regulating character of the economic system. Not that short term demand management and economic stability became the be-all and end-all of economic policy. The long run balance between the different components of aggregate demand had also to be considered. There was in addition, and always has been, something that we can call supply management which looks to the longer term, may conflict with demand management, and is usually a good deal more important.

The Keynesian approach to demand management adopted in the United Kingdom after the war was couched almost exclusively in terms of budgetary action. This emphasis derived largely from pre-war experience when it appeared that, once interest rates had been brought down to a low level and the banks had ample funds, not much more could be hoped for from monetary policy and any fresh stimulus would have to come via the budget. In such circumstances, with Bank Rate held constant at 2 per cent for nearly twenty years, monetary policy was largely passive. In wartime it had been a precept of policy to refrain from raising interest rates and so adding to the tax burden. Then, and in earlier years, Keynes lent his support to efforts to keep down the long term rate on the grounds that once investors were encouraged to think higher rates appropriate it would not be easy to induce them to return to a regime of cheap money and yet just such a regime might be required by a glut of capital.

When the war was over, fears of a higher debt burden and a possible slump again combined to induce the government to avoid the use of monetary weapons as a means of restricting demand. For this purpose it turned instead to large budget surpluses supported by rationing and other administrative controls. This preference for fiscal measures may have rested also on antipathy for the rentier and doubts as to the efficacy of high interest rates. There was an appearance of greater certainty about tax changes; Ministers could be offered a rough assessment of the magnitude of the impact of these changes on demand and output which no one would have dared to offer in respect of changes in monetary policy. When the Treasury first engaged in economic forecasting in wartime it did so in terms of an inflationary gap to be closed by budgetary, not monetary, measures. Money was left out of the picture, just as it had been in pre-war analyses of government-engineered expansions in demand and output like Lord Kahn's celebrated article in 1931 on the multiplier. In the increasingly sophisticated forecasting of postwar years this neglect of the monetary aspects of the forecast continued.

None the less, in the successive packages of measures introduced to deal with the long series of crises in the 1950s and 1960s it was usual to include a rise in Bank Rate and/or fresh guidance to the banks intended to curb the creation of credit in particular directions. The imposition of hire purchase restrictions, which was an equally regular component of the packages and often the most important, could also be regarded as a monetary measure designed to limit consumer credit. It would be going much too far to imply, therefore, that no regard was paid to monetary conditions; on the contrary, some care was taken to make monetary and fiscal policy pull in the same direction. Rarely, however, was there any government action aimed specifically at limiting the money supply; indeed, as Harry Johnson pointed out in 1959, there were no adequate figures of the money supply. The government was content to vary short term interest rates in sympathy with its fiscal stance. At the longer end of the market it took a fairly passive line, seeking to preserve stability in the market for government debt and make what sales of gilt-edged it could at prevailing interest rates.[1]

In those days it was possible to concentrate more or less exclusively on the 'real' economy, i.e. on income flows, without bothering too much about the financial aftermath of a budget surplus or deficit. The main aim of policy was to get the level of demand right, avoiding too much pressure or too little, and this aim could be fulfilled in different ways, depending on the use that was made of alternative instruments of policy. If there was pressure on the balance of payments, monetary weapons would be more likely to be brought into use. If importance was attached to a higher level of investment, monetary policy might be eased and fiscal policy tightened so as to maintain a constant pressure of demand. The choice of weapons was also affected by the urgency of the situation and the need for quick results. The monetary authorities were in a position to influence the situation more or less continuously while fiscal action was inevitably intermittent. But in a crisis both monetary and fiscal weapons were almost certain to be brought into use and to operate in the same direction in mutual support.[2]

MONETARISM

The subordination of monetary to fiscal policy came under challenge in the 1960s from a school of thought which inverted the relationship between the two, giving clear precedence to monetary policy. The need to control inflation was put in the forefront and demand management dismissed as superfluous if not actually damaging. Control of inflation could be secured by limiting the money supply and in no other way. Monetary policy, if aimed at the level of output rather than the level of prices, would be misapplied and in the long run ineffective. Fiscal policy should be such as to comply with the need to keep the money supply under firm control.

These are propositions that have much in common with pre-Keynesian thinking. The Treasury in the 1920s would have had no difficulty in accepting all of them. In those days unemployment was explained in terms that left out any reference to the level of effective demand and in any event effective demand was thought to be beyond the power of government to influence. Government borrowing to finance public investment was officially regarded as displacing or 'crowding out' an equal amount of private investment. The quantity theory of money went without question, usually in a form that linked prices and the money supply with only a passing reference to output. It was precisely these ideas that Keynes sought to overturn: not only sought to overturn but *did* overturn.

The resurrection of these propositions does not mean that they are generally accepted. On the contrary, most economists would dismiss them on much the same grounds as Keynes did: that the capital market and the labour market do not clear in the manner of an auction market. They would suspect that, whatever may be true in academic circles, the influence on governments of such ideas rests less on their intellectual merits than on the way they chime with the temper of the times: the disenchantment with government intervention, the recognition that intervention may not achieve its professed purpose, and the greater disposition to rely on market forces.

We have hear successive Prime Ministers denounce the idea that increased public expenditure can soften the impact on employment of a trade depression. We are told almost every day that an increase in the money supply would serve only to revive inflation and would damage the long term prospects for increased employment. We have seen an abandonment of direct intervention in the foreign exchange market in order to hold or vary the exchange rate and, what is more surprising, an abandonment of the idea that changes in real exchange rates can be accomplished by intervention. This is a retreat from demand management on the grand scale.

Of course, it is a retreat in principle only and what governments do in practice is very different. It has not resulted in balanced budgets or a steady growth in the money supply or a stable and predictable rate of exchange. The attempt to supersede discretionary government action on the level of effective demand by stated rules and targets governing the operations of the public authorities may have been intended to provide the private sector with a firm basis on which to plan ahead; but if so it has not succeeded.

The very fact that governments have adopted monetary targets and pursued fiscal policies that pay no regard to the current state of employment makes it evident that something has gone wrong with demand management. What is it that has gone wrong and how does it affect the choice of policy, if there is one, between fiscal and monetary instruments?

What has gone wrong is inflation and expectations of inflation, short-circuiting expansionary measures aimed at increasing employment and output on the one hand and outlasting contractionary measures aimed at reducing inflation on the other. The system of ideas underlying demand management originated in a world of underemployed economies in which the danger of inflation could be almost entirely ignored and higher prices would have been positively welcomed. It was a world in which a rapid increase in the money supply excited no alarm: as, for example, in the four months preceding the conversion of 5 per cent War Loan in 1932 when clearing bank deposits expanded by over 6 per cent (i.e. at over 18 per cent per annum) while money GNP remained steady or actually fell. With over two million workers unemployed an expansion in demand was unlikely to raise wages very much and such rise as did occur was quite consistent with a downward trend in wage costs. Import prices, too, were remarkably stable in spite of the depreciation of the pound; and the terms of trade, which have so often played a central part in the inflationary process, had swung in Britain's favour to an unparalleled extent – over 25 per cent – between 1929 and 1933.

LIMITATIONS OF DEMAND MANAGEMENT

Yet even in pre-war years it was possible to foresee some of the limitations of demand management. First, there was the difficulty that neither fiscal nor monetary policy was very effective in its impact on the level of costs. Money wages – the largest element in costs – were not sensitive to small changes in demand pressure, as later experience showed, except upwards and in the vicinity of full employment. Other elements in cost were at the mercy of changes in world markets and in the rate of exchange. It followed that demand management could not by itself protect the economy from the danger of inflation.

A second limitation that became apparent in the years before the war was that the available instruments of policy are insufficiently selective. It is not enough to aim at a general and widespread increase in the pressure of demand when the increased pressure is felt unevenly and resources are not fluid. There may be bottlenecks within the economy (for example, in the building industry) or at the level of the world economy (for example, in the markets in primary commodities). Such bottlenecks can generate price increases at strategic points in the economy and if the increases spread to adjoining markets they can rapidly breed a general inflation. Where the bottleneck is of such importance as energy supplies it is capable of thwarting the response in output to an expansion in demand and such an expansion may then produce nothing but inflation.

A rather similar result may follow an over-rapid expansion of demand which gives insufficient time for supply to respond. Pre-war literature dwelt on the case of a boom in private fixed investment that enlarged the flow of expenditure and forced up the price of consumer goods until the new equipment came into use or the financial strain broke the boom. But the danger of inflation from setting out on too steep a path of expansion is not confined to cases of this kind nor is it necessarily confined to situations in which there is little slack in the economy.

These limitations all have to do with maladjustments in the 'real' economy. They all relate to the danger of inflation or to the difficulty of combating inflation without a serious loss of output and employment. When a government is pursuing an expansionary policy the crux of the matter is how much of the expansion in nominal demand will be translated into additional output and how much will spend itself in raising the price level. The bottlenecks envisaged in the second and third limitations increase the upward slope of the supply curve and dissipate more of the increase in demand in higher prices. But the first limitation – the insensitivity of costs to changes in demand – brings into question the apparatus of thought enshrined in an aggregate supply curve. If wage earners react to a rise in the price level by claiming and obtaining a compensatory increase in money wages, costs and prices can rise progressively without any perceptible change in the level of output. If in course of time *expectations* of a rise in the price level begin to govern wage claims and wage settlements, again independently of the level of output, the notion of inflation as a movement along a rising supply curve of output becomes even more inappropriate.

In the first two decades or so after the war the interrelationship between prices, costs, and expectations did not greatly limit the effectiveness of demand management, although the pressure of demand was a good deal higher than it afterwards became. The period was one of uninterrupted and, by previous standards, very rapid inflation. But there never seemed much likelihood, except perhaps in 1950–1, that inflation would get out of hand and gather speed unpredictably at a rate that no one could afford to ignore. Once expectations became adjusted to a fairly steady rate of inflation, fiscal policy appeared to work in much the same way as it might be expected to in an underemployed, non-inflationary economy of the pre-war type. What changed matters in the 1970s was a series of jolts to the international economy that shook customary expectations and sent them into a new orbit.

JOLTS

The first such jolt was the change in the atmosphere of the labour market after the 'events' of May 1968 in Paris. A second jolt, in 1972–3, was partly financial, involving a flight from money into commodities, and partly real, marking the abrupt end of a long period in which the terms of trade moved against staple commodities on world markets. The quadrupling of oil prices at the end of 1973 carried the movement in the terms of trade further and at the same time threw the international economic and financial system out of balance. A further jolt was given to the system by the renewed rise in oil prices in 1979–80. All of these operated to produce rates of inflation in the United Kingdom and other industrial countries unheard of in peacetime. They also introduced major uncertainties as to the adjustments that would be made both in the immediate future and eventually. These uncertainties, and the expectations to which they gave birth, transformed the task of economic management.

On the one hand, wage earners, already reacting against the greater weight of taxation they were being asked to bear, found themselves faced with a much more rapid increase in prices, reflecting in large measure the higher cost of imports. Their expectations of real income were not adjusted to the fall by 25 per cent in the terms of trade; and their expectations of money income were adjusted sharply upwards by the observed rise in consumer prices and the uncertainty as to how they would move in future. At the same time, lenders and investors, alarmed by the way inflation was accelerating, were increasingly sensitive to any acts of government savouring of more rapid inflation. They were liable therefore to react strongly to government measures involving an increase in the supply of money or the PSBR and to the extent these reactions raised interest rates or pushed down the exchange rate they frustrated the expansionary intentions of the measures.

Opinion and expectations tended to be based on a perceived threat running from the PSBR to the money supply and from there to prices and the rate of inflation; and these expectations, like the expectations of wage earners, tended to be self-fulfilling. The fear of inflation discourages the holding of money and titles to money (i.e. debt) and encourages a switch into real assets, titles to real assets (equities) and foreign currencies. Such switches raise the price of assets and make imports dearer, laying the basis for a broader inflationary movement. At the same time, wage negotiators stick out for bigger increases in money wages that produce the very acceleration in prices against which they are seeking to guard.

The shocks to the system over the past decade, therefore, not only precipitated much higher rates of inflation but left it with a hangover that made treatment more difficult. The central issue no longer related to the pressure of demand but to how expectations could be changed. It was not at all clear that either fiscal or monetary policy was well adapted for such purposes. There was an obvious danger that if used to expand output they would be ineffective and if used to damp down inflation would involve a disproportionate loss in output.

Once the main object of policy is to change expectations – or, to use more old-fashioned language, to restore confidence – the issue ceases to be a technical one for economists to decide. It necessarily turns on what will sufficiently impress those whose expectations must be changed before the system can function again in a normal way. It may be necessary to pander to unfounded beliefs about the causes of inflation, to play for time so as to allow current expectations to die away, or to indulge in a show of strength that arouses expectations of a different kind.

THE POLICY MIX

Against this historical background it would be surprising if the same mix of monetary and fiscal policy was appropriate in all situations. Which instruments are preferred must depend on what objectives of policy have priority, whether circumstances favour the use of one set of instruments rather than the other, and how it is thought the economy works. If, for example, control of inflation takes priority over getting rid of unemployment, monetary weapons have the advantage that they have an immediate and direct effect on prices just as fiscal weapons have an immediate and direct effect on employment. But it is possible to imagine circumstances in which, with unchanged priorities, monetary policy might be more effective in coping with unemployment and fiscal policy – though this is less likely – in coping with inflation. If, for example, private investment is highly sensitive to small changes in interest rates, and interest rates in turn are highly sensitive to small changes in the money supply, it may be possible, as in 1932, to exert more leverage on employment by a policy of cheap money than would be exerted by higher deficit spending. Indeed, if financial markets interpret a move to balance the budget as pointing to lower interest rates and if lower rates would not provoke a large outflow of capital, a combination of cheap money and *lower* deficit spending might in some circumstances offer the best hope of expanding employment. *Per contra* it is arguable that in the early postwar years, with large excess liquidity that would have survived much higher interest rates, it was preferable to rely on large budget surpluses to keep inflation at bay.

Leaving aside differences in policy objectives and economic circumstances, there remains a sharp difference of view over the way in which fiscal and monetary policies should be combined. On the one view, control of the money supply is the necessary and sufficient instrument for tackling inflation and without such control not much can be done to get rid of unemployment. Without quite arguing that 'money is all that matters for changes in *nominal* income and for *short run* changes in real income', the monetarist school of thought holds that fiscal policy does not matter, or if it does, is monetary policy in disguise.[3] Neo-Keynesians, on the other hand, have been inclined to attribute prime importance to fiscal policy as a means of regulating employment and to look to some other instrument such as incomes policy for dealing with inflation. Even a neo-Keynesian would be obliged to concede, however, that if financial markets are strongly monetarist in their assessment of economic policy and if wage earners will brook no reduction in real wages in any circumstances, while at the same time inflationary expectations are firmly shared by both groups, there may be no way in which a government can expand the economy by fiscal (or perhaps any other) policy. A mixture of wrongheaded beliefs and confident expectations, dictating the conduct of capital and labour, would be quite sufficient to put an end to the present economic system.

For our purposes it is sufficient to recognize that policy has to deal both with unemployment *and* inflation and that neither fiscal nor monetary policy can be relied upon by itself to get rid of both of them. Monetarists argue that monetary policy could always get rid of inflation but this would be true only if no limit were set to the loss in output or the length of time required. They do not propose any new instrument of policy and see a curtailment of the supply of money both as more feasible and more effective than their critics.

The monetarists are right to emphasize that an expansion in the money supply affects prices in a way that fiscal policy does not. In their view of the inflationary process the line of causation runs from money to prices to costs. An increase in the money supply causes a shift in portfolios towards other assets and hence a rise in their price (including the price of houses, foreign exchange, and – in consequence – imported goods of all kinds). It is unlikely that in those circumstances wages will for long show no response and this will reinforce the rise in import costs. But the line of causation may equally well run in the opposite direction. An increase in wages may push up costs and this in turn will push up prices and raise the demand for money. We have to reckon with both possibilities and which is the more typical and the more important is largely an empirical matter.

Where the monetarists are on weaker ground is in assuming that the money supply can be regarded as exogenous and within the control of the authorities. Given that the authorities have to operate through interest rates and not directly on the money supply, they can only control the supply in so far as they correctly gauge the demand, which responds to every wind that blows throughout the economy and from other economies as well. The more they concentrate their efforts on some target for the money supply in face of the waywardness of demand, the more volatile become the terms and conditions of credit, although the stability of these terms and conditions has an importance of its own. If, as they are bound to do, they allow some weight to the need for an element of stability in interest rates, the money supply will to that extent reflect changes in demand and not simply the intentions of the authorities. Instead of being an instrument of control, it will be a symptom of the state of the economy, a bell-wether of inflationary pressures.

By making the growth in the money supply the touchstone of policy, and fiscal policy entirely subordinate to monetary policy and little more than an aspect of it, monetarism comes near to collapsing all aspects of macro-economic policy into one and disregarding the many facets of any single line of policy – monetary, fiscal, or other. To attach over-riding importance to the money supply, when the objectives of economic policy are complex and often conflicting, is to make the same mistake as to stick through thick and thin to a fixed rate of exchange and for much the same reason: that the movement of costs, especially wage costs, may not accommodate itself to some pre-arranged target. Inflexible commitments to such targets may prove very expensive: the same forces that make it difficult to go back to the gold standard or to balance the budget make it unwise in an uncertain world to put on the straitjacket of unconditional monetary targets.

It is necessary to insist that monetary policy cannot be reduced to the single dimension of the money supply any more than the thrust of fiscal policy can be narrowed to the purely financial consequences of a budget surplus or deficit. It is possible to read an extensive history of monetary policy such as Richard Sayers's three volumes on the Bank of England[4] without being troubled by the thought that nobody knew what was happening to the money supply. But it is impossible to do so without being impressed by the wide range of central banking operations that have little or nothing to do with the money supply. Both monetary and fiscal policy cover a wide spectrum of measures with very different impacts on the economy; and it would be a travesty to boil them down to a single measure of that impact, even when only the macro-economic aspect is under discussion. If one *were* obliged to think in terms of a single dimension, it would be no more reasonable to treat changes in the money supply as a measure of the stance of monetary policy than it is to treat changes in the budget surplus or deficit as a measure of the stance of fiscal policy. The changes occurring in the money supply are the end product of a highly complex process in which the developments set on foot by the monetary authorities spread throughout the economy. These developments include the repercussions on the rate of exchange and the balance of payments; on budgetary expenditure (e.g. higher interest payments) and tax revenue; on the lending policies of financial institutions; and on the demand for money throughout the economy. The intentions of the authorities, as expressed in the measures adopted, may differ widely from the final outcome and not necessarily in the same direction. There are good grounds for interpreting monetary policy in terms of what the authorities actually do rather than in terms of some target at which they profess to be aiming.

SYMBIOSIS OF MONETARY AND FISCAL POLICY

Just as it is not possible to regard fiscal policy as a mere adjunct of monetary policy or vice versa, so it is not possible to treat monetary and fiscal policy as if they were completely independent of one another. The different instruments of policy have to be used in combination with one another and the thrust of the various elements in the policy mix cannot be measured separately. All economic policy instruments interact. What happens when any one instrument is used depends on the setting of the other instruments of policy and the conditions prevailing at the time. The stimulus to output that follows an increase in government spending will depend on the kind of incomes policy adopted and the success attending it. The response to a change in the exchange rate will be affected by the fiscal measures with which it is accompanied. And so on.

The 'symbiosis', as it has been called, of monetary and fiscal policy is particularly close.[5] An increase in the budget deficit requires additional borrowing and this in turn affects interest rates, the money supply, and the exchange rate. A change in monetary policy taking the form, say, of higher interest rates involves a heavier burden on the Exchequer and has other effects on the fiscal balance through changes in public investment and, so far as the level of activity is reduced, through a fall in tax revenue.

These interactions are heightened in a world in which financial markets interpret a larger borrowing requirement or an increase in the money supply as inflationary and regard the second as an almost automatic outcome of the first. Under those conditions the announcement of an expansionary fiscal policy, even before any additional borrowing took place, would be sufficient to produce a rise in interest rates in anticipation, whether the government had it in mind to expand the money supply or not. Such a rise might also accompany an expansion in the money supply even if the government hoped by doing so to *lower* interest rates. Where markets are highly sensitive to the danger of inflation *any* move on the part of the government to expand demand could encounter strong, perverse market reactions. These would be the more important the more powerfully demand is influenced by changes in interest rates and credit conditions as compared with direct changes in income flows.

Although it can be difficult to disentangle monetary and fiscal policy there are clearly some objects of policy to which one set of instruments is more appropriate than the other. It has been usual, for example, to regard fiscal policy as governed mainly by domestic, and monetary policy by international, factors. This does not mean that foreign holders of sterling are oblivious to the state of the British budget or that governments feel debarred from announcing monetary targets related to purely domestic objectives. It is possible also for the budget to be used to procure balance of payments effects through taxes on foreign-held balances or, in opposite circumstances, on the return on British investments abroad: and for monetary restrictions to do duty for higher taxes when electoral considerations tell against additional burdens on the taxpayer. But the limits within which monetary policy can reconcile diverging national and international pressures are narrow. Just as it is difficult to control simultaneously the price *and* the quantity of money – interest rates *and* the money supply – so it is difficult to control simultaneously the quantity of money in Britain and the terms on which it can be exchanged into foreign money, i.e. the rate of exchange. If the money supply is overexpanded, some of the excess will overflow on to the foreign exchanges, pushing down the value of sterling and in this and other ways levering up domestic prices. A fall in interest rates, given high international capital mobility, will have similar – perhaps even more powerful – effects. Conversely, if the government fixes a monetary target involving high interest rates it is in no position to resist a rise in the exchange rate and an inflow of funds that helps to relieve the contrived shortage of money. In the absence of capital controls – and usually also in spite of them – there are limits to the power of any one country to loosen or tighten credit conditions in comparison with other countries. There is, however, enough friction in the system to afford some leeway and countries enjoy more independence in their monetary policies than much current theory allows.

International factors also limit the power of individual countries to make effective use of fiscal policy in order to stabilize demand. Fluctuations in the level of activity in the international economy are almost inevitably reflected in the domestic markets of the leading participants. If they seek to mitigate or offset the fluctuations within their own economy they cannot do so by fiscal action alone without taking liberties with their balance of payments. They can only escape their 'share' of an international depression if they are able to divert resources from international to domestic uses and, even if they have large reserves or can borrow abroad, the necessary switch may not be easy to bring about.

LIMITS TO EXPANSION

The limits to monetary expansion would appear to be fairly narrow in normal circumstances. The monetarists are right to draw attention to the possibility that an over-issue of money may drive up prices without first generating additional income. Whether the line of causation is through a rise in the price of domestic assets or a fall in the rate of exchange, monetary expansion carries with it a danger of inflation insufficiently recognized in the past and differentiating it from fiscal expansion. It is not possible to dismiss this danger with the argument that an over-issue cannot occur since the demand for money must at all times equal the supply and that if people find themselves with too much money they will get rid of it. No doubt they will: but it is the process of getting rid of it that makes prices rise.

On the other hand, it is equally wrong to think that any increase in the money supply faster than the increase in GNP is bound to prove inflationary. It may be true that there is quite a high degree of stability in the relationship between money balances and GNP and that it would require exceptional tightness or exceptional looseness for the ratio to vary by more than a few percentage points within the year. But that does not entitle us to assume that more money must mean higher prices rather than higher output or that the demand for money balances never changes at all. All we can say is that if the ratio does show a perceptible change this should serve as an alarm bell for those who manage the economy.

In the case of fiscal policy there are limits of a different kind. A large and persistent borrowing requirement adds to the total weight of debt. What effect this will have on the economy depends on a number of factors. First, it depends upon the extent to which it does no more than take the place of private debt creation and leaves the level of economic activity unchanged. In such circumstances there is no obvious reason why rates of interest should be much affected. Second, it depends on the income yielded by the assets created out of government borrowing and whether this is sufficient to cover the debt service or leaves a residue that will swell progressively and absorb an increasing proportion of government revenue. Third, it depends on the rate of inflation. This will undoubtedly cause interest rates to rise and so add to the budgetary interest charge but at the same time it will eat away some of the real burden of debt. A fourth factor to be considered is the addition made to the net wealth of the private sector and the repercussions of this addition on the rate of saving.

It will be apparent that the last two factors interact. There will be no addition to the net wealth of the private sector if the value of the outstanding debt in private hands is being diminished by inflation faster than new debt is being created and marketed to the public. Such a situation is by no means hypothetical. In spite of the large nominal additions to the national debt occasioned by the recurrent government deficits and heavy borrowing of recent years the real value of market holdings of government debt in the United Kingdom has been falling year after year. To a large extent the deficits themselves are spurious since they are inflated by the higher interest rates that have to be offered on new issues of debt because of the very inflation that depreciates outstanding debt.

Why then should governments hesitate to borrow more in a major recession? Not, presumably, because they hold monetarist views. There is nothing inconsistent with orthodox monetarist ideas in increasing the PSBR if, as has been true in this country for the past decade, such borrowing adds little or nothing to the money supply. The hesitations of government derive in part from fear of aggravating inflation and in part from anxiety not to raise interest rates. There are circumstances in which such scruples are well grounded. If, for example, the government misjudges the amount of slack in the economy – as it would appear to have done in 1972–3 – the higher borrowing requirement will be superimposed on capital requirements that already tax the available finance and will inflate demand when capacity limits have already been reached. But where there is ample slack, the effects on inflation should be rather different. As the economy expands from a low level of activity to a somewhat higher one, whatever the cause, there may well be additional pressure on prices and interest rates. But if wages rise no faster than they would otherwise, the extra pressure is likely to be small and quite different from the kind of rise occasioned by *continuing* pressure on the price level when demand becomes excessive in relation to capacity.

The effect on interest rates might be more perceptible. In the absence of an expansion in the money supply there would be a greater strain on available funds and some rise in rates might also be necessary sooner or later because of additional pressure on the exchange rate. In addition, if government spending acts as a substitute for private spending, the same level of activity may be regained only at a somewhat higher level of interest rates because the method of finance of the two kinds of spending is not the same. Private investment, especially in manufacturing, is largely financed out of profits and rarely involves extensive longterm borrowing. In a depression the profits disappear while the government's deficit spending comes from money raised in the gilt-edged market or, to a limited extent, on short term. Unless the authorities are willing to expand the money supply, therefore, interest rates are likely to be pushed up and some further 'crowding out' of private investment will then result. Normally, however, this will be no more than a partial offset to the initial government stimulus.

CONCLUSIONS

Thus the emphasis over the past fifty years has swung from monetary policy to fiscal policy and back again to monetary policy. The swing has gone with changes in the parameters of the economy, in the ideas of economists about how it works, in the aims of policy makers and in the attitudes and expectations to which the system responds. The old consensus has disappeared and no new consensus has yet been achieved. In this state of uncertainty it would be a mistake for the authorities to proceed with complete confidence in any one economic model or to give priority to any one instrument of policy. Different policies interact and their separate outcomes are almost impossible to measure. What is always required is a set of policies to suit the circumstances.

From this point of view we have to recognize that we lack an instrument for reducing inflation without loss of output and that if inflation is not reduced full employment is compromised. Both monetary and fiscal policy have severe limitations in an inflationary world but they come into their own again in a world of underemployment as it becomes purged of inflation. In such a world the prime requirement is stability in money wages; only if that condition is fulfilled is it possible to exert the necessary leverage on employment through monetary and fiscal policy.

There has to be somewhere in the system an element of constancy to set limits to its instability. That constancy was once sought in the gold standard, then a fixed exchange rate and now monetary targets. The first two have been abandoned and the third is not what is really required. What is needed in order to impart the necessary inertia is a settled arrangement designed to stabilize money wages. Without such stability the system itself will be unstable and the promise of full employment illusory. But if money wages are kept reasonably stable, fiscal and monetary policy can again combine to restore high levels of output and employment without the risk of insupportable inflation.

NOTES

1 See M. J. Artis, 'Monetary Policy', in *British Economic Policy 1960–74*, ed. F. T. Blackaby, (Cambridge University Press for National Institute of Economic and Social Research, Cambridge, 1978), esp. pp. 229–233.

2 These matters are discussed in detail in 'Demand management: monetary and fiscal policy' which forms chapter 6 of my *Essays in Economic Management* (Allen and Unwin, London, 1971).

3 A. S. Blinder and R. M. Solow, 'Analytical foundations of fiscal policy', in *The Economics of Public Finance*, (Brookings Institution, Washington, D.C., 1974), pp. 9, 59.

4 R. S. Sayers, *The Bank of England 1891–1944* (Cambridge University Press, Cambridge, 1976).

5 Ralph C. Bryant, *Money and Monetary Policy in Interdependent Nations* (Brookings Institution, Washington, D.C., 1981), p. 231.

11

The sterling rate of exchange as an instrument of policy

Since the beginning of this century the rate of exchange of the pound sterling has played many parts and its successive roles have been the subject of almost continuous controversy.

Before World War I it was universally accepted in the United Kingdom that a fixed rate of exchange tied to gold was the best of all systems. At that time sterling was not so much on a gold standard as gold on a sterling standard, with world prices largely determined in the London market. When the war was over there was a spell for a few years under a quite different regime of floating rates that some economists would have liked to prolong. In 1925 the Gold Standard was restored but lasted not much over six years before it was abandoned in a panic and succeeded by another spell of floating rates. A couple of years later, before the end of 1933, still floating, the pound was back up again above its previous parity with the dollar. It remained there, almost as stable as if it were fixed, until about a year before World War II. It was devalued in September 1939, devalued again in 1949 and devalued yet again in 1967. Between each of these devaluations and until 1972 – that is, for a period of thirty-three years – the rate of exchange was held at a fixed rate, supported initially by a whole battery of controls over international trade and throughout the period by various measures of exchange control.

In 1972 fixed rates were abandoned once again, ushering in a decade in which the sterling exchange rate first plunged downwards alarmingly then climbed equally dramatically. For about half the decade after 1972 the government intervened vigorously in the foreign exchange market; and for the other half it came much nearer to allowing a 'clean' float i.e. abstaining from such intervention. In 1979, forty years after its

A revised version of the Brooman Memorial Lecture, delivered to the Open University, May 1982.

introduction, exchange control was discontinued. Thus over the past half century or so, Britain has had experience of almost every kind of exchange rate regime except multiple exchange rates. Indeed, even multiple rates existed for much of the time, either in the black market when sterling was inconvertible into dollars (i.e. up to 1955 or even 1958) or in the market for investment currency (i.e. up to 1979).

Opinion has fluctuated with these experiences. The hopes placed in a particular type of regime, with rates fixed or floating, sterling convertible or inconvertible, stabilized in this way or that, have varied greatly. Initially, in revulsion against the experience of pre-war years, there was international agreement at Bretton Woods that countries should aim at keeping their exchange rates fixed with adjustments from time to time in par values to deal with 'fundamental disequilibrium'. Then, in the 1950s and 1960s, floating rates were recommended – in the United Kingdom at least – as a recipe for faster economic growth. Now this argument is rarely heard. At one time automatic acceptance of a fixed but adjustable rate was thought to be involved in membership of the Common Market. Voices have been raised occasionally in favour of a return to the Gold Standard. Battles over clean or dirty floating, over exchange control or no exchange control, over dollars or SDRs or some other international standard, wax and wane with circumstances as attention revives and dies away again. But the United Kingdom, except briefly in 1972, has remained aloof for many years from international obligations limiting fluctuations in sterling.

As we shall see, there have been other fluctuations in opinion about exchange rate policy: about whether the government has it in its power to control the rate and impose its view on the market; whether, if it can do this, will make any real difference in the management of the economy; and whether it might not be wiser after all to use some different instrument of policy such as import limitation.

EXCHANGE RATE POLICY

Before discussing these questions let me first explain what I take exchange rate policy to be about. The policy may have a modest objective such as smoothing the daily fluctuations in the rate and preserving an orderly market; or the aim may be to hold the rate more or less fixed for a time against market pressure in either directon; or the authorities may try quite deliberately to push the rate up or down. These aims require intervention in the exchange market on the part of the central bank by drawing on, or adding to, its reserves. Smoothing operations may require no other action and may have no implications for transactions outside the foreign exchange market. But holding to a fixed rate or, still more, trying to lever the rate up or down has implications for other instruments of policy. it is conceivable that simply by making use of their reserves the authorities may achieve their object; but they are likely to find that they are obliged to reinforce the use of reserves by trying to influence market opinion, or moving interest rates, or tightening exchange control or taking budgetary measures or other action designed to alter the balance of payments. They may have to make use of a package of supplementary measures that operate on the balance of supply and demand in the exchange market and not, like the use of reserves, directly on the rate of exchange.

Exchange rate policy includes everything in the package. That is, it includes all action taken to influence the balance of payments and either relieve the pressure on the rate when the aim is to hold it in a fixed position or bring pressure on it upwards or downwards when it is floating.

Now exchange rate policy is only a fragment of economic policy as a whole. The means by which the authorities seek to influence the rate may coincide with the instruments they use for the management of the economy. Their purposes in making use of exchange rate policy should tally with their purposes in managing the economy. They may regard a movement in the exchange rate as a threat to the stability of employment or the stability of prices and be anxious to prevent it; or they may actively seek a movement in the exchange rate so as to expand employment or accelerate economic growth or damp down inflation.

Underlying exchange rate policy there is an implicit theory of how exchange rates are determined. For a long time the generally accepted view was that exchange rates reflected the balance of payments on current account, which in turn was dominated by the movement of costs and prices compared with the movement in other countries. One expression of this view was the purchasing power parity theory which predicted that exchange rates would settle at a level reflecting the relative increase in the price level (or fall in purchasing power) compared with other countries. An alternative theory took the flow of capital rather than of goods and services to be the more important – in some versions the decisive – influence on the balance of payments and the rate of exchange. The monetary theory of the balance of payments, for example, treated the behaviour of the money supply as dictating the rate of inflation and hence, given the level of prices elsewhere, the exchange value of the currency. Nowadays account is taken of other financial assets that are traded between countries, not just money, and theory runs in terms of changes in the portfolio of financial assets held in any country as asset preferences change with varying perceptions of risk and probable yield, changing expectations of the course of exchange rates, and changes in the stock of financial assets (e.g. because of government borrowing to meet a deficit). In this portfolio balance theory the short term movements of the exchange rate are dominated by capital flows that are not readily predictable while long term equilibrium can only be reached if the current account is also (in some sense) in balance.[1]

These developments in theory, to which we return below, correspond to a shortening in the time horizon and to a vast expansion in international financial transactions. Where in the nineteenth century changes in exchange rates were comparatively rare events and capital flows took the form mainly of long term borrowing by foreign governments and enterprises in the London market, exchange rates now fluctuate widely from day to day and the flows of funds across the exchanges are largely unrelated to the procurement of finance for long term purposes. What theory seeks to explain, therefore, is no longer what governs a slowly changing equilibrium but the volatile oscillations that are now typical of exchange markets.

I do not propose to enter in detail into these theoretical issues beyond noting that whereas older theories concentrated on the goods market, as influenced by the behaviour of wages and costs, the more modern theories concentrate on the capital market, as influenced by interest rates, budget deficits and expectations. In modern theories the national economy is seen as dominated increasingly by the international economy and the scope for national economic policy shrinks correspondingly. Exchange rate policy in particular can be made to appear as no more than a rather feeble instrument for warding off international influences on domestic activity. At one extreme are those who regard the money supply as governing both the domestic and the external value of the currency and distrust direct government intervention to steady the exchange rate as calculated to reduce its control over the money supply. Any of the familiar instruments of economic policy, including exchange rate and fiscal policy are seen either as superfluous, because they are really monetary policy in disguise, or as futile, because they change nothing unless the money supply changes too. At the other extreme one may take a more hopeful view of the way in which the exchange rate interacts with the rest of the economy and think of it as an important weapon of economic management in its own right, with powerful effects on the level of employment, the growth and distribution of income and the terms of trade with other countries. Whatever view one takes, one has to be ready to modify it if the economic forces at work change and the economy begins to function in a different way, with more or less controls, more or less inflation, more of less integration between national economies.

THE SCOPE FOR POLICY

The general presumption until recently has been that the exchange rate is a powerful instrument, to be ranked alongside other policy instruments of the highest importance, such as the budget or interest rates. Economists have given it comparable attention particularly when they were discussing macro-economic policy from an international point of view. They have frequently turned to the exchange rate to explain how one country might preserve a stability in prices or output which its neighbours were failing to achieve or to account for the superior growth performance of a country like Germany or Japan. The doctrine of export-led growth, for example, seems to imply that the exchange rate can be systematically undervalued so as to give exports a highly competitive edge and allow of continuous expansion unconstrained by balance of payments difficulties. Economists may be wrong in attaching so much importance to the exchange rate but the tradition is that it can make a big difference to the prosperity of a country if it is either too high or too low.

There is also, however, another traditional line of thought which counsels a country to make the best of the rate if already has. This comes out most strikingly in arguments over devaluation. Sir Stafford Cripps, for example, who was Chancellor of the Exchequer at the time of the 1949 devaluation, thought that it was wrong in principle to devalue and that the right thing to do was to use whatever controls were necessary to keep the rate pegged at the existing parity. Sir Ralph Hawtrey, in his day the most distinguished economist in the Treasury, dismissed the 1949 devaluation as inappropriate and costly. Sir Roy Harrod thought it 'an unfortunate incident' which had 'very severe effects, both on demand and cost inflation'.

There is no doubt that a fall in the exchange rate can have severe inflationary effects and we do well to remember this when devaluation is proposed. But this is not to say, as some economists now argue, that as soon as the nominal rate of exchange tumbles, the forces brought into play necessarily push up prices across the board until before very long the effective rate of exchange is no more competitive than it was. There are circumstances in which that may happen; but if it does the country has a problem for which devaluation is not the cure.

The view that devaluation changes nothing is far removed from the working hypothesis that guided economic policy after 1945. Immediately after the war, the government had control over all outgoings in foreign currency across the exchanges and over a very high proportion of total economic activity. It would have been astonished to be told that it did not lie within its power to move the rate of exchange up or down without inviting an offsetting movement in domestic prices. And it would have been still more astonished to have this impotence attributed to changes in the money supply when the whole economy was awash with excess liquidity throughout the postwar years.

Further back, in the 1920s, Keynes would have been equally astonished to be told that the nominal exchange rate hardly mattered. He spent a good part of that decade arguing about the exchange rate, warning against a premature return to gold at too high a parity and attacking the decision when it was taken: in short, treating exchange rate management as the most important current issue of economic policy. Was he deluding himself? Was it quite unimportant what happened to the nominal rate because price movements would ensure that the effective rate would finish up at much the same level anyhow?

Or if we move on to the successive devaluations with all the brouhaha in 1931 and 1949 and 1967, was the excitement really misconceived? Whatever may be true in the 1980s these devaluations did exercise a major influence on the economy of the kind economists would have predicted.

Yet the world has changed greatly since 1967. The international economy exercises a more and more powerful influence on national economies, imposing constraints on their freedom to choose policies appropriate to their circumstances. In particular, capital flows between countries are now on a scale far beyond that of the flow of goods and services. Exchange rates tend to be dominated by those unpredictable flows, which are governed by the volatile expectations of financial markets rather than by the more stable and predictable flows of goods and services. These changes in financial conditions greatly limit the scope for an active exchange rate policy.

Let us turn now to the practical issues of policy that governments have to decide.

ALTERNATIVE EXCHANGE RATE REGIMES

The first such issue is whether to aim at a fixed rate of exchange. At one time this would have meant deciding to fix the price of gold and observe the rules of the gold standard. In the postwar period it would have meant accepting the Bretton Woods arrangements and, in effect, pegging the currency to the dollar. In the 1980s it would be likely to mean joining the European Monetary System. Fixity even of one exchange rate involves two countries, not just one, and a system of fixed exchange rates involves all the countries that are members of the system. A country can only have fixed rates with the countries that have fixed rates with it and, by implication, with one another. No one country can create fixed rates. All it can do is to peg its rate to some other currency which may itself be floating or join a group of countries committed to arrangements for holding exchange rates fixed. Where there is already an international system of fixed exchange rates, it can adhere to the system and accept its rules.

In practice a commitment to a fixed rate is not absolute and it is not irrevocable. It is not absolute because the rate is usually allowed to vary within set limits, not held at a fixed point; and it is not irrevocable since countries may from time to time announce a new parity, devaluing or revaluing their currency. Further decisions are necessary therefore as to the permitted limits of fluctuation and the conditions under which the parity will be changed. The choice is not between an absolutely fixed rate and one that is allowed to float entirely freely: there are many gradations between the two. At one extreme the authorities may refrain from intervention of any kind in the foreign exchange market. At the other they may announce narrow and fixed limits to the fluctuations they will allow and enforce these limits by intervention that is, in principle, unlimited. Between these extremes there may be set limits that are wider or narrower, shifting or fixed, announced in advance or known only to the authorities; and there may be occasional or day to day intervention, on a small scale or on a large scale, aimed merely at smoothing random fluctuations and preserving an orderly market or at imposing on the market the government's own view of what the underlying trend is or should be.

This last choice is one that is inescapable in the management of a floating rate. With a fixed rate there is no choice: the government *has* to decide on the appropriate rate and defend it. But whatever the regime, there is a question how readily the government should yield to market forces and how far it should go in imposing its view and using its power over the rate as an instrument of policy.

At this point a rather different decision arises. The government can operate on the rate either directly by buying or selling foreign exchange or indirectly by seeking to affect the balance of payments. Unless it has very large reserves or can borrow freely abroad it is unlikely to limit itself to direct intervention in face of sustained pressure. If the authorities want to exercise more than a transitory influence on the rate they will find themselves obliged to reinforce direct intervention by other measures. Here again they have a choice. In seeking to improve the balance of payments they can use: (a) direct measures to limit imports (e.g. through quota restrictions) or boost exports (e.g. by setting targets backed up by controls and subsidies), as well as measures of exchange control that affect a wider range of international transactions; (b) traditional financial weapons such as Bank Rate that affect the flow of funds from one country to another; and (c) measures designed to improve the balance of payments by operating on the level of demand, the relative attractiveness of imported goods and services and the allocation of resources between domestic and international markets.

When devaluation takes place, for example, one of the key questions is what supplementary action the government can bring itself to take so as to consolidate the change in the rate.

Similarly when the government is resisting devaluation, one of the key questions is what measures for strengthening the balance of payments it is willing to take and how effective these measures are likely to be. The issue is rarely the simple one: shall we devalue or not? It usually takes the form: what package of measures would allow us to maintain the rate and how does that package compare with the package that would have to accompany devaluation? Each of the packages has to be assessed in terms not just of its probable effects on the balance of payments but of its total impact on the economy; and in the light of that necessarily very uncertain assessment, its political acceptability has then to be weighed up.

MARKET REACTIONS AND GOVERNMENT CONTROLS

At least that would be the rational way to proceed. But in a near-devaluation situation neither the government nor the market is conspicuously rational. The government may be so obsessed with matters of political acceptability that it attaches little importance to any economic assessment, particularly one that is bound to be open to question. The market has to size up which way the government will jump and may come to attach extravagant importance to symbolic acts such as changes in the rate of unemployment pay that have little direct effect on the balance of payments. It may also draw rather a sharp distinction between some forms of corrective action of which it approves and others of which it disapproves. The legitimacy of the distinction is less important than the size of the speculative transfers of funds to which it gives rise. It is these speculative transfers of short term funds that commonly overwhelm the last defences of any fixed rate, whatever may have occurred earlier to weaken the current or long term capital account.

But what are these distrinctions that the market draws? On the one hand the market rarely welcomes measures such as an import surcharge, import deposits, quota restrictions, or a tightening of exchange control and tends to dismiss them as incapable of remedying what is seen as an unstable situation. On the other hand, higher interest rates, tighter money, a firmer budgetary policy are commonly regarded as proper and effective ways of restoring equilibrium. There is some validity in this distinction: deflationary action not only improves the balance of payments directly but it may also in the longer run check any upward drift in costs and effect a continuing improvement in competitiveness. This is more than can be claimed for import controls; but they do buy time (which may be all that is needed) and they avoid the loss of output that deflation usually produces. As for exchange control it is difficult to make it effective and it may become less effective through time as ways are found round the regulations. British experience was that some forms of exchange control had little effect; others depended on making it more expensive to borrow in the United Kingdom than elsewhere and at high rates of interest were largely redundant; the largest shifts in funds usually took place in commercial credit through leads and lags and these were unaffected by exchange control. Nevertheless there were some large capital flows – purchases of foreign securities, for example – where the controls remained effective even after forty years. It is not possible to dismiss the use of exchange control to limit or halt such flows as illegitimate or ineffective.

Deflation and import or exchange control are only two of the various measures that governments can take to strengthen the balance of payments and maintain the rate of exchange. There are many other weapons at the government's disposal. The controls it can impose are not limited to direct controls over exchange transactions: other controls can be devised that procure similar results. Transactions that are costly in foreign exchange may be highly taxed. Activities that seem likely to save foreign exchange can be subsidized. The government may regulate its own transactions in foreign exchange so as to avoid undue pressure on the rate. It may engage in large borrowing operations in foreign currencies or encourage such borrowing by subordinate authorities or nationalized industries; or it may advance the timing of repayments of outstanding debt to foreign creditors. In an economy where the government spends half the national income it is impossible for it to avoid affecting the rate of exchange intentionally or unintentionally. If it does not consciously entertain a view as to the direction in which it would like the rate to move, such a view is implicit in the complex of policies it pursues.

I am not suggesting that the government should necessarily pile on one control after another in order to allow it to peg the exchange rate. It is a nice question how far it should go along that road. Many economists would argue that it should not even start. But the option is there and governments do avail themselves of it – sometimes, in my view, with success and sometimes not. By success I mean that the rate is held long enough for the pressures on it to die away and there is no reason in retrospect to regret that the rate was not changed in response to market pressure.

AUTOMATICITY AND MANAGEMENT

All this is clear enough when the rate of exchange is fixed. If the government's policy is to maintain a fixed rate then it must so conduct the whole of its policies that they are consistent with this aim. Once the government accepts *any* point of constancy, whether it is the price of gold, or the quantity of money, or a balanced budget it has to gear its policies to that constancy. Now it may be argued that, in gold standard conditions, there is no need for such policies because the exchanges will be self-regulating. If the balance of payments goes into deficit, the foreign exchanges will sink to the gold point, gold will be demanded from the central bank and will drain out of the reserves, the monetary base will contract and in due course the balance of payments will swing round as interest rates rise and economic activity falls off. The government has no need to do anything, provided it is willing to let things work themselves out – not, it need hardly be said, an unimportant proviso. Similarly, if the government is willing to allow a 'clean' float, the rate of exchange will again be likely to move in such a way as to extinguish any deficit, provided the government does nothing to aggravate matters. But when one is relying on automatic, self-correcting, economic forces it is as well to understand how these forces operate and whether in restoring balance in the international accounts they may not prove unnecessarily harsh. The fact that it may be possible to dispense with government intervention does not demonstrate the superiority of self-regulating mechanisms over deliberate policy.

The first coherent modern exposition of the case for management of the exchanges as against automaticity was that of Keynes in the 1920s. He pointed out that the gold standard mechanism of adjustment was far from painless. If a country like the United Kingdom went back to gold at too high a parity – as he was convinced had occurred in 1925 – it would find the exchanges moving against it and gold moving out. This would oblige it to raise interest rates and dear money would continue until the level of costs dropped far enough to restore the competitive position and remove the pressure on the exchanges. But in the short run the level of costs meant fundamentally the level of money wages and it might be a very long time before money wages could be reduced. Higher rates of interest would not do this automatically. They might help with the capital account by cutting foreign lending or attracting funds from abroad; they might help with the current account to the extent that dear money brought business depression and lower imports; but, given 'the virtual impossibility' of reducing money wages, they could not be relied upon to bring domestic costs into line with costs abroad. So the economy might remain underemployed for a very long time unless a rise in costs and prices abroad came to the rescue.

This view of exchange rates makes their behaviour turn largely on the movement in money wages. Essentially Keynes was arguing that it was better to adjust the exchange rate to the level of money wages than try to make money wages adjust to the exchange rate. Other economists have taken a very different point of view. Some of them regard a fixed exchange rate as one of the few available instruments of policy for putting a damper on increases in money wages. To adjust the exchange rate when money wages and other costs are clearly out of line with the levels in other countries can be justified, they would argue, only if it is a rare event. It would be wrong to give way too readily and still more wrong to announce in advance an intention to give way. To validate a rise in costs and prices by altering the exchange rate is on a par, in their view, with validating an increase in costs and prices by expanding the money supply.

Some of them – the so-called international monetarists – go further and see virtue in a high rate of exchange as a means of lowering the rate of inflation. Since international prices expressed in other currencies will not be much affected by an appreciation of sterling the price in pounds of all traded goods will be forced down. If, for example, sterling moved from $1 to £1 to $2 to £1 and the dollar price of wheat remained constant, the sterling price of wheat would be likely to fall by 50 per cent. This would certainly moderate inflation. But forcing up the value of a currency is a dangerous game unless the balance of payments is strong. Even then, unless other prices, and particularly wages, are also forced down, the country's competitive position is weakened and it may be obliged to backtrack by the repercussion of the high rate, first on its exports, next on profits in all activities that have to meet foreign competition, and finally on the level of employment and output in those activities. If it does have to backtrack, the attack on inflation through the exchange rate will have proved a costly failure.

A more extreme claim is that raising the exchange rate may start off a virtuous circle of falling costs, greater efficiency and increased competitiveness. This was the claim made, for example, in the British Green Paper in 1978 on the European Monetary System. Exports might initially become dearer to foreigners but imports would be cheaper to us, the cost of living would rise more slowly, and so, it was argued, would nominal wages. The pressure of a high exchange rate on costs would stimulate cost saving and greater efficiency and these gains would compensate for the handicap to exporters of the high rate while at the same time raising real incomes all round. It is a prospectus that sounds as attractive as the earlier prospectus in the 1960s that prescribed a *fall* in the exchange rate as the way into a virtuous circle. Neither rise nor fall seems to have brought the promised blessings. If raising the rate helps to stem inflation, it destroys business profits, creates industrial depression and unemployment and lays up trouble when the time comes to return to a more realistic rate.

THE ROLE OF THE MONEY SUPPLY

Some of the conflict of view between economists over exchange rate policy is simply a byproduct of the conflict of view between them over the significance of changes in the money supply. Monetarists would regard control over the money supply as carrying with it control over money wages and at the same time over the exchange rate. Keynesians would turn things round the other way and think of the money supply as largely governed by money wages, the exchange rate interacting with both.

Suppose, for example, that, unlike the situation in the 1920s, there is continuous full employment and a straightforward monetary inflation. How would we then account for the movement of the exchange rate? The explanation, in terms of the monetary theory of the balance of payments, would start from what was taken to be the root cause of the inflation, the oversupply of money. The public would seek to unload their excess money balances partly in buying additional goods and services which, given full employment, would have to be imported or held back from exports, and partly by a portfolio adjustment between cash balances and other assets. These assets would include foreign securities and foreign currencies. There would thus be a capital outflow which would put pressure on the exchange rate simultaneously with the pressure exerted on the current account by increased spending. If the exchange rate was fixed, the deficit in the balance of payments would be met from the reserves and would represent that part of the excess in money balances that had been exported. If the exchange rate was floating, it would be depressed until the various shifts in the current account, in cash holdings and in portfolios balanced one another.

Under the conditions assumed, this is an illuminating explanation. It provides one reason why, for example, the exchange rate is usually driven down faster by inflation than domestic prices are driven up. If the money supply is being expanded at a rate that arouses expectations of further inflation, people will try to reduce their holdings of money and this will make commodity prices outrun the money supply; and they will try to hold foreign money in place of domestic money, so producing an outflow of speculative funds and a fall in the exchange rate faster even than the rise in commodity prices. This picture of the inflationary process supplements the traditional purchasing power parity theory which has nothing to say about different speeds of adjustment but warns us that at the end of a period of inflation the external value of a currency and its domestic value will eventually show changes of the same order of magnitude.

All this, however, relates to rather special circumstances. We have to ask ourselves what happens when there is a fair amount of slack in the economy and the danger of inflation, if there is one, does not arise from the pumping out of more money. The exchange rate may continue to fluctuate within wide limits and the monetary theory of the balance of payments, even if logically valid, may throw very little light on the reasons for the fluctuations.

In each of the three major devaluations of sterling in peacetime, there is no evidence that the behaviour of the money supply played much of a part. The run on the pound in 1931 was partly due to distrust on the part of foreign bankers in the British government's budgetary policy but probably more to the publicity given in the summer of 1931 to the size of the banking funds held in London in relation to the liquid assets held abroad by London, i.e. to the dangerously illiquid position that seemed to have developed. The devaluation in 1949 followed a drain on the reserves that had its origin in a depression in the United States and took place *after* a very large improvement in the balance of payments over the postwar years. In 1967 and only in 1967 was there any marked expansion in the money supply. But even then, monetary developments were of very secondary importance in comparison with a sudden weakening in the balance of payments that could be readily traced to a temporary check to the growth of world markets on the one hand and a surge in public spending on the other.

The distrust that some economists have in any attempt by governments to influence the rate of exchange rests on one or more of four grounds:

1. the government is pretty sure to get it wrong;
2. even if the government gets it right, the market has more power over the rate and its view will prevail;
3. even if the government is successful in influencing the rate it will serve no useful purpose;

4 even if it does serve a useful purpose, there are other and better ways of proceeding.

Let us take these in turn.

No one can claim that governments are infallible but one can go too far in the opposite direction. In the matter of exchange rates there is no objective way of settling who is right and who is wrong. No doubt it could be argued – indeed it has been argued – that the way in which the rate moves is determined by actual transactions, not by armchair pronouncements, and that it therefore reflects the considered view of those who are most willing to back their judgement financially. If they were not proved right oftener than wrong they would fail to gain a livelihood from market operations and be driven out of business. Governments, however, can go on making mistakes with impunity.

This is not a convincing line of argument. Business transactors, as company accounts make plain, do lose money and so do many speculators. But that is really beside the point. The foreign exchange market is not a guessing game in which those who guess correctly are right in any other sense. The question is rather: whose judgement of a *sustainable* rate is most likely to prove correct? What is sustainable may diverge quite markedly from current market rates and depends on the pressures likely to develop over time. Market operators who have a very considerable flair for sensing how things will develop from day to day may have no gift at all for judging the underlying pressures. In arriving at a judgement they have to go through exactly the same process of reasoning as an economist and although they are likely to be better acquainted with some of the facts than an onlooker, they have no great claim to superior wisdom in judging long term developments. If the government and the central bank do not intervene, the rate must be from day to day what the market makes it and in that sense the market can claim infallibility. But if in the longer run, still without government intervention or any notable change in circumstances, the rate drifts into a quite different position it is reasonable to ask whether that does not indicate short-sightedness or error in market judgement.

The market does make mistakes. In 1949, for example, pressure on sterling was resumed very soon after a devaluation by 30 per cent that should have been seen as sufficient and proved in fact more than sufficient. It was well into 1950, when the reserves had already been recovering for some months, before the market regained confidence. The 1967 devaluation gave more grounds for hesitation over the outcome but by the end of 1968 there was strong evidence that the balance of payments was swinging round. Yet it was not until 1970, when the current account had been in surplus for a year, that the spot rate against the dollar rose above par. Similarly, it is hard to see how the market can have been right both in pushing up the dollar rate from $2 to £1 at the beginning of 1979 to $2.40 at the beginning of 1981 and bringing it down again to $1.80 in a little over six months.

Even more striking was the high value of the dollar in the first half of the 1980s when the current account of the United States was in increasingly heavy deficit. The greater the prospective deficit the more likely was the dollar to *appreciate* since it could be taken for granted that American interest rates would rise and the flow of funds into the American market would grow. The market sustained the dollar year after year at a level that was quite evidently at odds with the long term prospects of the American economy since America could not borrow indefinitely without some fall in the dollar and equally could not reduce her borrowing unless the rate fell. Only a major American slump could prolong the high rate and the issue by 1986 had become whether such a slump would be forced on America by the high interest rates needed to attract foreign capital or avoided by a sharp fall in the dollar rate of exchange.

The fallibility of the market does not make the government infallible. On the contrary it is prone to error for obvious reasons. Governments feel compelled, particularly with a fixed rate, to take up a position and have difficulty in abandoning it later. In Britain they have been consistently reluctant to devalue, sometimes for good reasons but usually for bad. Ministers are reluctant to accept market verdicts on their performance and overestimate their ability to make use of political power to suppress or over-ride market forces, dismissing unwelcome trends in financial markets as the work of speculators.

With a fluctuating rate many of these difficulties cease to apply if only because there is no public commitment that the government must either honour or repudiate. The government can give ground without embarrassment or high drama such as devaluation involves, and can vary the scale of its intervention to match the pressures it encounters. It is likely to hand over all except a few strategic decisions to the central bank and leave it free to make purely technical judgements. But even with the greater flexibility that comes with floating rates, governments may still make mistakes.

It is simply not possible on grounds of pure logic to demonstrate that the market or the government is the more likely to be right. Experience suggests that both can err and that there can be no presumption in favour of one or the other without regard to the circumstances of time and place. There are, however, some grounds for expecting governmental errors to be more frequent and more serious with fixed than with floating exchange rates because of the inflexibility of the commitment that a fixed rate involves.

The second line of argument – that market power is stronger than government power – is a persuasive one. When one looks back at the exiguous gold reserves of the Bank of England before World War I it seems inconceivable that a few million pounds of free reserves could have guaranteed the parity of sterling, a currency in which one-third or more of the world's dealings were conducted. But at that time the Bank could operate on the large amount of commercial credit extended to other countries in the form of sterling bills of exchange. An increase of 1 per cent in Bank Rate could bring gold from all ends of the world.

Since that time, although central banks have greatly increased their reserves, private commercial and financial companies throughout the world have added to their financial resources on a still bigger scale. The mobility of their funds has also increased as they have organized themselves to guard against changes in exchange rates. The Eurodollar market which is not controlled by any government or central bank now disposes of funds vastly exceeding those available in liquid form to any government. The proportion of the world's business that takes the form of transactions between countries continues to increase and is now 25 per cent or more. The information services at the disposal of those holding foreign currencies or with liabilities in foreign currencies have developed out of all recognition.

If, therefore, the exchange rate of a currency is called in question, market opinion has the means to assert its judgement against the central bank and government of the country concerned. As far back as August 1931 Keynes told the Prime Minister, Ramsay MacDonald: 'When doubts as to the prospects of a currency, such as now exist about sterling, have come into existence, the game is up'.[2]

In 1949 Stafford Cripps said much the same thing before throwing in the sponge. He told the Cabinet in August, when the decision to devalue was confirmed, that: 'An atmosphere has . . . been created . . . in which the pound could not reach stability without devaluation'.

In 1967 the government backed the existing parity with £1500 million of borrowed money together with forward contracts that may have exceeded £2000 million. But it was not enough; and although the possibility of further borrowing was mooted, the government had little option but to accept the market's verdict.

In 1976 there were two further demonstrations of the power of financial markets. The first occurred in the spring of 1976 when the Bank of England appeared to be engineering a gradual depreciation of the pound from the rate of $2 to the £1 at which it stood in the early months of the year. This excited such distrust in the market that the depreciation soon exceeded anything the authorities may have contemplated. A fresh crisis broke out in the autumn with the pound falling by 5 cents in a day and rumours circulating that the IMF thought the appropriate rate no more than $1.50 to £1. There were dire predictions that the fall would continue until the pound was worth no more than a dollar but in fact it touched bottom at $1.55½. In April and May it took just over two months for the pound to drop 20 cents; in October it took just over a month.

It is clear that the authorities were more or less powerless to stop these movements once they had gathered momentum. In the single month of October the Bank of England drew down the official reserves by $455 million but this did not stop a 20 cent drop in the rate.

The reverse movement then took place. After the fall from over $2 to $1.55½ in eight months in 1976 the pound took just over two months to recover 15 cents to $1.70½ at the beginning of 1977. In the course of that year the monetary authorities took no less than £9600 million into the reserves in an effort to hold down the rate – an average of £800 million a month. Even so, the effective rate against other currencies rose steadily throughout the second half of the year, ending up nearly 7 per cent above the starting rate at the beginning of the year.

The experience of 1977 appeared at the time as the final proof of the irresistibility of the market. No further sustained effort was made by the authorities to hold down the value of the currency. In the next three years it was allowed to rise against the dollar from $1.92 to $2.40 – a rate last seen in 1975. If fluctuations on that scale are truly irresistible the scope for any exchange rate policy is obviously very limited. Yet when one observed the dollar rate tumble from $2.40 in January 1981 to $1.80 in August one was bound to ask whether, in so volatile a market, somewhat greater stability was unachievable. It is true that the fluctuations in sterling were powerfully reinforced by fluctuations in the dollar so that the volatility was not altogether in one currency. The effective rate for sterling, measured against other currencies and not just the dollar, was 14 per cent lower in August 1981, not 25 per cent. But there must be some doubt whether the final appreciation of sterling in 1979–80 was irresistible. A government determined to keep the rate within reach of the mid-1979 rate, even if it meant adding extensively to the reserves, could surely have succeeded and would have proved in the end a better judge of a sustainable rate than the market has turned out to be. A government less determined to impress market opinion with the tightness of its monetary policy and more willing to express its concern over the rise in the rate could have given a lead to the market and enlisted its strength in holding down the rate.

If there is some doubt as to the power of the monetary authorities to impose their will on the market, even when their aims are modest, there can be little doubt that the fluctuations occurring in exchange rates do exercise real effects. This is shown by the movement in real rates of exchange, i.e. the movement in rates adjusted for changes in domestic costs and prices. When the pound appreciated from $1.80 to $2.40 this was not made up for by a rise in costs in the United States well above the rate in the United Kingdom. On the contrary, costs rose a good deal faster in the United Kingdom, reinforcing the competitive handicap of the high exchange rate. The subsequent fall in the dollar rate was not accompanied by a widening of the difference in inflation rates between the UK and the US: on the contrary, they came closer together.

Similarly, if one goes back over the more dramatic changes in exchange rates in the past such as the devaluations in 1931, 1949 and 1967 there is no sign that any competitive advantage was quickly lost because of a sharp rise in wages and other costs. After the 1931 devaluation, as it happens, prices continued to fall for another year and the rise in money wages from 1932 onwards averaged about 1–1.5 per cent a year. The feedback of the devaluation on prices was quite the opposite of what was widely expected because the countries supplying the United Kingdom with food and materials devalued simultaneously and had to accept lower sterling prices for a time as the depression deepened and their market contracted. After the 1949 devaluation of sterling by 30 per cent, once the Korean war was over, there proved to be very little difference between the rise in prices in the United Kingdom and in the United States. The American GDP deflator in 1954 was up by 13 per cent on 1949 and in Britain the rise was 16 per cent. As after 1931, the cost advantage of devaluation was substantially retained in succeeding years. Even after 1967 wages rose no faster in the next two years then they had done in the years before devaluation. It is true that there was a sharper increase in 1970, attributable to the removal of wage restraint; but estimates of the net effect of the devaluation on wages and consumer prices from 1967 up to 1971 show a rise of an extra 6 or 7 per cent – less than half the devaluation.

It is always possible that things might work out differently at other times and in other circumstances. The effects of a devaluation may be blunted in a highly inflationary atmosphere. More important, the effects depend on the other action taken by the authorities. If there is initially a deficit and the adjustment has to be made on current account, there has necessarily to be a reduction in absorption in relation to income. Devaluation by itself will not effect that reduction. Resources have to be released by action to reduce final demand and reabsorbed in improving the current account. If there is no reduction in final demand then the competition between home and foreign demand will simply become more intense and generate enough inflation to squeeze out the extra foreign demand.

Devaluation usually reflects some underlying disequilibrium and the measure of its effectiveness is whether the disequilibrium is removed or reduced. It is important, therefore, to identify the cause of the disequilibrium and establish whether it can be removed in some other way, whether it will remain in operation after devaluation or whether it will be no longer active. If it is assumed that the economy was in equilibrium to start with, then there is no point in the devaluation and it would not be surprising if it merely led back to the pre-existing price relationships. If the devaluation was brought on by inflation and the inflationary forces remained unchecked then again devaluation would do nothing to remove the source of the trouble. But if the situation is one in which disequilibrium has no single, remediable cause and the price structure has become seriously distorted, devaluation may be the most effective and acceptable way of getting rid of the distortions and restoring the basis on which the economy can remain in balance.

We are not dealing with long run relationships that can be assumed to remain unchanged from one state of equilibrium to another. We are necessarily dealing with a short run that may last for several years in which all kinds of price relationships are changed when the exchange rate moves. First of all, traded goods change in price relatively to non-traded goods. With devaluation, imports and exports both go up in price and each of these changes operates on the balance of trade. If the elasticities of demand are large enough, the balance of trade will improve. But the price structure will begin to revert towards its earlier shape. If exports are fetching higher prices relatively to goods sold on the home market there will be some tendency for the two to come closer together. The rise in the price of imports will affect home market sales in the same way by easing the pressure of competition on the price of home produced goods. But the idea that all three sets of prices will be closely governed by world prices and undergo only a fleeting change of relationship is not borne out by such studies as have been made. On the contrary these show that domestic prices have far more inertia than traded goods and that even traded goods, particularly manufactures, do not change to the full extent of the change in the exchange rate. Devaluation effects changes in the structure of prices that persist; and these in turn cause shifts in output between domestic and international markets.

Secondly, the change in the prices of traded goods is not accompanied by equal changes in wages. There is a Scandinavian theory that when devaluation makes traded goods rise in price, wages in the industries affected also rise soon afterwards, either because employers bid for more labour or because workers become more demanding when they see higher profits being made. The increase in wages then spreads across the economy and the wage and price structures are re-established at a higher level. This theory may apply to a small, open economy but it does not seem to apply more than partially to the United Kingdom. Wages do not keep closely in step with export or import prices.

Moreover, when the rate of exchange is put up instead of down the connection between prices and wages becomes a great deal more tenuous. A fall in the price of traded goods may have very little effect on wage negotiations in the industries affected. The failure of wages to reflect the reduction in prices and profits may lead to an increase in unemployment and this may depress earnings and, over a period of years, wage rates as well. But even when the export industries negotiate lower wages other industries and occupations may go on paying unchanged rates. The contrast between sheltered and unsheltered industries in the 1920s and 1930s lasted throughout the interwar period and was not a matter of transitional divergences. The wage settlements in manufacturing in the past year or two have again shown how wages in activities exposed to foreign competition do not necessarily move in parallel with wages in activities sheltered from such competition.

What is much more difficult to generalize about is the impact of exchange rate changes on capital movements. These are likely to be rather different after a devaluation – i.e. a downward adjustment of a parity – than after a sharp fall in a floating rate. The devaluation may restore confidence and produce a return of speculative funds in a way that is unlikely to follow a dip in the floating rate. Much ingenuity has gone into explaining how expectations will be affected in various circumstances. But is is doubtful whether there is any simple theory that covers all the possibilities. For one thing it obviously makes a difference what causes the rate to move in the first place. One can probably count on an eventual transfer into a currency that has fallen in value if there is convincing evidence that the fall has improved the current account: and one can count on it with greater confidence if, as is likely, the improvement is a sign that prices have not increased to the full extent of the depreciation.

There remains a final line of argument against relying on variations in the exchange rate as an instrument of policy. Why, it is argued, try to remedy a balance of payments deficit by letting the exchange rate fall when this has two major undesirable consequences. The first is the acceptance of less favourable terms of trade; the second is an aggravation of inflation. Why not simply exclude the imports we can't afford? When unemployment is high this will create more jobs; and since there will be a multiplier effect as the newly employed spend their higher incomes the community will be richer and will want to buy more from abroad. So the import restrictions need not in the end mean fewer jobs abroad. The higher level of income and spending can overflow the barriers against imports, maintaining the previous volume, so that trading partners have no real cause for complaint.

It is an alluring picture for a country with a large external deficit and high unemployment. It is not a new picture: it was drawn more or less in these terms fifty years ago by Lord Kahn in his celebrated article on 'the multiplier'. But there are snags particularly if other countries have high unemployment too and if their external deficits are even larger. We shall come to the further complication of North Sea oil presently.

It may be agreed first of all that a change in the rate of exchange is not the only, and not necessarily the best, way of dealing with a balance of payments deficit, even when the deficit seems to be a lasting one. When the rate of exchange is held constant, there *have* to be other ways of removing the deficit; it is usually only as a last resort, when other remedies have failed or are judged to be even more painful, that the rate is allowed to depreciate. With floating rates the priorities may be reversed: the rate is allowed to take the strain and other remedies are called in aid only when the swings in the rate are judged to be intolerable. There is always *some* alternative to relying on a change in the rate and the possible alternatives always need systematic review. Moreover, even if no other line of action is judged to be as attractive as a change in the rate, the best results may be obtainable only by combining such a change with other measures that form a partial alternative.

There are many such options, from an open or concealed widening of the gold points (or the limits within which the rate is free to move) to quotas on imports and a tightening of controls over foreign lending and investment. Some of these may have to be ruled out on political grounds or because of international agreements. It may be judged impolitic to make use of quotas on those grounds. They cannot be used against other members of the European Community and if used against other countries would be open to the charge of discrimination, both by trading groups and by country. Even if the total volume of imports did not suffer, the import bill would be redistributed between different suppliers. Assurances that imports would be maintained would therefore cut little ice or do much to prevent retaliation.

Making use of changes in exchange rates does not altogether avoid political obstacles: here too other countries may raise objections. They may deliberately create uncertainty as to their reactions in the event of devaluation or threaten to devalue themselves if the change in parity exceeds what they think reasonable. Curiously enough, although such a change affects different countries in different ways, it is rarely represented as discriminatory. On the contrary, over the postwar period the trend has been towards increasing and exclusive reliance on exchange rate movements as the internationally acceptable way of dealing with external imbalance. Not only so, but clean floats are often recommended in preference to 'dirty' floats: even the use of reserves and *a fortiori* of funds borrowed from abroad to support the rate tends to be frowned upon. This represents the apotheosis of market forces: the belief that the rate of exchange should be left to those forces without any attempt to use it as an instrument of policy.

So long as such views are strongly held in the exchange markets of the world, the attempt to find surrogates for exchange rate changes is severely handicapped. Any measures introduced for strengthening the balance of payments other than the classic devices of higher interest rates and general deflation will be discounted as 'artificial' and taken as symptoms of the government's reluctance to use 'fundamental' remedies. Under such conditions the pressures on the exchange rate may partake more of psychological warfare than the forces of supply and demand approved of by market operators. The rate ceases to be what ordinary business dealings would make it and moves towards whatever figure the market thinks appropriate.

In these circumstances the mere introduction of quotas on a comprehensive basis might prove, not a substitute for a fall in the exchange rate, but the cause of one. The market would judge that the expansionary policies about to be introduced were such as to involve depreciation of the currency in the absence of quotas and would conclude that by the time the quotas were withdrawn, no smaller depreciation would meet the case. The rate would therefore begin to fall immediately.

But why, in any event, should quotas be preferable to a fall in the rate? There are good arguments for quotas in wartime or in emergency when foreign exchange has to be rationed and such rationing can be satisfactorily handled by quantitative limitations rather than by price. But such circumstances are far behind us. In 1980, for example, it made no sense to argue against driving down the dollar rate of exchange when it had reached $2.40 to the £1. When the rate fell to $1.80 the fears previously expressed that this would bring on severe inflation proved to have been grossly exaggerated. Later, with unemployment in excess of three million, and wage settlements moving down, it was not easy to see why a further devaluation should have any larger impact on wages and prices than import quotas and why it should be necessary to make use of such a professedly temporary device.

One reason why it might be necessary would be if the rate kept floating up on North Sea oil and would not fall below a rate consistent with renewed industrial expansion. It is sometimes argued that the strength of sterling in 1980–81 reflected the support brought to the balance of payments by North Sea oil and that the larger this contribution the more other elements in the balance of payments such as exports of manufactures would be squeezed out. This would be true if the rate of exchange were governed by the purely trade elements in the international accounts and if economic activity in total remained steady. Under those conditions there is no doubt that the more oil was exported the higher the rate would go until other exports fell off. But this is neither how rates of exchange are actually determined in normal times nor how they are determined in a slump. The United Kingdom in 1980–81 ran into a deeper recession than other industrial countries and the income effects of this on the level of imports completely swamped any simultaneous changes in the trade in oil. Imports fell heavily, the balance of payments swung into surplus and the surplus grew as the depression deepened. That by itself was a powerful prop to the rate of exchange in 1980 but did not prevent a sharp fall in 1981. The main influence on the rate, however, is usually not the balance of trade but the capital items. These are powerfully affected by market sentiment and, as is clear from the rise of 10 per cent in the two months after the Conservative Party's first budget in May 1979, it was the market's perception of the government's economic policy – and particularly its monetary policy – that started off the extraordinary rise in the sterling exchange rate in 1979. There is no doubt that the rise in the price of oil at the end of the year also helped. But the evolution of the rate between May 1979 and the peak in January 1981 suggests that monetary factors in Britain, the United States and elsewhere played the more important part.

When we look at the decline in manufacturing activity, the same general conclusion emerges. The decline had proceeded a long way before the discovery of oil had any perceptible influence – no such influence was visible in the crisis of 1976, for example, and by that time manufacturing employment had already fallen by 17 per cent from its peak in 1966. The almost equally large fall from 1979 to 1982 was no doubt associated with the rise in the rate of exchange and the damage done to the competitive position of manufacturing industry by that rise. But as events have shown, the rise in the exchange rate to January 1981 was not something dictated by irreversible forces such as an expanding supply of North Sea oil: it had more to do with the high rate of interest and the swing of the balance of payments into surplus as the depression deepened.

When we take a longer view of the matter we have to take account of long term as well as short term capital movements. The removal of exchange control in 1979 transformed the relative attractiveness of domestic and foreign securities by putting an end to the premium paid for investment currency. There was a consequent shift in asset preferences in favour of foreign securities and an outflow of capital into those securities on a large scale. This outflow may have reflected a once-for-all shift in preferences but the shift in practice was spread over several years. Moreover the greater ease of transfer tended to magnify fluctuations in capital movements produced by movements and expected movements in the exchange rate. A further depreciation of the pound would raise the sterling price of overseas assets, including foreign securities, and discourage the outflow of capital. Any response in the exchange rate to lower export proceeds from oil, in other words, might provoke an offsetting reduction in the outflow of capital and vice versa.

Consciously or unconsciously, therefore, the rate of exchange forms one of the key elements in any government's economic strategy. It exerts its most powerful influence when it is not used at all but remains fixed, since then all other elements revolve round it as round a sun. If left to float, it may appear to leave economic policy free from external constraints but these constraints, driven out of the exchange rate door reappear at the window of inflation. The exchange rate, as the bridge between the domestic and the international economy, cannot be jettisoned as an element in policy except in conditions of autarchy. Every divergence between what is happening at home and what is happening abroad tends to register as pressure on the exchange rate in one direction or the other. If the government holds the rate steady and takes no further action, the economy will behave like any other fragment of a single international economy: expansion and contraction, inflation and deflation, will roll across the exchange rate bridge without impediment as they would from England into Wales or Scotland. There are those who doubt whether a government can do much to prevent subordination to the impulses coming from the world economy. But so long as a national government seeks to make it possible for the domestic economy to go its own way it must feel free to operate on its exchange rate, not only directly in the foreign exchange market but indirectly through its influence on the various elements that go to make up the balance of payments.

NOTES

1 For a useful summary of the present state of theory see 'Exchange rate determination: the dollar - a study', *Midland Bank Review*, Winter 1985.

2 S. Howson and D. Winch, *The Economic Advisory Council 1930–1939*, (Cambridge University Press, Cambridge, 1977), p. 89.

12

The rise and fall of employment policy

No economic problem between the two World Wars excited so much public interest or presented such a challenge to the emerging profession of economists as how to grapple with unemployment. The literature of the interwar period is saturated with a sense of frustration and anxiety: frustration because no way could be found to provide opportunities of employment for the whole working population; and anxiety over the consequences of this failure, national and international. In Britain in particular, where severe unemployment lasted throughout the entire period, the unemployment problem dominated debate.

Few people at that time thought that it was possible to have full employment as we have known it since 1945. Lord Beveridge in an extensive analysis of the problem in 1936 concluded that even in favourable circumstances unemployment in the United Kingdom was unlikely to fall below 10 to 12 per cent. The following year, when unemployment had only just fallen to a million and a half, Keynes was worried that the economy would overheat in a rearmament boom. In the middle of the Battle of Britain in the summer of 1940 there were still nearly a million people out of work. Yet within a few years the level of unemployment had fallen to a mere 70,000 – well under 0.5 per cent.

Postwar experience in Britain has been at the opposite extreme. Instead of starting off with unemployment at 3 million as in 1931 and ending up at 70,000 as in 1944 or 300,000 as in the early postwar years, unemployment has climbed back to over 3 million in the 1980s. When Beveridge in 1945 put forward 3 per cent as a reasonable target for postwar governments, even Keynes thought that this was too optimistic and expressed scepticism as to its feasibility. But for twenty years after the war unemployment hardly ever rose above 2 per cent, much less 3 per

Revised version of a lecture delivered at Washington University, St Louis, in 1982, and subsequently at the Universities of Calgary and British Columbia.

cent. By the 1960s 3 per cent had come to seem disastrously high and enough to bring down a government.

There were, of course, mild cyclical fluctuations in which unemployment alternately rose and fell by 100,000 or so. Throughout the 1950s it consistently returned to much the same level of about 300,000. In the 1960s it became clear that this was no longer happening. From one cycle to the next the average level of unemployment was rising slowly but steadily. In 1950–54 – a fairly typical postwar period – unemployment averaged just over 300,000. In 1960–64 the average was just over 400,000. By 1970–74 it had risen to 690,000 or just under 3 per cent. Then began a sustained increase from 1974 onwards, with only a slight dip in 1978–79, and by 1980–84 the average had become 2,500,000 – well over 10 per cent. Unemployment reached 1,300,000 at the end of 1976. It was still at that level when the new Conservative Government came into office in 1979 but shot up over the next few years, doubling by 1982, rising to over 3 million soon afterwards, and staying there. Thus unemployment in Britain in the mid-1980s was ten times what had come to be accepted as normal in the postwar decade.

The increase from the mid-1970s to the mid-1980s was much larger than in other countries. In the United States unemployment was perceptibly lower in 1985 than at the previous peak in 1975 and less than twice the level aimed at twenty years before in the expansionary days of the New Frontier. In Continental Europe the rise was a good deal bigger: unemployment there doubled on the average over the ten years after the earlier peak in 1975. But in no other European country was the rise in unemployment quite so persistent and dramatic as in the United Kingdom.

The experience of the United Kingdom is of particular interest since it shows not only a wide swing in the level of unemployment but a much wider swing in policy. There, too, the wheel has come full circle. The acceptance by the Coalition Government in 1944 of responsibility for the level of unemployment was a revolutionary change in policy, marking official acceptance of the ideas of Lord Keynes. The repudiation of these ideas and of that responsibility by the Conservative Government that took office in 1979 was an equally decisive break with the past. In what I have to say about these two revolutions in thinking I shall touch lightly on the rightness or wrongness of the doctrines by which policy was guided, though I shall not conceal my own adherence to the essentials of what I take to be the neo-Keynesian position. I shall touch even more lightly on the extent to which policy controlled the march of events. It is all too easy when events are in tune with policy statements to assume that it is the policies that govern events: that when there is full employment under a government proclaiming full employment it must all be the government's doing because it says so; and that when there is heavy unemployment under a government disclaiming responsibility for safeguarding the level of employment, the slump can be laid at the government's door as the necessary consequence of its policies. I shall concentrate, not on these matters, but on the development of policy and the thinking behind it.

THE WHITE PAPER ON EMPLOYMENT POLICY

Employment policy in Britain goes back to the White Paper of May 1944 which set out: 'the course of policy which the Government propose to follow internally in order to maintain the highest possible level of employment'.

Unlike the American Employment Act of 1946 the White Paper was never embodied in legislation but it represented just as firm an acknowledgment of the Government's responsibility for the level of employment. It was careful, however, not to commit the Government to anything carrying the label 'Full Employment'; a 'high and stable level of employment' was the aim.

The authors of the White Paper offered no guarantee that the aim would be achieved. In the very first paragraph they emphasized the dependence of employment on foreign trade and conditions abroad. The loss of foreign investments in wartime would make it more difficult to pay for imports and success in doing so would be contingent on a large increase in the volume of exports above their pre-war level. 'Collaboration among the nations' was indispensable to the expansion in trade required. This could help to ensure reasonably stable rates of exchange, check the swings in world commodity prices and allow countries 'faced with temporary difficulties in their balance of payments . . . both to take exceptional measures to regulate their imports [by which was meant import quotas] and to call on other nations, as good neighbours, to come to their help'.

The Government accepted that when a trade depression occurred, recovery would not happen of itself or at least the process of recovery in a complex industrial society like Britain's: 'if effective at all, is likely to be extremely prolonged and to be accompanied by widespread distress'.

The Government was prepared, therefore: 'to accept the responsibility for taking action at the earliest possible stage to arrest a threatened slump'. As to how this was to be done, the Government put its faith in the management of demand: 'Total expenditure on goods and services', it argued, 'must be prevented from falling to a level where general unemployment appears'.

Four guiding principles of demand management were laid down. First, it would be necessary to avoid an unfavourable *foreign balance* (on current account). Although fluctuations in the foreign balance were recognized to be one of the two main sources of instability, no very clear indication was given of the action that might limit or offset them other than unspecified international measures undertaken in conjunction with other countries. If British exports fell off sharply: 'an expansion of internal demand would not alone be an appropriate remedy and indeed . . . might lead to inflation'. The only positive suggestion made was that exports would have to be much larger than before the war.

Swings in *private investment* – the second major volatile element – would have to be damped down. Since it was intended to pursue a policy of cheap money after the war, variations in interest rates would not be used at first though they might be brought into use later. Instead – and this was the third guiding principle – the Government proposed to rely on planning *public investment* over the five years ahead so that it could be slowed down or accelerated to offset opposite swings in private investment. At the same time they hoped to persuade privately owned enterprises to plan their capital expenditure on the same principle 'in conformity with a general stabilization policy'.

Fourthly, it would be necessary to check and reverse such changes in *consumers' expenditure* as normally followed fluctuations in private investment (fluctuations in exports were for some reason disregarded at this point in the argument). What was required was 'some corrective influence which would come into play automatically – on the analogy of a thermostatic control – in accordance with rules determined in advance and well understood by the public'.

The built-in stabilizer favoured by the Government – it was the invention of James Meade – was a scheme for varying, 'in sympathy with the state of employment' the weekly social security contributions paid by employers and employed. Another, more tentative, suggestion involved 'regulating hire purchase transactions according to the state of trade'. The possibility of running a budget surplus from time to time and refunding the excess to taxpayers in bad times was mentioned hesitantly as something that 'might well become a matter for consideration'. But the Treasury insisted that there must be no 'deliberate planning for a deficit in the National Budget in years of sub-normal trade activity'.

The White Paper made it clear that demand management in conformity with these general principles was not by itself enough. There had to be 'mobility of workers between occupations and localities' and measures to ensure balanced regional development. It was also 'essential that employers and workers should exercise moderation in wages matters so that increased expenditure provided at the onset of a depression may go to increase the volume of employment . . . Increases in the general level of wage rates must be related to increased productivity due to increased efficiency and effort'.

The White Paper regarded the stability of prices and wages as 'a condition vital to the success of employment policy', and went on to insist that 'workers must examine their trade practices and customs' to ensure that they would not impede expansion and 'defeat the object of a full employment programme' while restrictive agreements on the part of employers would be the subject of 'appropriate action' by the Government.

On the administrative machinery necessary for employment policy the Government expressed its determination to learn from experience and 'improve the instruments of our new policy as we move forward'. There was to be 'a small central staff qualified to measure and analyse economic trends and submit appreciations to the Ministers concerned . . . Many of the decisions required . . . will depend on quick and accurate diagnosis . . . Questions of timing will be equally delicate: it is no easy matter to judge when a period of growing prosperity has reached its climax . . . and requires corrective action'. Exact quantitative information would be needed about current economic movements; and the Paper concluded by prescribing what amounted to a revolution in official economic statistics.

These passages give a reasonably accurate picture of the state of opinion as the war was drawing to an end. The Government's commitment to stablization policy was still somewhat hesitant. The aim of regulating employment was more firmly grasped than the methods by which it was to be achieved. The stress laid on the balance of payments, on stability in prices and incomes, on localized unemployment and on the need for accurate and up to date information have all stood the test of time. These have indeed been ever present problems.

INADEQUACY OF THE INSTRUMENTS

What seems in retrospect most curious is the almost complete absence from the picture of the role that fiscal and monetary policy came to play. So far as fiscal policy is concerned, it is fair to say that the line taken by the White Paper was neither in accord with the way budgets were already being planned nor with the ideas of the economists who prepared the document. Monetary policy, however, was generally thought to be ineffective, particularly in a controlled economy. Since the proposal to vary social security contributions was never adopted and the idea of offsetting fluctuations in private investment by contrived, opposing fluctuations in public investment did not make a great deal of headway, the methods suggested for the regulation of demand now seem quite inadequate to such a major undertaking. As for the problems of diagnosis and timing, these assumed an importance far greater than the brief treatment in the White Paper seemed to imply.

It is very doubtful whether there was any clear understanding on the part of Ministers of the task they faced. They had become used in wartime to economic planning supported by controls of all kinds so that expenditure was limited and directed by administrative decisions rather than by financial considerations. The budget was only one, and by no means the most important, of the controls over consumer spending and capital investment. When officials at the end of 1945 analysed the problems facing the economy in financial terms in a draft *Economic Survey*, much as they did in later years, their report was set aside by Ministers who were baffled by the whole system of thought and conditioned to think in terms of balances of men and materials rather than of cash. A second *Economic* Survey in 1946 which also treated the budget as the relevant instrument for planning a peacetime economy was rejected in its turn. Monetary policy was given even shorter shrift as an instrument of employment policy. The first Labour Chancellor of the Exchequer after the war, Hugh Dalton, a former Professor of Economics at the London School of Economics, aimed at pushing long term interest rates down in a booming economy and was successful for a short time in reducing the rate on government bonds as low as 2.5 per cent. Bank Rate, which controlled short term interest rates, remained at 2 per cent from 1932 to 1951. A third instrument of policy, the exchange rate, was brought into play once only in the first twenty years after the war, in the devaluation of 1949; and when the devaluation took place there was hardly a single Minister who saw it as fulfilling any useful purpose and several, including the Chancellor, Stafford Cripps, who regarded the move as the antithesis of planning.

If in these early years there was continuous full employment it was not because of skilful demand management. It was simply because there was no lack of demand, for reasons that had very little to do with British policy. There was the pent-up demand from wartime, backed by the savings and excess liquidity accumulated in the war years. There was the wartime destruction to be made good, in Britain and abroad. There was the additional investment needed to match the higher level of spending and demand. There was the enormous increase in demand abroad after six years of war and the need to expand exports fivefold from the low point in 1944 in order to pay for necessary imports. The problem was not one of maintaining full employment but of avoiding inflation and getting back into external balance in dealings with other countries. But since there *was* full employment and the government claimed responsibility for the level of employment, the public was happy to give the government the credit for what it had not done and accept as axiomatic that in future it would have equal success.

What the government did do, and with great success, was to restore external balance. The United Kingdom, for the second time in half a century, emerged from a prolonged and devastating war with a heavy external load of debt, and greatly diminished external assets. It was necessary to economize severely on imports and keep them below their pre-war level for ten years after the war. In spite of Britain's dependence on imported food and materials, the necessary degree of economy was accomplished without damage to employment and exports rose fast enough to restore external balance by 1948.

The control of inflation rested heavily on the goodwill of the unions, coupled with food subsidies that held down the cost of living. In the first five years after the war, with unemployment about one-fifth of its pre-war level, weekly wages rose at 4 per cent per annum–no more than twice as fast as in the depression years in the mid-1930s. Labour Ministers were able to persuade union leaders in 1949 when the pound was devalued by 30 per cent not to press for higher wages unless the cost of living rose by over 5 per cent (and in fact it rose a good deal less).

Employment policy was not really tested until the 1950s and even then not very severely. In the middle of a world boom it would have been surprising if Britain alone had experienced a recession of any depth. But as the various controls surviving from the war were abandoned one by one, with monetary policy largely in abeyance, the government found that the instruments at its disposal for regulating demand were narrowing down to one only: the budget. The budget became the focus of policy not only for adjusting the pressure of demand and the level of employment but for the whole array of the government's economic objectives from stable costs and prices to balance in the international accounts, the encouragement of productive investment and greater economic equality. There were clearly too many different objectives for a single instrument of policy to carry.

Reliance on the budget had the great disadvantage that there was only one budget a year so that the judgement that it embodied could not be corrected until another year had passed. This made policy highly dependent on a forecast of events up to a year away when the forecast itself was based on information that related to a period six months or so in the past. The government therefore sought other weapons that could be used more flexibly. It began to make use of control of bank credit, not by operating on the monetary base but by letters issued to the banks by the Governor of the Bank of England asking for their cooperation. It also made use in nearly every crisis of restrictions on consumer credit prescribing minimum down-payments or maximum periods for paying off the balance. Then in 1961 it sought powers to vary indirect taxation between budgets through the use of two 'regulators' as they were called. One, which revived the idea of varying social service contributions, was quickly dropped but the other, the Customs and Excise Regulator, which allowed the government to vary a wide range of indirect taxes up or down by up to 10 per cent, has been used on several occasions. In addition to these powers, the British Government, unlike most other governments, could bring most budget changes into effect immediately without waiting for the Finance Bill to be enacted. Hence although its ability to influence demand and employment was limited, it could give effect to its judgement, once formed, with a promptitude that is normally associated with banking rather than budgetary policy.

Powers were one thing: judgement was another. It remained extremely difficult to decide when to intervene. This became a little easier as a result of the progress made in the 1950s with the collection and analysis of the the economic statistics necessary for employment policy. The technique of economic forecasting became increasingly sophisticated. The difficulty remained, however, that the available data could never be up to date, were inevitably conflicting and of doubtful reliability, and were often open to widely different interpretations. Similarly the models on which the forecasts rested might easily mis-specify the underlying relationships and these relationships themselves were undergoing changes which might take the model builders by surprise.

STOP–GO

The timing of intervention came in for an increasing volume of criticism. The complaint began to be heard at the end of the 1950s that demand management was producing fluctuations in economic activity instead of preventing them. At first this took the form of agitation over 'stop–go' policies. It was argued that the government seemed to time its intervention so that as soon as the economy had begun to get up some momentum measures were taken to withdraw purchasing power or restrict credit and bring the expansion to a complete stop. Alternatively, the government was accused of hitting the economy when it was already going down. It is certainly true that production in the 1950s did not rise smoothly from year to year along the line of trend but grew in short bursts, punctuated by intermediate spells of stagnation in output. This gave the impression that the government was holding back the growth of the economy and that if it simply refrained from action – though how it could do so was never explained – there would be more stability and faster growth.

These are very doubtful propositions. In any economy there are bound to be fluctuations of some kind and comparisons between experience in Britain and other countries suggest that such fluctuations were as common and of the same magnitude elsewhere. The main difference was that because growth was slower in Britain a check to expansion looked more severe because it completely arrested the expansion instead of merely slowing it down. Whether stop–go policies were responsible for the slower rate of growth is open to question. Of course, a smooth continuous expansion would have allowed business to plan ahead more efficiently. But that was something no country enjoyed; fast growth was just as erratic as slow. On the other hand, if expansion had been allowed to proceed unchecked, when there was so small a margin of spare capacity even in the 'stop' phases of the cycle, there was a very real risk that inflation would speed up and the balance of payments move into heavy deficit. As the government learned very quickly, the level of employment was not the only thing that mattered. It was necessary at some point to take account of other dangers that might affect the balance of the economy.

Nevertheless concern over 'stop–go' brought pressure on the government to take a longer view of developments. The British public suddenly became aware of the more rapid progress made since the war in continental economies and were particularly struck by the changes in France under General de Gaulle. These they attributed for some reason to French planning which they took to be the antithesis of 'stop–go'. What appealed to them in planning was the steady pursuit of fixed objectives against longer term perspectives without the rather fidgety 'fine tuning', as it was called, of demand management.

A change in the same direction had already been proposed in relation to control of public expenditure. The Government sought in the course of the 1960s to introduce a system of control under which Departments were asked to submit expenditure programmes covering the next five years and these were reviewed together in relation to the resources likely to be available to meet the expenditure over that period. While this seemed a business-like way of proceeding it was not without its difficulties especially if Departments took it to imply that they could plan ahead for up to five years without fear of having to cut back from time to time under the compulsions of each year's budgetary problems. In any event, the attempt to keep public spending, and with it public investment, on a steady course immune from the fluctuations in the rest of the economy, meant the abandonment of the White Paper's 'guiding principle' that public investment should, so far as possible, be made to fluctuate so as to offset equal and opposite fluctuations in private investment.

What had happened since 1944 made this seem an increasingly unreal objective. As the White Paper itself recognized, a large part of the Government's spending programme is dictated by 'urgent public needs' and cannot be easily trimmed or enlarged to meet conjunctural requirements. Moreover, the Government's powers over local authorities, nationalized industries and other spending agencies are limited. Above all, government decisions tend to lag behind events and take time to come into effect so that by the time public investment responds to efforts to control it the situation may have changed quite radically and call for adjustment in the opposite direction. This is not mere hypothesis. There were times in the 1960s when large capital projects that had been sanctioned in an effort to relieve local unemployment were finally begun just as unemployment was disappearing at the peak of a boom two or three years later.

The vogue for planning in the early 1960s, culminating in the National Plan of 1965, was short-lived. It did not so much represent a reaction against short term economic management as demonstrate that full employment had come to be taken for granted so that it was not endangered by the pursuit of other objectives such as economic growth. There was, however, an increasing tendency to dwell on conflicts between short term and long term aims of policy and argue for a more relaxed attitude to transitional forms of instability. One example of this was the growing influence of monetarist ideas, beginning with a conference in 1968 at the Treasury between government officials and a team of economists from the IMF.

CHANGING ATTITUDES IN THE 1970S

The big change in official and Ministerial thinking did not take place until the 1970s. The way in which the government arrived at a judgement of the economic situation and the measures that it thought appropriate were not very different in 1970 from what they had been fifteen years earlier. More notice, it is true, was taken of the money supply or of the new-fangled concept, domestic credit expansion. There was also some doubt about the interpretation to be put on the gradual increase in unemployment over the previous decade since it had not been accompanied by a similar change in other measures of the tightness of the labour market. But by 1970 unemployment had been steady for three years, the balance of payments had swung at last into substantial surplus after the devaluation of 1967 and prices, though rising rather faster than before devaluation, had shown an average increase of under 6 per cent a year in the three years following devaluation. Employment policy was still near its zenith.

The change in attitude over the next ten years was remarkable. It can be traced partly to events and partly to the influence of new theories of how the economic system functions. What has been called 'the searing experience' of the early 1970s was the extraordinary acceleration of inflation in those years. Consumer prices had risen in the 1960s at an average of 3.8 per cent per annum. In the 1970s that became 13 per cent, more than three times the previous rate. But, much worse, prices in 1974–75 were rising at over 20 per cent per annum and touched a peak of over 36 per cent per annum in the second quarter of 1975. Added to that, public expenditure seemed to be out of control, the balance of payments was in heavy deficit, the foreign exchange reserves were draining away, the exchange rate itself was falling and unemployment was mounting to a level without precedent since the war.

These events, which led up to a major crisis in the autumn of 1976, were alarming enough in themselves. But what made Ministers desperate for new ideas was that conventional methods of demand management seemed impotent to deal with the situation. As Mr Callaghan declared to the Labour Party Conference in September 1976 in a much quoted speech:

> We used to think that you could just spend your way out of a recession, and increase employment, by cutting taxes and boosting government spending. I tell you in all candour that that option no longer exists, and that in so far as it ever did exist, it worked by injecting inflation into the economy. And each time that happened, the average level of unemployment has risen. Higher inflation, followed by higher unemployment. That is the history of the last twenty years.

Mr Callaghan's version of history is open to question but his perception of the difficulties of demand management in highly inflationary conditions would be widely shared. The revolution in thinking that gave rise to demand management rested on the denial of the proposition that supply creates its own demand; what happened in the 1970s was a denial of the converse proposition that demand automatically creates its own supply. Instead it may, as Mr Callaghan contended, merely push up prices or push down the rate of exchange and the price of government bonds.

The events of 1972–75 are open to conflicting interpretations. Some economists have argued that the root of the trouble lay in the very large increase in the money supply in 1972–73 after the introduction of a more relaxed system of credit control. It was this increase in the money supply, they suggest, that two years later worked its way through to the price level and created the inflation that reduced the government to impotence. Much better, therefore, to keep an eye on the money supply and forget about regulating spending through the budget. In any event, some would say, there is really no need to regulate spending: the economy will regulate itself if the government contents itself with sound money policies. Unemployment will sink back to its 'natural' level and output expand at a 'natural' rate.

These are not views that have won general acceptance. Most British economists are apt to ask for a figure to be put to the idea of a 'natural' rate of unemployment and point to estimates varying from less than 2 to more than 10 per cent. When they are assured that any excess above the natural rate is voluntary, they express some scepticism that a million more people can be voluntarily unemployed in 1981 than in 1980, when presumably the natural rate was no different but the level of unemployment was a million less. As for the part played by the money supply, they recall that there was far more excess liquidity in the economy in 1945 than there ever was in the early 1970s and yet prices rose very little in the first period and very fast in the second. The rise in 1974–75, which the Conservative government attributed after 1979 to the lax monetary policies in 1972–73 of an earlier government of the same political colour, can be explained in quite different terms. Every other country in 1974–75 suffered an inflation of some kind and, if it was worse in Britain, that had presumably as much to do with the 25 per cent adverse shift in the terms of trade as with anything else. British policy played little or no part in the big rise in world commodity prices in 1972–73 or the dramatic increase in the price of oil in 1973–74. If it proved specially vulnerable to these increases it was not primarily because of mistaken monetary policies two years before.

The new ideas, right or wrong, exercised an increasing influence. The Labour government introduced monetary targets as far back as 1976 and targets have continued in use ever since. By themselves these targets imply that what happens to the money supply is more important than what happens to employment or real GNP, especially if there is no corresponding target for employment enjoying equal status. The introduction of monetary targets, therefore, represented a downgrading of employment policy. The Labour government of 1974–79 did not explicitly abandon employment policy but it took no vigorous action to reduce unemployment although it doubled during its term of office.

A NEW ECONOMIC PHILOSOPHY

The Conservative government that came into office in 1979 was not doing anything new, therefore, in relying on monetary targets. What *was* new was the economic philosophy in which the targets were embedded: the view that control of the money supply was the key to control of inflation and would have little effect on output and employment. The government showed no interest in 'a high and stable level of employment' and although it subsequently took action to mitigate the effects of unemployment through job creation schemes and in other ways the level of employment did not figure at any point in its economic strategy. Instead, that strategy was conceived almost exclusively in terms of the money supply, the public sector borrowing requirement (PSBR) and latterly the exchange rate. This did not fully emerge in 1979 but in the budget of 1980 a Medium Term Financial Strategy was announced which provided for a reduction, year by year, over the next four years in the rate of growth of the money supply and sketched a corresponding fall in the PSBR to ensure that interest rates were not pressed upwards. These changes were to take precedence over any other elements in policy. In 1980 and again in 1981 when it was universally expected that, in the absence of changes in policy, output would fall and unemployment rise, the net effect of the measures taken was deflationary. On the government's own showing, the 1980 budget was calculated to deflate demand by £1 billion at a time when a severe recession was in prospect: it has to be remembered that an actual fall in total output is a very rare occurrence in the postwar world and implies a major slackening in economic activity. In 1981 with unemployment up by 1 million, another deflationary budget was introduced. Even in 1982 after another rise of ½ million in unemployment the budget gave only the slightest of nudges towards expansion and for the fourth time running no mention was made in the budget speech of the probable change in unemployment that it implied.

What had happened, therefore, by 1981 was tantamount to an abandonment of the entire tradition of postwar economic policy. It was not an abandonment welcomed by the economics profession in the United Kingdom, many of whom signed a letter of protest to *The Times* at that stage. It was also not a general abandonment by all the political parties – a counterpart to the general acceptance of postwar employment policy at the time of its announcement by the Coalition Government in 1944. It is not even certain that the Conservative Party will continue to support the ideas behind existing policies. These ideas changed substantially after the Party took office and there have also been some striking divergences between what is said and what is done, as well as between what is intended and what actually happens. On these divergences I will not enlarge.

SOME QUESTIONS FOR THE FUTURE

What may be of more interest are three general points with which I will conclude.

First of all, it is natural to ask what happens if there is no fresh consensus and one party remains wedded to what one may still describe as monetarist ideas while the others subscribe to neo-Keynesian policy prescriptions? We have had plenty of experience in the United Kingdom of the influence of ideology on economic affairs and there are some directions in which this influence is not easily reconciled with the two party system. We have seen industries nationalized, denationalized and renationalized. We have seen Prices and Incomes Boards appointed, wound up, recreated and again wound up. There seems no limit to the number and variety of institutions that one party will create and another disband. But at least an institution has limits. What is to happen if a government that subordinates the whole of its policy to the money supply or the PSBR is succeeded by a government that attaches no special importance to either of these and overwhelming importance to getting unemployment down?

It may be that this first problem will yield to experience. The age-old gravitation towards the centre may dispose the parties to work towards a common framework of thought even if there is no sharing of priorities. In that event the new party that has come on the scene – the SDP – might have an important role to play. But there may be no centre, no oscillation between policies leaning first in one direction then in the other within accepted limits. In the past the swings in the stance of fiscal and monetary policy, as one party took over from the other, were not closely related to the general party line: if anything it was the Conservative Party that proved the more recklessly expansionist and the Labour Party that found itself obliged to follow a cautious restrictive tack. All that may now be changed. We could swing from the kind of extreme non-intervention of the Thatcher government to an attempt to supersede financial controls by administrative action that became increasingly comprehensive as in the days of the New Deal. If the main parties identify themselves with widely differing views as to how the economy works, and neither really knows, all hope of stability in employment (and in much else) would go out of the window.

A second question relates to the way in which incomes are fixed and the role of the trade unions in fixing them. The fundamental division of opinion a few years ago was between those who thought that inflation was largely the work of the trade unions and those who thought that it echoed the behaviour of the money supply. It was possible to see prices dancing to the tune set by wages or alternatively wages doing no more than follow prices in the ritual dance. The present government started from a position in which they absolved the trade unions of all responsibility and almost openly encouraged them to squeeze all they could from their employers. That line of talk has died away. The government and the unions have been locked in more than one prolonged and costly struggle over wages and the need for moderate wage settlements is a frequent theme. But neither of the two traditional parties shows much enthusiasm for incomes policy and the Conservative Party is dead against it. Wage settlements have in fact moderated under the influence of massive redundancies and a drastic fall in manufacturing output. But wages are still moving up at a rate that would have produced consternation in almost any of the first 25 years after the war. Most economists, therefore, would be inclined to agree that incomes policy in some form is indispensable if inflation is to continue to ebb and employment must be made to expand. They are painfully aware, however, that no policy that has so far been put into operation has proved to be acceptable, effective and lasting and that every imaginary incomes policy is likely to prove full of holes.

In the background is a question even more fundamental than any relating to employment or inflation. It is this: how are we to restore hope in the future? It is not just a matter of jobs. Young people in Britain now have little or nothing to lift their eyes from a sombre and darkening present to a compelling vision of the future. There is no British Empire; no crusade like the Spanish Civil War in my generation; no Hitlers and Mussolinis against whom they are invited to fight. They feel the bomb hanging over them and over the whole human race so that its survival is in doubt. In the past there always seemed to be some cause to fight for, some group to admire, some Utopia lying ahead. Now the causes are compromised, the groups blown upon, and the Utopias have turned into science fiction accounts of Armageddon or the end of the world. Ideals give way to a chilling sense of futility.

Without vision the people perish, says the Psalmist. But perhaps they turn violent and destructive first. There have been riots already in England and there will undoubtedly be more. There is also a rising tide of sheer vandalism. We all remember what was born in Europe from the mass unemployment of the early 1930s. It is natural to feel some alarm at the prospect of a similar decade of unemployment ahead of us when the very idea of employment policy that once gave us hope is now openly scouted and spurned.

13

Is employment policy a thing of the past?

It is nearly forty years since the publication by the wartime Coalition Government of the White Paper on Employment Policy. The economic philosophy of that historic document persisted under governments of different political persuasions until at least 1976 and was rejected outright only in 1979.

The theme of the White Paper was the acceptance of responsibility by government for the level of employment. There may be room for doubt whether the methods outlined in the White Paper for securing 'a high and stable level of employment' were adequate for the discharge of that responsibility. But the commitment to full employment (or something very like it) was itself a powerful weapon not to be lightly abandoned. The British government was the first in the world to make that commitment. Now it would seem to be a thing of the past.

Full employment was never, as in the United States, made part of the law of the land and it was not necessary therefore to repeal any legislation to escape from responsibility for it. All that was necessary was to give priority to some other objective such as controlling inflation. In other countries where there was a formal requirement to pursue an employment policy, the same reversal has occurred. Governments have tended to wash their hands of responsibility for the level of employment and treat efforts to reduce unemployment as futile so long as inflation is still acute. The break with the past may not have been as decisive as in the United Kingdom but it is associated with very similar ideas.

If one looks at what has been happening to unemployment, this revolution in ideas is strangely timed. The common experience over the past half century has embraced a gradual fall in unemployment from the

From *The Three Banks Review*, September 1983.

very high levels reached in the early thirties, its virtual disappearance in World War II, its comparatively low level for nearly thirty years thereafter, and its subsequent rise to levels that in some countries are comparable with the highest levels reached in the 1930s. In the United Kingdom, for example, recorded unemployment has oscillated between three million in 1931–32, an all-time low of 70,000 in 1944 (coinciding with the publication of the White Paper) and over three million again in 1986, with a labour force 20–25 per cent bigger than fifty years ago. In other countries the swing has been less pronounced and the change over the last few years later and less steep. Whereas in the United Kingdom unemployment has trebled since 1975, in the main Continental countries it has doubled and in the United States it is not very much higher than in 1975 and not a great deal more than twice the level regarded as optimal twenty years ago in the days of the New Frontier. Nevertheless, unemployment is everywhere on a scale where it would be natural to expect immediate government action rather than declarations of impotence or disclaimers of responsibility.

Why is such action not taken? Why is it that governments acquiesce in such high levels of unemployment and the enormous loss of output and income that accompanies them? Why have we had a revolution in ideas that has produced the *abandonment* of employment policy when a similar situation fifty years ago led eventually to the deliberate *adoption* of employment policy? In addressing these questions my object will be to offer some explanation for what, in the perspective of history, is a very puzzling turn of events, not to suggest that the explanation justifies inaction. On the contrary I shall be outlining arguments and describing attitudes with which I am very much out of sympathy.

A ROSIER VIEW OF MARKET FORCES

Part of the explanation of the present situation lies in a change in attitudes towards government intervention of any kind. There is less disposition in most countries to turn to government to put things right, less faith that governments know what to do or how to do it, more anxiety to set some limit to the role of government and the size of the government machine. This goes with a revolt of the taxpayer and an attack on the increasing demands of the welfare state. The counterpart is a rosier view of market forces, a recognition of the power of those forces and doubts whether government efforts to control them are based on a genuine understanding of how they operate. The upshot is a willingness to accept that government intervention in the market place may merely serve to make matters worse or prove entirely ineffective.

This change in public attitudes has coincided with the emergence of a school of thought which seeks to demonstrate that in any event intervention is not necessary. The economy is fundamentally self-regulating, so it is argued, and will return without government action to a level of employment consistent with the underlying preferences of the labour force. Of course, mistakes may arise for one reason or another because market signals are misread, and these may give rise to fluctuations in employment. But these fluctuations around what is misleadingly called 'the natural rate of unemployment' will be short-lived and self-correcting.

This view is buttressed by attempts to demonstrate that any *sustained* rise in unemployment is likely to be voluntary. Either it results from efforts by workers to secure higher real wages than employers can afford – in which case workers are 'pricing themselves out of a job' – or it is an indication that workers prefer to be idle and draw unemployment benefit to working for a rate of pay that is not sufficiently higher to make the exertion worthwhile.

These propositions are not new since the same kind of arguments used to be heard in the 1930s. There was a famous argument between Keynes and Jacques Rueff in 1930–31 over the contribution made by 'high' wages and the 'dole' to the heavy unemployment of those years. A rather similar controversy was launched a few years ago by Benjamin and Kochin in the Chicago *Journal of Political Economy*, and is still raging, over the extent to which unemployment in Britain in the thirties was voluntary.[1] But anyone who lives in a country where unemployment has oscillated between three million and 70,000 and back again in his own lifetime, and has seen unemployment double in a matter of months and stay over 10 per cent for years on end, must rub his eyes a little at learned demonstrations that unemployment is almost entirely voluntary and that governments can do nothing about it.[2]

Admittedly, there is evidence that the level of unemployment at which labour shortages begin to make their appearance on a scale sufficient to upset the balance of the labour market has gradually increased in many countries over the past couple of decades. It is not altogether clear why this should be so. In the United Kingdom the unemployment figures behaved qute differently in the 1970s from all other labour market indicators such as vacancies, overtime, turnover, and reported shortages of skilled and unskilled labour: so much so that while the other indicators agree in pointing to a situation in the spring of 1979, for example, very similar to that in the spring of 1972, the unemployment figures show an increase over that period of 100 per cent. White it may be possible to account for some of this as a symptom of an increasing mismatching between labour supply and labour requirements, it is also possible that there has been a change of attitude towards paid work and that the terms on which workers will accept the jobs on offer have stiffened. Some younger workers seem to have become more ready to mix spells in a job and spells without one. No such change of attitude, however, could possibly account for the large and sudden increase in unemployment that began in 1979.

THE 'SEARING EXPERIENCE' OF INFLATION

A second, even more powerful, influence on thinking about unemployment has been inflation. So long as the rate of inflation was comparatively modest, governments could ignore it or make only spasmodic efforts to control it. But when it increased in the 1970s to 10, 20, or even 30 per cent, they felt obliged to give anti-inflationary measures priority over all other objectives, including that of full employment. For them the 'searing experience' of the 1970s was inflation just as in the 1930s it had been unemployment.

All the expedients to which they had turned in the past had failed to get rid of inflation and they felt the need, therefore, for a new and more resolute approach. Such an approach was confidently offered by economists who regarded control of the money supply as a necessary and sufficient instrument for the purpose. This approach was again not new: it stretches back through the long history of the quantity theory of money to David Hume in the eighteenth century. It seemed also to accord with common sense that the more money there is around the less value it will have. What more natural than to conclude that the more tightly the money supply is controlled the less the likelihood of inflation? Unfortunately, it may be the level of output that falls rather than the rate of inflation; and with falling output goes rising unemployment.

In the course of the 1970s there was a steady increase in most countries in the emphasis put by governments of all persuasions, first on the need to control inflation and second on limiting the growth of the money supply as a means of achieving that control. Indeed, as time went on, monetary targets came to be no longer a means but an end in themselves even when they proved to be misleading indicators of financial stringency. Sometimes it came to seem as if governments were willing to allow all other major objectives of economic policy to be over-ridden by the imperative of their monetary targets. The United Kingdom, for example, announced in 1980 a medium term financial strategy covering the next four years in which the centrepiece of policy over the whole of that period was a series of steadily diminishing targets for the growth of the money supply. At the same time fiscal policy was relegated to a purely supporting role with the object of reducing the strain that a tight monetary policy might throw on interest rates. The purpose of the strategy was to change expectations by bringing home the determination of the government 'to squeeze inflation permanently out of the system' and impose constraints on the functioning of the system that would ensure that result. Other countries have indulged similar hopes and relied on similar weapons.

Policies of this kind, whatever their intellectual merits and whatever their ultimate effects, necessarily imply a downgrading of previous objectives such as full employment. Control of inflation is given precedence. But the change in policy goes far beyond this. Inflation comes first and employment nowhere at all. Operation on the money supply is expected to get rid of inflation and to have little effect on output and employment. There may be some transitional difficulties in what is represented as a stabilization crisis; but these will be no more than withdrawal symptoms on the way to the restoration of a healthy, inflationless economy and, it is argued, will be over quickly. The greater certainty that attends economic transactions in a world of stable prices, interest rates, exchange rates and, by implication, money wage rates will ultimately improve the performance of the economy and allow output to expand. Whatever happens to unemployment, it is inflation that governments should seek to influence. As has become increasingly apparent, however, the methods adopted by governments to lower the rate of inflation have taken effect mainly by boosting the level of unemployment.

To anyone who holds the views in which I was brought up there is nothing very surprising in such an outcome. The money supply is not, except in special circumstances, the cause of inflation in a modern credit economy so much as a symptom of it. The causes generally lie deeper in the intransigence of organized groups either of workers or of suppliers of energy, raw materials or finance. Such groups are in a position to force up the level of costs and to resist downward adjustments whether the level of demand warrants a corresponding movement in prices or not. The pressure they exert can squeeze profits if resisted and so make current levels of activity unprofitable and unsustainable; or if not resisted the pressure will be reflected in higher prices and, if on a sufficient scale, in inflation. One form of acquiescence in the pressure from the side of costs is to let the money supply increase; one form of resistance is to hold down the money supply, usually through higher interest rates. If the supply of finance *is* restricted and becomes more costly, employers find it harder to put up prices but face an undiminished pressure on their costs, including the extra pressure of more costly finance. It is then employment and output that give: any relief on the side of inflation is accompanied by what may be a quite catastrophic loss on the side of economic activity and employment.

It would not be possible for me to deal comprehensively here with the causes of inflation, monetarism in its various forms and the rationale of macro-economic policy. My concern is with the changes in objectives and ideas that have followed the inflationary surge of the 1970s: the displacement of employment policy by inflation policy as the centrepiece of government action in the leading industrial countries and the emphasis on the supply of money and monetary targets as the instruments of inflation policy. These changes are tantamount to an abandonment of the entire tradition of postwar economic policy. It would have been unthinkable a few years ago that governments should give no clue in their budgets to the employment implications of the measures taken. But the British government in particular has been conspicuously silent since 1979 in budget after budget, issuing no forecasts of unemployment then or at any other time and treating the future level of unemployment almost as a forbidden subject, like devaluation in the mid-1960s.

SHOULD INFLATION TAKE PRIORITY OVER UNEMPLOYMENT?

Yet if one asks why inflation should take priority over unemployment as the focus of economic policy there is no very convincing answer. What matters is surely the level of output, employment and the standard of living more than changes in the value of money. If inflation and monetary instability make it necessary to acquiesce for a time in a retreat from full employment this is primarily because of the threat of a more disastrous breakdown in economic activity eventually if inflation goes unchecked. If inflation could continue indefinitely without doing any appreciable damage to the level of output or the chances of steady employment, getting rid of it would not rank nearly so high as an object of policy. The distributive injustices that accompany inflation would not by themselves be enough to give disinflation priority over employment policy since they could be dealt with at much less cost than the losses in output we are now suffering. It is the danger of heavy unemployment at a later stage that is the compelling reason for immediate action. But if this were recognized, the ultimate target would still be an employment target, not a target for inflation, still less a monetary target.

If I have dwelt on inflation and on monetarist ideas about inflation, it is because these constitute a major impediment to economic recovery. Governments that are willing to pursue deflationary policies while unemployment goes on increasing to 10 per cent or more are unlikely to make violent changes in the opposite direction just because the rate of inflation has come down from 20 per cent to 10 or 5 per cent. If they adopt an extreme monetarist position, they may either take for granted that unemployment will go away by itself or become wedded to rising unemployment as the only effective means of checking wage inflation. Either way, they will *never* see any need to pursue expansionist policies. Instead they will take a 'soup-kitchens and relief works' view of unemployment and try to make it a little less painful and dispiriting. Or if they take the hard-boiled view that the unemployed are simply too well off to see any need to work, they may cut or tax unemployment benefit to make unemployment less attractive.

THE LIMITS TO EXPANSIONARY POLICIES

But suppose the government was anxious to encourage expansion and was not obsessed by the money supply, what then? What could it hope to achieve?

First of all, it might still scruple to increase the pressure of demand by whatever means were available to it because this would add to the danger of inflation. This line of argument is not the same as one highlighting the quantity of money as the cause of inflation since it relates to the level of demand not to the money supply. It rests on the proposition that the higher the level of output the greater the pressure on scarce resources of labour and materials and the greater the risk that these might rise more steeply in price. But are we to conclude from this that it is safe to re-expand only when prices are actually falling? The risk of excessive pressure is very different when unemployment is negligible and when it runs into millions. Even if inflation were visibly ebbing away, it could always be contended that *any* generation of additional demand would slow down the process. This would be true whether the extra demand was of the government's creation or came about spontaneously through increased private spending. Once inflation becomes the touchstone of demand management we may have to wait a very long time, and see employment fall a very long way, before governments will contemplate an expansionary programme.

This is the more likely because it is not at all clear that changes in the general level of demand have a very marked impact on the rate of inflation. No doubt at high levels of activity additional pressure has a perceptible effect on wages and prices; but when there is already an enormous margin of spare capacity and a high level of unemployment throughout the world the impact of a moderate expansion could hardly be very great. The very fact that inflation continues at a relatively high rate when economic activity is already falling should make one sceptical of a determinate relationship between the two.

I hope at least that no one now tries to explain the behaviour of wages, which are the largest element in costs and prices, in terms of the Phillips curve which seeks to establish a functional relationship between the level of unemployment and the rate of increase in wages. More unemployment does not necessarily slow down the rise in wages and so in prices. The labour market is far too complex to be summed up in a single equation. It takes time for wage bargains to move down to a level that is compatible with stable or fairly stable prices, and it may well also involve changes in the whole machinery of collective bargaining. But neither of these things should be allowed to hold up recovery.

What this comes to is that, when there is already so much slack, governments should not hesitate to expand demand because of the repercussions this might have on wage settlements or on other elements in cost. The chances are that wage settlements at high levels of unemployment would be little affected while the gains in productive efficiency associated with a higher turnover would more than offset any increase in the cost of materials.

BALANCE OF PAYMENTS DIFFICULTIES

But this is not the end of the matter. What if one country expands and others do not join in? Might it not be forced to backtrack because of balance of payments difficulties? Some of the expansion in demand would overflow on to imports and there might well be reactions in financial markets that produced an outflow of capital and pressure on the exchange rate. These risks are particularly evident in a country like the United Kingdom with a high income elasticity of demand for imports and a strong propensity to invest abroad.

Any one country is a fragment of the world economy and is bound increasingly to its neighbours in ways that limit its freedom of action. Unless it started out with a favourable balance of payments and substantial reserves or was prepared to use import quotas or other restrictions, it could be difficult for a single country to embark alone on economic expansion. Of course, it could try to shelter behind a falling exchange rate. But that would involve other risks. It would raise import prices and might, in spite of high unemployment, stiffen wage demands so that there was a real setback to the fight against inflation. These are not inevitable consequences. In some countries a lower rate of exchange might be desirable in itself and not a valid reason for hesitating to expand. In others, wage demands might be unaffected. But the need to maintain external balance could in any circumstances dampen enthusiasm for a programme of solitary expansion.

The stresses produced by differences in the economic situation in different countries make nonsense of a monetary policy conceived in purely national terms and the setting of monetary targets without regard to international influences on interest and exchange rates. If a large country like the United States has to finance high budget deficits that seem likely to outgrow its savings potential it may only be able to cover these deficits by letting interest rates rise and sucking in funds from other countries much as it did in other circumstances in 1929. The resulting high rates of interest may then spread to other countries where they are quite inappropriate and extremely damaging unless these countries are willing to let their exchange rates slide and face the danger of renewed inflation. In the management of their economies, governments need the support of other governments just as they need the support of the groups exercising economic power within their territory.

The fact that countries are increasingly interdependent may limit their freedom of initiative. But it puts a heavier responsibility on the more favourably placed among them to take the lead. There is no longer a single dominant power committed to expansionist policies and providing simultaneously a stimulus and a safety net that allow other countries to pursue similar policies. It is necessary instead to make headway in a fragmented world economy where national differences have to be composed and the self-interest of each by no means ensures the prosperity of all. One can but hope that countries will learn to make less use of instruments of policy such as high interest rates that do the maximum of damage to their neighbours; and that the strongest among them will cooperate with one another to reinforce, not thwart, a renewal of economic expansion wherever it occurs.

BOTTLENECKS

Next, there is the argument that expansion would encounter bottlenecks and be held up by weaknesses of industrial structure. That there are bottlenecks is always true. There were acute bottlenecks in the building and engineering industries in the United Kingdom in the mid-1930s when unemployment was over two million and some of the worst bottlenecks were in areas like Clydeside where unemployment was most acute. Old skills become obsolete and new skills have to be acquired whatever the level of employment. Industrial capacity also becomes obsolescent and new capacity has to be created in its place to take advantage of technical change or shifts in costs and prices such as are involved in the emergence of new sources of supply and new consumer needs. The process of structural adjustment takes time and requires investment; and while it is taking place an expansion in demand is ineffective and does little or nothing to add to employment. It is, therefore, of cardinal importance whether an increase in output is held up by a general deficiency of demand or by delays in structural adjustment.

Now there are many reasons that can be advanced for supposing that a substantial element in current unemployment is structural. Some economists point to the rise in energy costs and argue that this has rendered much existing equipment obsolete – cars, houses, industrial plant – and that the process of adaptation is bound to be extensive and protracted. There may be something in this as an explanation of the sustained high level of investment in the United States but I have yet to see any evidence that accelerated obsolescence resulting from the energy crisis has made a perceptible contribution to unemployment.

NON-WAGE LABOUR COSTS

On the European continent the more general argument has been advanced that investment is currently too low to provide the capacity necessary to restore employment to its previous level. The lack of investment in turn is explained in terms of low profits and profit expectations and these in their turn to the burdens imposed by the state in social security contributions and other labour costs. How much there is in all this is hard to say: we are in an area where assertion is easy but demonstration difficult. There is no doubt that non-wage labour costs are very high in Continental Europe: but so they were long before 1983 without producing heavy unemployment. There were even those who in the 1960s were in favour of making labour expensive in just such a way in order to speed up the substitution of new, labour saving machinery for old, high cost, labour intensive machinery. There is also no doubt that profits are low: but that is usual in a slump and tells us more about the state of demand than about the level of costs. As for the shortage of capacity on which the whole argument revolves, it has rarely been impossible, even under boom conditions in the 1950s and 1960s, to squeeze more output from existing capacity when the demand was there. In the United Kingdom the National Institute has suggested that it would be possible to expand industrial production by up to 15 per cent from existing capacity but also, one must admit, without any great increase in employment. For a really big increase in employment it would certainly be necessary to add substantially to capacity; and this would be likely to require both higher investment and the creation of a large number of new enterprises to meet demands that can at present be only dimly foreseen.

Another line of argument that is frequently developed is that the old centres of production in the industrial countries are now being challenged by the new industrializing countries of Asia and Latin America and that manufacturing employment will increasingly move to the second group of countries, leaving a rising total of unemployment in the first. The challenge is real enough. But it does not go very far to explain current levels of unemployment. Imports from the developing countries supply only about 3 per cent on the average of the market for manufactures in the developed countries and this percentage is rising at quite a slow pace. Over the past decade, moreover, the increase in exports of manufactures to the developing countries has far exceeded the simultaneous increase in imports from them. It is just not true that the so-called 'erosion of the industrial base' in the developed countries takes the form of a large scale shift of industrial activity from these countries to the developing countries. The wound is self-inflicted.

STRUCTURAL OBSTACLES TO EXPANSION

In any event, structural limitations do not condemn us to the indefinite continuation of unemployment on its present scale. Unless it is thought that *all* unemployment is structural they do no more than set limits to the pace of expansion. They oblige us to acquiesce in a prolonged spell of high unemployment. This might be reduced by foresight if workers were trained and capacity created in the right directions ahead of demand. But whatever is done in advance there is a kind of logistic limit to the rate of expansion which is set initially by the succession of bottlenecks that arise in the mobilization of additional resources where they are needed and the time lags that this involves.

Nevertheless, even if unemployment fell by no more than 1 percentage point per annum the difference that this could make to output and employment could be very substantial. The working rule in the British Treasury in the 1960s was that a drop in unemployment by 1 percentage point would go with a rise in employment of 3 per cent and an increase in output by 5 per cent. Obviously these relationships, which applied in the vicinity of full employment many years ago, do not hold now in an economy where unemployment is of the order of 13 per cent. But it is entirely possible that output varies, not five times but, say, twice as much as unemployment so that if unemployment were reduced by 5 per cent to the level in the autumn of 1980 there would be a 10 per cent gain in GNP, quite apart from any gain resulting from the secular improvement in productivity. Some of the present difficulties of governments (and families) in making ends meet would be a great deal less pressing if we could get GNP up even if there was no corresponding change in unemployment.

Of course it could turn out that there were structural changes of a different kind. Employers might have made up their minds, for example, never again to take on more workers than they currently employed. They might do so from fear that a larger staff would make them more vulnerable to strikes and labour trouble or because legislation made it more difficult to cut down the workforce again or simply because they had lost any inclination to expand their business. The only way to increase employment would then be through self-employment or more government employment or, in some circumstances, by cutting hours of work, and sharing out both the work and the pay. No country has quite reached that stage yet. But in all countries employers do show reluctance to recruit more staff if they think labour too expensive; and this more usual ground for reluctance is frequently alleged. There are some countries where an increase in real wages has coincided with rising unemployment and this could certainly slow down expansion. The argument here differs from one that simply points to high burdens on the employer of a kind that he has borne for many years. If real wages go on increasing in a depression this may reflect an unwillingness on the part of workers to acquiesce in the conditions called for by an expanding volume of employment. Some increase in real wages could take place because of a fall in demand and in profit margins. But if workers held out for increases in nominal wages that prevented a readjustment in real wages when efforts were made to increase demand – if there were so-called 'real wage resistance' in face of less favourable market conditions of employment – they could indeed price themselves out of jobs.

We can disregard as unlikely to contribute to our understanding of the present situation the popular view that the increase in unemployment has been brought about by new labour saving devices – computers, micro-electronics, robots and the rest. These may be tending all the time to reduce the demand for unskilled labour relatively to skilled and to make current relationships between the pay of the two groups increasingly inappropriate. But until the past year or two there has been no sudden increase in labour productivity such as would be implied if labour saving methods of production had led to major economies in labour. On the contrary the complaint everywhere has been that labour productivity has improved much more slowly than in the days of full employment before the oil shocks.

Whatever the structural obstacles to expansion in the industrial countries or to the pace of expansion, most of the increase in unemployment over the past few years reflects a deficiency of demand of exactly the kind experienced in the 1930s. It would be wise to proceed with some caution in expanding demand; and it is unlikely that we shall see unemployment fall to the low level of ten years ago within the present decade. But that is no reason for doing nothing and putting off an effort to make what progress is possible.

DIFFICULTIES IN EXPANDING DEMAND

I have assumed so far that there is no difficulty about increasing demand and that the government knows what action to take for the purpose. But the matter is not quite so straightforward. One way of operating on demand is for the government to spend more or tax less. If either of these courses is pursued far enough, however, it is bound to result in a budget deficit or, if the budget is in deficit to start with, a larger budget deficit. Now there are always people who think budget deficits wrong in principle and a great many other people who think governments far too apt to run deficits already, without encouragement from economists. When the British government issued its White Paper on Employment Policy in 1944 there was a long argument inside the government over what was to be said about the use of the budget in regulating employment and the Treasury set its face against any general commitment to run a deficit as a means of increasing effective demand. Instead it was content to see the government commit itself to full employment through the use of a series of devices that were about as adequate for the task as trying to climb Mount Everest on a bicycle. In due course the British government did turn to fiscal policy as its main instrument of demand management but there was always some doubt how far it would go in running a budget deficit; and any doubts one might feel about the British government were as nothing compared with the doubts evoked by other countries.

The reluctance of governments to rely on fiscal policy if it might mean substantial deficits was understandable. The deficits had to be financed; and in going to the market for finance the government put itself at its mercy. If market opinion regarded budget deficits as inherently inflationary or, as in the United States, foresaw a succession of still larger deficits ahead, the price of government bonds would be likely to be marked down and interest rates would rise correspondingly. This would mean that some at least of the fiscal stimulus to demand would be offset by the increased cost of money, not just to the government but to industrial and private borrowers as well. Even if market opinion did not equate budget deficits with inflation, a government which did might expect the market to share its view and doubt whether much was to be gained by way of increased demand by adding to its deficit. In other words, there is first a danger that markets may be perverse and then a danger that governments may be perverse. It is then no comfort to demonstrate that in a depression, budget deficits need not be inflationary. The point is that either form of perversity can get in the way of expanding demand.

The same applies to the second main instrument of demand management, monetary policy. If the market has been taught to regard an expansion in the money supply, whatever the circumstances, whatever the simultaneous change in the demand for money balances, as a sure sign of future inflation, the expansion may be prevented from taking effect on demand by the reactions of the market. The expectation of inflation will again raise interest rates and act as a brake on expansion. In addition some of the additional money may be transferred into other currencies, not just because there will be a natural overflow but because of the expectation of inflation that has been created. These transfers across the exchanges will tend to force down the exchange rate and raise the price of imports in the local currency. This rise may then spread to other goods and eventually encourage larger wage claims until in the end the inflation feared by the market becomes a reality. Once again, action to stimulate demand is short-circuited, largely by perverse market reactions.

These reactions were familiar to Keynes in the 1930s and are discussed in his writings. But in a world in which inflation is endemic they assume much more importance than they did then. Keynes occupied himself in establishing that supply does not automatically create its own demand and that we have to reckon with the possibility of a deficiency of demand. He did not dwell on the converse proposition that demand does not automatically create an equivalent response in supply but may be thwarted by market reactions or spend itself on pushing up prices instead of output.

Thus the path of recovery may lie between the Scylla of real wage resistance and the Charybdis of market perversity. In principle – though not, I think, in practice – the two together could destroy the present economic system with workers striking doggedly for higher wages and owners of capital striking against expansionary policies. The two groups, in apparent pursuit of their own self-interest, could undoubtedly perpetuate a severe slump and so defeat their own true interests by holding down the national income out of which wages and the return on capital are paid.

Wage earners, by prolonging inflation, could end up with fewer opportunities of employment, lower real wages or both while capitalists could see profits disappear and any higher interest they receive clawed back in taxation by the governments that pay out most of it.

But one does not have to take a fatalistic view of the behaviour of markets or of labour organizations. On the contrary, both can be influenced by a determined and clear-headed government. If I have laid stress on the perversities of markets it is mainly because I believe that the monetarist case rests on these perversities, not on the virtues of markets as depicted by the monetarists. How markets react and how labour organizations react depends quite heavily on their reading of the economic situation and their assessment of what the government intends. If we are ever to get out of the present mess there will have to be more agreement between all parties over the conditions of recovery, and confidence that governments will seek to maintain these conditions.

One ingredient in that agreement will have to be a more expansionary budget. The large deficit which inhibits the government from spending more, or reducing taxation, is entirely phoney: with proper inflation accounting it would disappear. Instead of sticking doggedly to its Procrustean task of adapting its spending to a shrinking, underemployed economy, the government should be reviewing how it could usefully add to its spending, preferably for capital purposes. With public investment 40 per cent lower than ten years ago there is ample scope for an increase.

In the end we cannot escape from the present depression without a large increase in demand and there is no likelihood of such an increase without an initiative on the part of governments. It is pure fantasy to suppose that output will recover of itself: that amid the scenes of industrial collapse, new businesses will be founded and flourish in the number required, while old businesses take heart and invest as never before. On the contrary, in a business environment conditioned by tight money, high real rates of interest, and determined efforts to put an end to budget deficits, what incentive is there to launch new businesses and embark on new projects? And if that is so, what prospect is there for the recovery we are so often promised and the fall in unemployment which is so plainly necessary?

NOTES

1 Among comments on this article is one by P. A. Ormerod and G. D. N. Worswick, 'Unemployment in inter-war Britain', *Journal of Political Economy*, April 1982, pp. 400–409. The same issue carries a lengthy rejoinder by Benjamin and Kochin, 'Unemployment and unemployment benefit in twentieth century Britain: a reply to our critics', pp. 410–436. Discussions on the incentive

to seek employment in present day Britain include S. J. Nickell, 'The effect of unemployment and related benefits on the duration of unemployment', *Economic Journal*, March 1979, pp. 34–49; G. Trinder, 'Income in work and when unemployed', *National Institute Economic Review*, February 1983, pp. 56–61; and an exchange between P. Minford and others and J. A. Kay and C. N. Morris in *Fiscal Studies*, February 1983, pp. 66–73.

2 It is of course true that in one sense all unemployment can be dismissed as voluntary: any individual worker can improve his chances of employment by offering to take a cut in his pay or by being less exigent about working conditions. But whether *total* employment can be expanded by a general cut in money wages or acceptance of less favourable working conditions is a very different question. Cuts in money wages may leave real wages unaffected if the flow of spending falls off correspondingly and employers cut prices in line with the fall in their costs. It is only if *demand* increases (including overseas demand) that employment will expand.

Index